BANGKOK

Written and Edited by Steve Van Beek
Directed and Designed by Hans Hoefer
Produced by Geoffrey Eu
Photography by Luca Invernizzi Tettoni

APA PUBLICATIONS

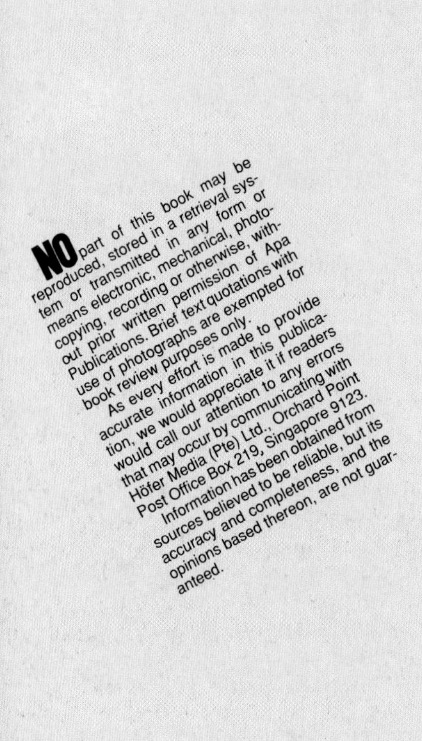

BANGKOK

Second Edition

Printed in Singapore by Höfer Press Pte. Ltd

ABOUT THIS BOOK

When a traveller returneth home, let him not leave the countries where he hath travelled altogether behind him.

—Francis Bacon, Essays, 1597-1625

Encapsulating a city as complex as Bangkok between the covers of a single book is an audacious and daunting task. With a wealth of attractions to choose from, the problem lies in deciding which items to weed out to keep the book from becoming unwieldy, yet allow the end result to serve the broad range of readers who have come to depend on APA's *Insight Guides* as their indispensable travel companions.

The book must provide background information that gives the traveler a greater appreciation of the things he experiences. It must also serve Mr. Bacon's assertion so that when the traveler returns home, he can flip through its pages and recall or perhaps more completely understand some of the exotic mysteries he has witnessed and share them with those who were not lucky enough to travel with him.

This was the challenge that faced the editors and writers of *Cityguide: Bangkok*. They responded as they have since *Insight Guides* were first launched in 1970. Being an Asian-based publishing company gave them a special advantage. With their familiarity with the region, they could tap the talents and knowledge of long-time residents to gather information and shape it into usable yet entertaining form, knowing what to retain, what to discard. Their experience in exploring Bangkok was poured into the pages of a book which conveys the true flavor of the City of Angels, warts and all.

It is fitting that *Cityguide: Bangkok* should be one of the first in APA's *Cityguides* series. In 1973, Thailand, a country that has always held particular fascination for the publishers, was the subject of one of the first *Insight Guides*, following the successes of the *Bali* (1970), *Singapore* (1971) and, *Malaysia* (1972) guides.

Cityguide: Bangkok is the creation of APA publisher and founder **Hans Höfer**, editorial director **Geoffrey Eu** and author/editor **Steve Van Beek**, a resident of Bangkok and writer on historical, cultural and social subjects. The team was augmented by the talents of photographer, **Luca Invernizzi Tettoni**, also a Bangkok resident with whom Van Beek had collaborated on several other books, an important symbiosis which benefitted the overall look of the book. A second writer, **Robert Halliday**, was commissioned to provide the insightful comments on Thai food and sweets.

The backbone of the creative team included **Savika Srisawat** and **Siripimporn Phoosomporn**, who had the unenviable task of checking and double-checking every fact, a vital necessity in the Travel Tips section. **Gayle Miller** and **Sara Lai** acted as litmus paper for the final text by checking its assertions against their own and friends' experiences both in touring Bangkok and in looking after the multitude of guests who continually drop out of the sky and want to be told where to go and what to do.

The concept of a photo-guide is a simple one easily visualized in the abstract but eminently more difficult to realize in book form. It requires succinct text backed by striking photographs that not so much illustrate each attraction as recreate the city's

Van Beek

Tettoni

Eu

atmosphere, conveying its essence in 150 or so arresting images.

Project coordinator Geoffrey Eu was the linchpin of *Cityguide: Bangkok*. His editorial judgement and calm guidance ensured that it would serve the double purpose of being factual and looking good. Eu brought to his job double-barrelled qualifications rare in travel publishing. He is both a graduate of the School of Travel Industry Management at the University of Hawaii and holder of a Master's degree from the Medill School of Journalism at Northwestern University. His credentials have been augmented by his experience in editing APA's *East Asia* and *South Asia* guides, each of which called for him to compact travel highlights of several destinations into a readable volume.

American-born writer/editor Steve Van Beek arrived in Asia in 1966 to live in a small Nepalese village as a development worker for the Peace Corps. He moved to Bangkok in 1969 where, aside from brief residences elsewhere, he has lived ever since. He gained his foundation in Thai culture by living in a stilted house in the Chao Phya River opposite the Grand Palace for 11 years and by serving as the editor of various cultural magazines. Since 1977, he has worked as a freelance writer for Asian and American magazines and written and produced more than 20 films. He is the author of *The Arts of Thailand*, *Bangkok Only Yesterday* and half a dozen other books on Thailand.

Fellow American Robert Halliday arrived in Bangkok in 1969. He has periodically left to live in Washington D.C. but the lure of Bangkok, particularly its food, is too great to resist and he keeps coming back to live. He presently works as an editor for the *Bangkok Post* newspaper when he isn't prowling the markets and foodstalls in search of new sensations to tempt his tastebuds.

Luca Invernizzi Tettoni's name is synonymous with Thailand, as a major portion of the excellent photographs (and books containing them) on Thailand have come from his practised eye. Born in northern Italy, he studied archaelogy and in pursuit of his studies found it useful to photograph what he saw. This practical talent grew into a profession that has earned him accolades, especially for his fine work in recording old architecture, ceremonies and arts, many of them threatened with extinction. Resident in Bangkok since 1977, his books include *The Arts of Thailand*, *Legendary Thailand* and numerous other titles on Thailand and Southeast Asia.

Savika Srisawat brought her experience as a reseacher plus her training as a tour guide to the benefit of the book. It was her task to check every fact, not an easy job in a city which continously changes business and residential telephone numbers as it expands its communications system.

Siripimporn Phoosomporn undertook the major task of assembling the key elements of the Travel Tips section, notably the shopping and restaurant guides. A graduate of San Diego State University, she utilized her training as a graphic artist to draw the initial design for the many maps in the book and to ensure both their visual and factual accuracy. The result is now in your hands. We hope you like it.

—APA PUBLICATIONS

Srisawat

Phoosomporn

CONTENTS

SIGHTS AND SITES

THAI CUISINE

ACCOMMODATION AND TREATS

TRAVEL TIPS

ธนาคารไทยพาณิชย์

BANGKOK: CITY OF ANGELS

Few cities fire the traveler's imaginations with as many exotic images as Bangkok does. Golden temple spires, palm-shaded canals, costumed classical dancers with fingers bent back at impossible angles, brilliant smiles, all the evocative images that look out from postcards and picture books of the City of Angels.

Yet Bangkok is more than a treat for the eyes. It is a sensual feast that envelopes you from the moment you set foot in it: Tiny temple chimes set tinkling by a breeze, an April sky filled with brightly-colored kites, the aroma of chicken being roasted by a sidewalk vendor, fragrant garlands, orchids in rainbow colors, pungent incense smoke spiraling out of a Chinese shrine, saffron-robed monks chanting ancient sutras in the pale morning light and, above all, the Thai smile and gracious manner. All these are Bangkok, one of the few Asian cities that has retained its "Asianess" in a rapidly-changing world.

Not that its charms are immediately apparent. The sights that greet the first-time visitor are hardly likely to enchant him. Ribbons of concrete plunge like daggers through the city's heart, tall buildings dwarf the Buddhist stupas, the sounds of a gentle people are lost beneath the roar of traffic. On first encounter, it seems to be a city strangling in the throes of development. Except for a few sections, it looks very much like any other modern city. Plunked down in a busy thoroughfare hemmed by tall buildings, one is hard to put to know where he is; only the curly-que lettering on the signs tells him he isn't in Los Angeles or some other Western metropolis.

In 1902, intrepid traveler J.G.D. Campbell expressed feelings that are just as appropriate today: "The expectant visitor...will probably derive much disappointment from his first experience of Bangkok. His earliest acquaintance will most probably be with a long, dingy, squalid road running for several miles lined on both sides with third-rate Chinese shops and thronged with Asiatics of every hue and costume, a perfect bedlam...(Yet) with further knowledge, Bangkok will win his affections." Not a lot has changed in the years since, including the postscript which reveals the author's ultimate feelings and sums up Bangkok for most visitors.

As Mr. Campbell discovered, Bangkok is not a philosopher's city, it is a realm of the senses. Those who surrender to their senses, who ignore the surface and thereby pass through walls, are rewarded by a wealth of sensations. Its layout, its edifices ancient and

Preceding pages: Monks gather at Wat Thammakai to observe Visakha Puja, which celebrates the birth, death and enlightenment of Buddha; the Royal Family at Wat Phra Kaew, collecting donations for their charity projects; the pageantry of the Royal Barge is still unsurpassed among the spectacles Bangkok has to offer; well-preserved mural in the Buddhaisawn Chapel; Bangkok's growth in the past five years has been tremendous. Left, trumpeting the King's Birthday, in front of the Giant Swing.

modern, its pursuits, its whole existence seems to have been dictated by whim and a sense of fun, a concept which seems to define most of its activities and makes exploring a journey of sweet anticipation.

The mundane facts reveal little about Bangkok. It covers an area of 626.1 square miles (1,565.2 square km) and has a population of 5,468,915 souls (1986 statistics). Located 14 degrees north of the equator, it lies on the same latitude as Madras, Khartoum, Guatemala City, Guam and Manila. Like them, its climate ranges from tepid to torrid. The sun in its eternal peregrinations is the single most important element shaping the moods and modes of its people and daily life. Since 1782, Bangkok has been Thailand's capital.

But these facts tell you little. Bangkok is a city of extremes and superlatives, a city you do not react to indifferently. Recently declared the world's hottest city by the World Meteorological Organization, it also boasts the world's longest name—*Krung-thep-maha-nakorn-boworn-ratana-kosin:mahintar-ayudhya-amaha-dilok-pop-nopa-ratana-rajthani-burirom-udom-rajniwes-maha-satarn-amorn-pimarn-avatar-satit-sakattiya-visanukam.* Not surprisingly, only a handful of Thais can remember such a mouthful, although the abbreviated translation of the whole is a relatively brief "jewelled city of the god Indra." However, most Thais simply refer to it as *Krung Thep*, City of Angels.

Bangkok is unique among Thai towns. It is as far removed from the rest of Thailand as, say, New York City is from Dubuque, Iowa. It is an island in a sea of green rice fields, a Mont St. Michel surrounded by hinterlands. Understanding it will help little in understanding the rest of Thailand.

If Thailand is shaped like an elephant's head, then Bangkok is the beast's gold tooth. It is figuratively and literally the epicenter of the nation. With a population 50 times greater that the country's second largest city, it dominates all political, commercial, religious and social activity in Thailand. Few capital cities enjoy such primacy.

The seasons run from hot (March-June), to monsoon (July-November) to blissfully cool (December-February). The air is perpetually humid but its hothouse climate makes possible its lush plant life and the flowers that perfume the night air. Its warmth makes pleasant an evening in a garden restaurant, suffuses the golden temples with glowing beauty and permeates the sunny dispositions of its people.

What is it about Bangkok that fascinates visitors? Its color, its chaos, its contrasts. It is the highs of temple architecture and graceful dances, the lows of the rawest forms of nightlife. It is the fabulous variety of food and the appealing differences between a rowdy city and a gentle people.

Bangkok explodes around you, challenging each of your senses, involving you in a way that few cities can. You are never at a loss

Right, dressing up comes naturally to this youngster.

for things to do in it. It is a hedonist's delight that can be explored on a number of levels, from the exalted to the mundane. It is a city of rich and poor people, of fragrances, flowers and the fetid stench of stagnant canals. It is the pleasure of an afternoon by the pool and the discomfort of the searing heat that burns the air and bakes the pavements.

In short, it is an experience you cannot ignore. Mr. Campbell was right on target all those years ago—Bangkok is a city that doesn't really try to, but ultimately wins your affections nevertheless. And, as you discover long after you have returned home, the feeling pervades your very being, its heart becoming your heart.

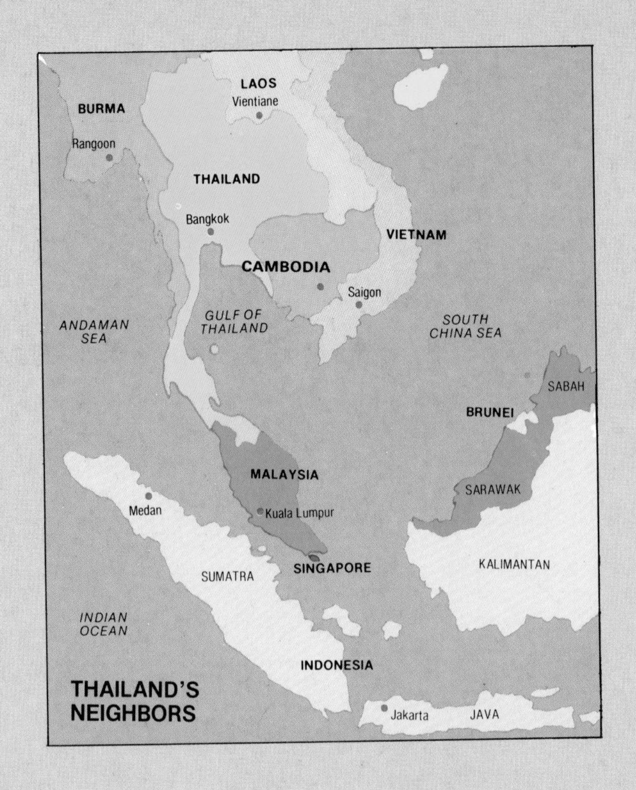

Right, the presiding Buddha Image at Wat Benjamabophit.

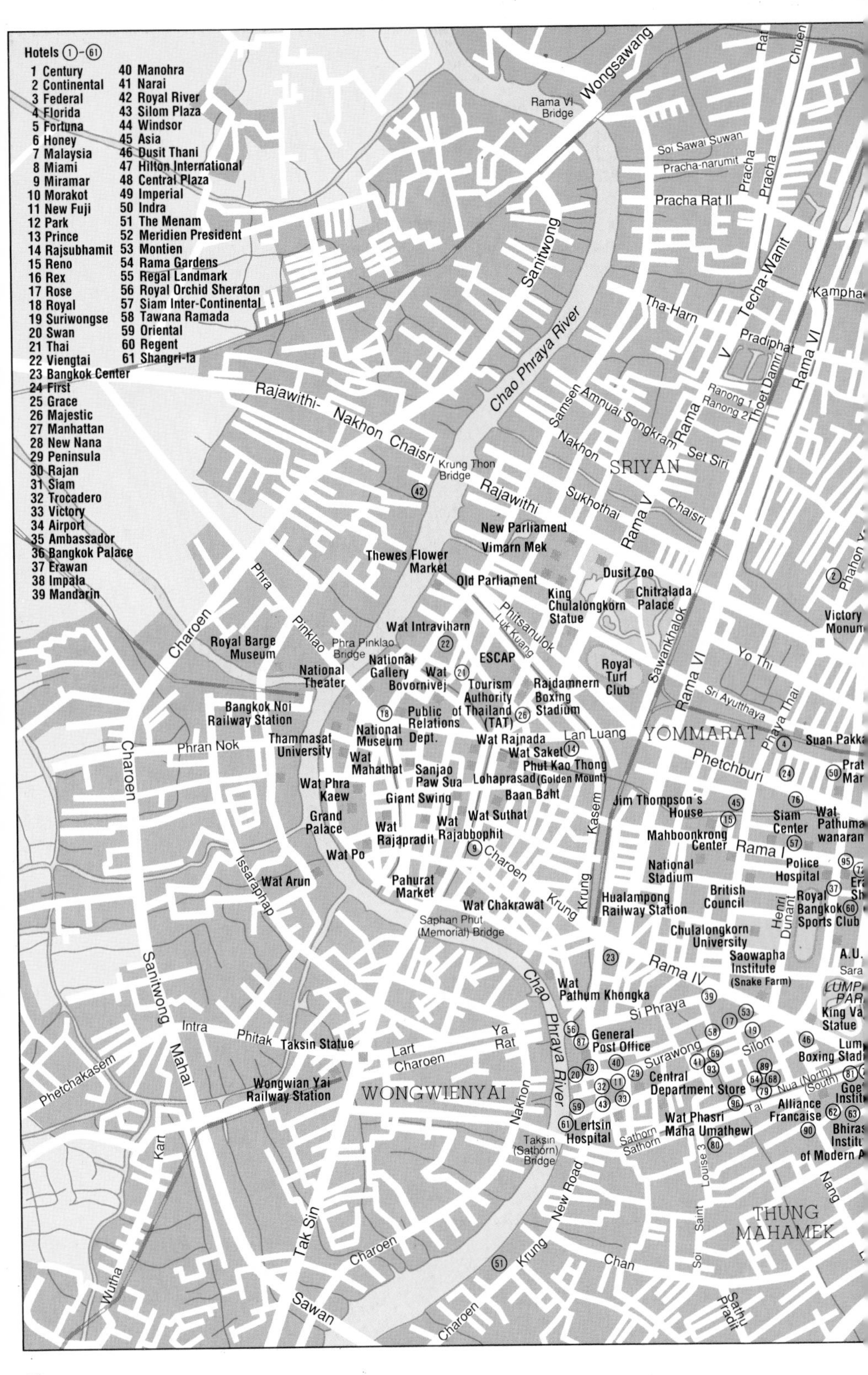
Hotels 1-61
1 Century
2 Continental
3 Federal
4 Florida
5 Fortuna
6 Honey
7 Malaysia
8 Miami
9 Miramar
10 Morakot
11 New Fuji
12 Park
13 Prince
14 Rajsubhamit
15 Reno
16 Rex
17 Rose
18 Royal
19 Suriwongse
20 Swan
21 Thai
22 Viengtai
23 Bangkok Center
24 First
25 Grace
26 Majestic
27 Manhattan
28 New Nana
29 Peninsula
30 Rajan
31 Siam
32 Trocadero
33 Victory
34 Airport
35 Ambassador
36 Bangkok Palace
37 Erawan
38 Impala
39 Mandarin
40 Manohra
41 Narai
42 Royal River
43 Silom Plaza
44 Windsor
45 Asia
46 Dusit Thani
47 Hilton International
48 Central Plaza
49 Imperial
50 Indra
51 The Menam
52 Meridien President
53 Montien
54 Rama Gardens
55 Regal Landmark
56 Royal Orchid Sheraton
57 Siam Inter-Continental
58 Tawana Ramada
59 Oriental
60 Regent
61 Shangri-la
Wongsawang
Rama VI Bridge
Soi Sawai Suwan
Pracha-narumit
Pracha Rat II
Pracha
Techa-Wanit
Sanitwong
Chao Phraya River
Tha-Harn
Pradiphat
Rama VI
Ranong 1
Ranong 2
Thoet Damri
Rama V
Samsen
Amnuai Songkram
Set Siri
Nakhon
SRIYAN
Rajawithi-
Nakhon Chaisri
Krung Thon Bridge
Rajawithi
Sukhothai
Chaisri
New Parliament
Vimarn Mek
Thewes Flower Market
Old Parliament
Dusit Zoo
Chitralada Palace
King Chulalongkorn Statue
Phitsanulok
Luk Kuang
Sawankhalok
Victory Monument
Phra
Pinklao
Charoen
Royal Barge Museum
Phra Pinklao Bridge
Wat Intraviharn
ESCAP
Royal Turf Club
Yo Thi
National Theater
National Gallery
Wat Bovornivej
Tourism Authority of Thailand (TAT)
Rajdamnern Boxing Stadium
Sri Ayutthaya
Phaya Thai
Bangkok Noi Railway Station
Public Relations Dept.
Lan Luang
YOMMARAT
Suan Pakkad
Phran Nok
Thammasat University
National Museum
Wat Rajnada
Wat Saket
Petchburi
Wat Mahathat
Sanjao Paw Sua
Phut Kao Thong
Lohaprasad (Golden Mount)
Wat Phra Kaew
Giant Swing
Baan Baht
Jim Thompson's House
Grand Palace
Wat Rajapradit
Wat Rajabbophit
Wat Suthat
Kasem
Mahboonkrong Center
Rama I
Siam Center
Wat Pathumawanaram
Wat Po
Issaraphap
Charoen Krung
National Stadium
Police Hospital
Wat Arun
Pahurat Market
Wat Chakrawat
Hualampong Railway Station
British Council
Royal Bangkok Sports Club
Henri Dunant
Saphan Phut (Memorial) Bridge
Chulalongkorn University
Saowapha Institute (Snake Farm)
Rama IV
Wat Pathum Khongka
Si Phraya
King Vajiravudh Statue
Sanitwong
Intra
Phitak
Taksin Statue
Ya Rat
General Post Office
Surawong
Silom
Boxing Stadium
Lart Charoen
Phetchakasem
Wongwian Yai Railway Station
WONGWIENYAI
Central Department Store
Nua (North)
Tai (South)
Alliance Francaise
Mahai
Nakhon
Lertsin Hospital
Wat Phasri Maha Umathewi
Sathorn
Taksin (Sathorn) Bridge
Louise 3
Kart
New Road
Nang
Soi Saint
THUNG MAHAMEK
Tak Sin
Charoen
Krung
Chan
Wutha
Sawan
Sathu Pradit

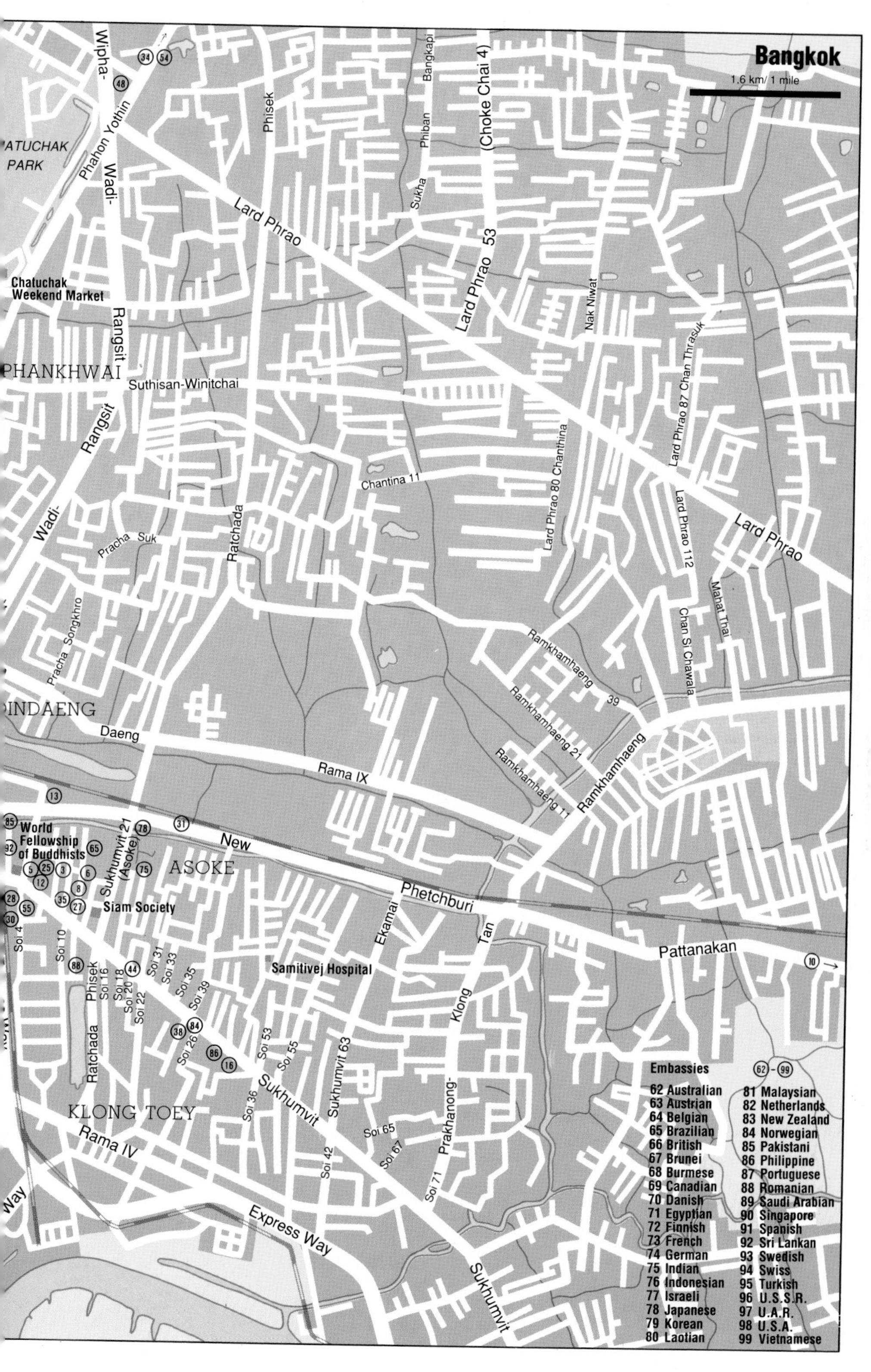
Bangkok
1.6 km/ 1 mile
CHATUCHAK PARK
Chatuchak Weekend Market
Phahon Yothin
Wipha-
Wadi-
Rangsit
Phisek
Lard Phrao
Sukha
Phiban
Bangkapi
(Choke Chai 4)
Lard Phrao 53
Nak Niwat
Lard Phrao 87 Chan Thrasuk
Lard Phrao 80 Chanthina
Lard Phrao 112
PHANKHWAI
Suthisan-Winitchai
Chantina 11
Pracha Suk
Ratchada
Pracha Songkhro
Mahat Thai
Chan Si Chawala
Ramkhamhaeng 39
Ramkhamhaeng 21
Ramkhamhaeng 11
Ramkhamhaeng
DINDAENG
Daeng
Rama IX
World Fellowship of Buddhists
Sukhumvit 21 (Asoke)
ASOKE
New Phetchburi
Siam Society
Ekamai
Tan
Pattanakan
Samitivej Hospital
Klong
Prakhanong-
Soi 4
Soi 10
Phisek
Soi 16
Soi 18
Soi 20
Soi 22
Soi 31
Soi 33
Soi 35
Soi 39
Soi 26
Soi 53
Soi 55
Sukhumvit 63
Soi 36
Sukhumvit
Soi 42
Soi 65
Soi 67
Soi 71
Ratchada
KLONG TOEY
Rama IV
Express Way
Way
Embassies
62 - 99
62 Australian
63 Austrian
64 Belgian
65 Brazilian
66 British
67 Brunei
68 Burmese
69 Canadian
70 Danish
71 Egyptian
72 Finnish
73 French
74 German
75 Indian
76 Indonesian
77 Israeli
78 Japanese
79 Korean
80 Laotian
81 Malaysian
82 Netherlands
83 New Zealand
84 Norwegian
85 Pakistani
86 Philippine
87 Portuguese
88 Romanian
89 Saudi Arabian
90 Singapore
91 Spanish
92 Sri Lankan
93 Swedish
94 Swiss
95 Turkish
96 U.S.S.R.
97 U.A.R.
98 U.S.A.
99 Vietnamese

A Date With Destiny

Bangkok is a young city with an old history. This seeming contradiction gives it a dual character unique among Asian capitals. It is a young, vibrant, dynamic metropolis and at the same time, a city steeped in centuries of tradition. Although an important town for hundreds of years, it sat on the sidelines, watching history pass up and down the Chao Phya River on its way between the ancient capital of Ayutthaya and the world beyond the seas. It was only by accident of history that nearly destroyed the Thai nation that Bangkok was suddenly called upon to become the stage on which Thailand's destiny would be played out.

As old as the hills: The story of Bangkok begins in the far north of Thailand. The soil from which tall buildings now sprout once provided sustenance for rice shoots. At that time, as little as 1,500 years ago, the future capital city lay beneath the ocean's waters. Each monsoon season, the powerful currents of the Chao Phya River swept southwards, carrying eroded farmland into the sea, each year nudging the shoreline a little further into the Gulf of Thailand.

Eventually, the mudbanks rose above the waterline, the mangrove trees took root and the lungfish moved in. Soon, houses rose on stilts above the tidal mudflats. Their inhabitants used their self-made islands as bases for fishing expeditions into the nearby sea. Each year, the river added more soil until the delta was high enough that farmers could till it and plant rice in it. From the fields that once nurtured rice, grew villages, then towns, and finally a city.

Because it originated in an alluvial plain, Bangkok today is a flat city, with no natural point more than a meter or two above any other. As a reminder of its aquatic origins, Bangkok each October returns to the sea. The Chao Phya River, swollen with the abundance of monsoon rains, meets the incoming tide and spills over its banks into the streets, turning Bangkok into a veritable Venice, its avenues plied by boats and inhabited by fish.

Village in the plum-olive trees: Bangkok's history as a town began in the 16th century when King Phrajai (1534-1546) commanded that a 1.2-mile-long (two-km) canal be dug across the neck of a 10-mile (17-km) loop of the river to cut the distance between the sea and Ayutthaya. The annual monsoon floodtides scoured the banks of the canal like sandpaper until, eventually, the canal widened to become the main course of the river. On its banks rose two towns, trading posts on the route to Ayutthaya, some 47 miles (76 km) up the winding river. On the sunset bank lay Thonburi and across the river Bangkok.

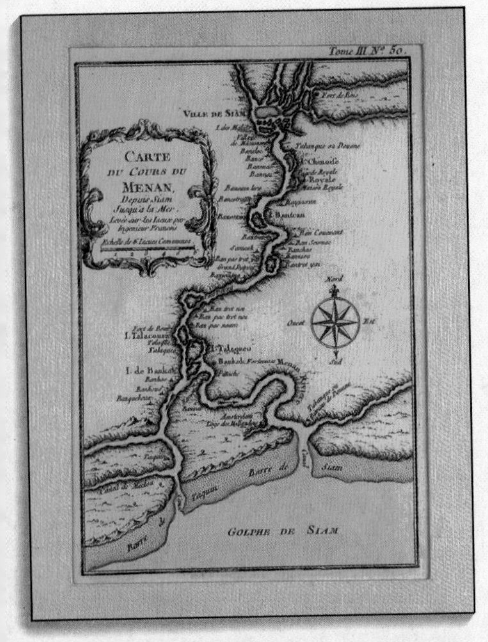

At the time, Bangkok was little more than a village (*bang*) in an orchard of trees whose fruit has stumped botanists to the point they cannot decide if they are olives or plums, settling instead for the Thai compromise word *kok* (plum-olive). Hence, the town's name, Bangkok.

During the 17th century, the town was inhabited by a few Chinese merchants and farmers who tended their *kok* trees on low ground which was subject to flooding and therefore with little commercial potential nor reason to grow. But grow it did, "becoming" one of Asia's grandest cities, an accident of history, a bit of a miracle and a testament to the tenacity and regenerative powers of its inhabitants.

To understand why Bangkok developed as it did, one must look to its antecedents. Thailand's history began in its northeastern region where a Bronze Age culture flourished between 2,000 and 250 B.C. There is a gap of 500 years until the third century A.D., when annals note the presence of Indian missionaries and merchants in Central Thailand and in the far south. There are seventh-century accounts of religious communities at Nakhon Pathom to the west of present-day Bangkok, and in Lopburi 95 miles (153 km) to the north in the lush Central Plains.

Stirrings of nationhood: During the latter half of the first millennium, the far northern hills were populated by indigenous tribes and by ancestors of the Thais who in the eighth century had begun drifting south from China to settle on Thailand's hills and valleys. In the 10th and 11th centuries the area was in the political grip of the brilliant Khmer civilization that built Angkor Wat.

By the 12th century, Khmer power began to wane and it began retreating to its original borders. The principalities that formerly paid allegiance to the Khmers felt bold enough to establish their own political dominance, forging a federation of small Thai kingdoms to fill the vacuum left by the departing Khmers. In 1238, 23 years after the signing of the Magna Carta in England, they established the kingdom of Sukhothai and, with it, the Thai nation.

Sukhothai, formerly a Khmer city, ruled Siam, (as Thailand was called until the 1930s) for a little over a century. By 1350, however, it had become pre-occupied with religion to the detriment of politics with the result that a city further down river seized the reins of power. This new city, Ayutthaya, was destined to rule the country for 400 years and to serve as the model upon which Bangkok would be built.

From humble beginnings, Ayutthaya grew in power. By the 15th century, it had

Preceding pages: Bangkok in 1900, seen from the Golden Mount. Left, this 18th-century French map charts the lower course of the Menam Chao Phya. Right, Siamese 'angels'.

annexed vast territory and overrun Angkor Wat, the former Khmer stronghold. By the 17th century, it was one of Asia's richest cities. War victories against Burma to the west and Cambodia to the east plus the creation of a prosperous economy founded on rich harvests had combined to create a city of unrivalled brilliance. The journals and letters of 17th-century European travelers speak of a splendid city of palaces and pagodas, a city of more than 2,000 gold statues of Buddha and gold-tipped spires visible from great distances. It was known as *Krung Thep*, City of Angels.

Ayutthaya was sited on an island guarded by a natural moat formed by three rivers. Its army was complemented by mercenary soldiers recruited from as far away as Persia and Japan. Ayutthaya's wealth attracted merchants from England, Portugal, Holland and France who built small communities outside the city walls. Thai envoys from time to time paid official visits to the court of France's King Louis XIV.

Gateway to a celestial city: Far to the south, Bangkok, and to a greater extent Thonburi (Money Town), guarded the portals to the upper reaches of the river where Ayutthaya lay. These twin sentinels on either side of the river with their French-built star-shaped fortresses bristling with cannon were formidable barriers to discourage potential invaders from intervening into the heart of the realm.

Thonburi served as a customs port and as a point for large European and Chinese ships to transfer their cargoes to shallow-draft boats for the journey upriver to Ayutthaya. At that time, however, Bangkok was still little more than a village set amidst orchards with a few old temples—Wat Po, Wat Saket, Wat Samplum and Wat Sampeng—homes and some shops, giving little hint of Bangkok's future importance.

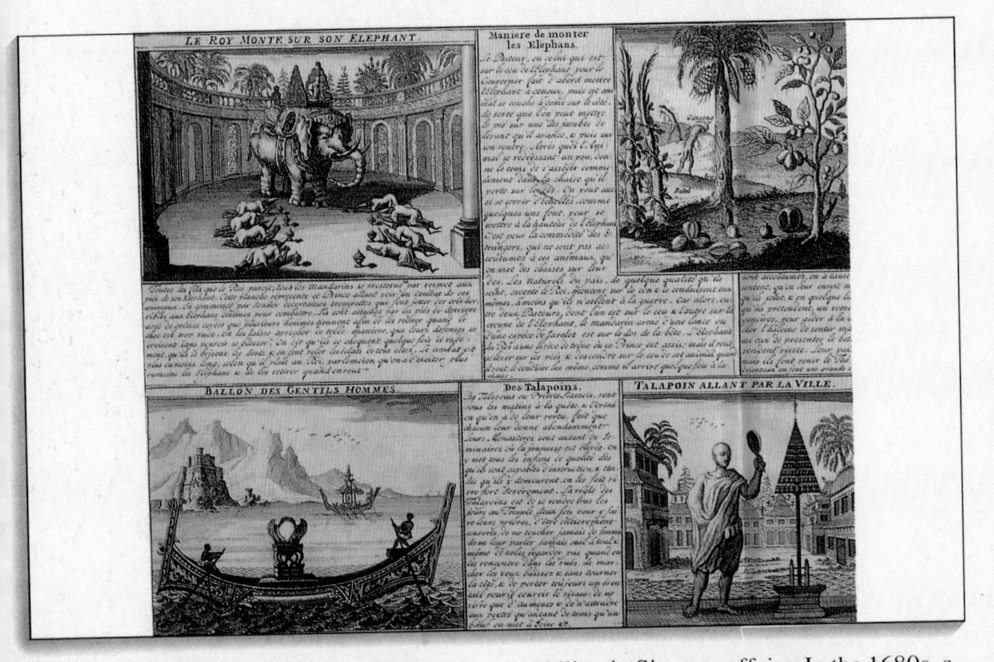

Late in the 17th century, Europeans began meddling in Siamese affairs. In the 1680s, a Greek adventurer named Constance Phaulkon rose to high rank in the Siamese court of King Narai. Phaulkon connived with the French to convert the country to Catholicism and thus ensure French dominance of trade, a fore-doomed attempt which he, with his wide experience, should have been astute enough to foresee. Unfortunately, King Narai died in 1688 and in retaliation the Siamese nobles executed Phaulkon, expelled all Europeans, and closed Siam's doors to European merchants for the next 150 years.

From 1688, Ayutthaya settled into complacency. Neighboring Burmese had long coveted its wealth and sent army after army against its battlements in the vain hope of overrunning the city. Ayutthaya's architecture saved it each time.

In 1767, however, it is said that treacherous elements within the city opened the gates to the Burmese who went on a rampage of destruction. They sacked the city, stripping it of its wealth. Its inhabitants were killed, scattered or taken back to Burma to serve as slaves. In an instant, a fabled city of one million, larger than contemporary London, became a ghost town of 10,000 souls living in the shadows of ruined spires and the ashes of greatness.

From the ashes of defeat: The remnants of the Siamese army re-grouped and a few months later drove the Burmese garrison forces from the city. A quick survey of the ruined city convinced Siamese leaders that Ayutthaya had no future. They took to their boats and moved downriver.

The leader of the Siamese army, Phya Taksin, chose Thonburi as his headquarters to wage war on Siam's enemies. For nearly 15 years, Thailand was engaged in constant warfare against the Burmese, the Laotians and the Vietnamese. It is a testament to the Thai thirst for independence and an ability to rebound from disaster that by 1780, Siam held more territory than it had at the height of Ayutthaya's power.

The warfare, however, distracted Taksin from the task of building a proper capital city. When in Thonburi he lived and held court in the former town governor's house in a temple compound just south of the Temple of Dawn (Wat Arun).

It is said that the demands of leadership and the constant worries about provisioning and arming his soldiers unhinged Taksin's mind and he began abusing those about him, including Buddhist monks. It finally became too much for the lords of the realm and they conspired to have him removed. He was tried and executed. A new ruler was picked from among the leading nobles, a general with the title of *Chakri* (military commander). This man, General Thong Duang, had amassed a considerable reputation for his prowess as a tactician, notably against the armies of Laos from whom he captured the Emerald Buddha, a small jade image of

Left, illustrated accounts of the first French visitors to Siam. Right, reenactment of the war against the Burmese.

surpassing power, providing divine protection to any city which owned it. Thus, in the year 1782, the triumphant *Chakri* was invited by the Siamese nobles to become the King of Thailand.

The former *Chakri* took the name of Ramathibodi, a 14th century Thai king. One of his descendents, King Vajiravudh (1910-1925) would later simplify the multiplicity of names by which *Chakri* kings were known by giving to each member of the dynasty the name *Rama*, the name of the ancient god-warrior of the Indian literary classic, the *Ramayana*. Thus, King Ramathibodi is also known as King Rama I, just as succeeding kings have been known as Rama II, Rama III, etc.

A new City of Angels rises: King Rama I was an ambitious man eager to re-establish the Thai people as a dominant civilization. He saw that Thonburi was too confined to create the capital city he envisioned. He had something grander in mind, an evocation of the glory of Ayutthaya, a new *Krung Thep* or "City of Angels" as the former capital had been known.

Choicer land lay to the east of the river among the *kok* trees. He ordered the digging of a canal across a neck of land to create an island and define an inner city. This canal, Klong Lawd, runs north from Pak Klong Talat market to the approach of the Phra Pinklao Bridge. This watery ribbon served as a boundary, a moat and, literally, as an artery along which communication and commerce could flow.

Rama I saw this "island" as the core of his new capital. He was profoundly aware of the power of symbols in uniting a people and focussing their attention on a single site. He was likely aware of the powerful religious significance of the island's shape, that of a sacred conch shell, which had defined the contours of many antique Thai towns. Here, within its rim, he would concentrate the principal components of the Thai nation: religion, monarchy and administration. To underscore his recognition of the power of the country's principal Buddha image, he called this island *Ratanakosin*, meaning "Resting Place of the Emerald Buddha."

To dedicate the ground solely to the purposes of statecraft and religion, he formally requested that the Chinese living there move to an area to the southeast. This new district soon sprouted thriving shops and busy streets. Known as Sampeng, it quickly became the commercial heart of the city and the center of what is now known as Chinatown. Now, nothing could come between Rama I and his goal.

On April 6, 1782, at a time and place chosen by geomancers and astrologers, the new monarch proclaimed both the establishment of a new City of Angels (still known to modern Thais as *Krung Thep*; only foreigners call it Bangkok) and of a dynasty called Chakri, which today is a partner in the constitutional monarchy which rules the nation.

On the morning of April 21, 1782, 54 minutes after the sun crested the horizon as decreed by the court astrologers, Lak Muang, a sacred pillar honoring the Hindu god Siva, was dedicated as proof of the god's divine protection over the city.

The new king's first task was to make the city secure from attack by enemies still lurking in the hinterlands. His model for its

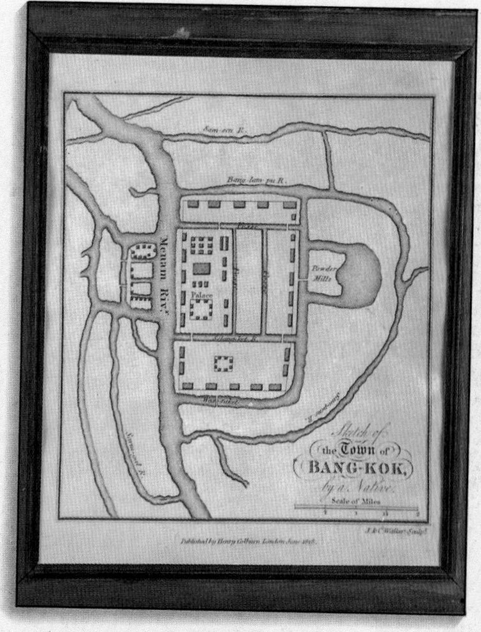

Left, the Golden Mount was the highest point in Bangkok at the end of the last century. Right, an early map of the city emphasizes its waterways.

defenses was Ayutthaya. Recognizing that Bangkok would need room to expand, he ordered 10,000 Cambodian captives to dig a second canal in a concentric arc some 2,640 feet (800 meters) east of Klong Lawd.

To gird and guard the city, 5,000 Laotian captives built a high stout wall along the inner banks of the second canal and the river and punctuated it with 14 octagonal watchtowers, only two of which remain today.

A practical man and one fully aware of symbolic significance, Rama I sent his workers north to Ayutthaya to dismantle the ruined city's buildings. The bricks were transported downriver to Bangkok and cemented together to form the wall. By doing so, Rama I ensured that Bangkok would be imbued by the spirit of ancient Ayutthaya, irrefutably establishing Bangkok in his subjects' minds as the soul of the nation. Just as diverse elements were fused into the new city, the Cambodian and Laotian captives were gradually assimilated into the populace as free men.

The Dynastic Chronicles suggest that Rama I was not without a touch of sentimentality. Near the present Golden Mount, he had Klong Mahanak dug in a straight line to the east both as a highway deep into the eastern region and as "a place where the people of the capital city could go boating, singing and reciting poems during the high-water season just like the custom observed in the former capital of Ayutthaya."

As the city grew, a third canal was dug a further 2,640 feet (800 meters) east, again in a concentric arc. A labyrinthine network of canals was dug to connect them. These capillaries of the great watery arteries were plied by thousands of small boats. Many of the city's houses were rafts. When the monsoon rains came, no one worried; the houses rose with the tide and life continued as before.

Indeed, in the early days the city had only three dirt tracks: Bamrungmuang, an elephant path running east from the city wall; a road circling the outside of the city wall; and a third one inside the wall. It would be 80 years before Bangkok would have its first paved road. By the middle of this century, most of the canals had been filled in to make roads. Today, when the city floods, chaos ensues.

Rivalling Ayutthaya's brilliance: Rama I then turned his attention to constructing the royal island's principal buildings. One would think that he would first build his own palace. He recognized, however, that it was more important to construct a home for the Emerald Buddha, the most sacred Buddha image in the realm, which until then had rested in a temple in Thonburi.

Two years later in 1784, the glittering complex of buildings, *stupas* (called *chedi* in Thai) and monuments known as Wat Phra Kaew was completed. Amid the blare of conch shells and with the air resonating with the chants of saffron-robed Buddhist priests, the Emerald Buddha was carried in august ceremony across the river and installed in the central temple. It was only after he had completed Wat Phra Kaew (the Temple of the Emerald Buddha) that he turned his attention to building a palace for himself.

The Grand Palace was more than a home; it was a center of government. It contained buildings for receiving royal visitors and debating matters of state. It was built piece by piece as and when there was a need. The last building, the Chakri Mahaprasad with its triple crowns, was not erected until late in the 19th century.

These two complexes were the core structures of Rama I's new royal enclave. Thus, Ratanakosin Island is the epicenter of the nation's religion and monarchy, holding the Temple of the Emerald Buddha and the Grand Palace which, until 1946, was home to Thailand's kings.

It also contains Wat Po; the National Museum; the Royal Institute; one of the nation's two most prestigious universities, Thammasat University; the National Theater; the Fine Arts University; the Ministry of Finance; the Ministry of Justice; the Ministry of Interior; and the Ministry of Defence. In short, it is the very heart of the city.

If Rama I laid the foundations of Bangkok, it was Rama II (1809-1824) who instilled it with the spirit of the past. He recognized the vital importance of recreating the literature lost in the destruction of Ayutthaya. He gathered about him the kingdom's leading poets and together they set down from memory the classical works, the dramas, and poems that had been destroyed in the fires of Ayutthaya.

Rama II was also a gifted artist who carved the ornate doors on Wat Suthat, cutting fully two inches (five centimeters) into the thick teak with special chisels he created for the work and which afterwards he threw into the river to keep others from duplicating his feat.

Rama III (1825-1851) opened Thailand's

Scenes of early Bangkok, from the murals of Wat Rajapradit (left) and Wat Thong Thammachat (right).

doors to foreigners once again, setting in motion forces which would change the kingdom. He signed a trade treaty with Britain in 1826 and with the United States in 1833. The wars with neighboring countries tapered off and by the middle of his reign, ceased altogether. Thailand would not be threatened by invaders until World War II, leaving the country free to concentrate on the task of development and the combating of a more subtle enemy, colonialism.

Transformation begins: Rapid development began with the reign of King Rama IV (1851-1868), one of the most remarkable rulers of 19th century Asia. Known as King Mongkut and to the West as the monarch of the film (still banned in Thailand) *The King and I*, he was a highly intelligent man, for the most part self-educated. It is unfortunate that a disturbed woman named Anna Leonowens should write a book which maligned him so badly because it has prevented outsiders from appreciating his true genius.

During his short reign, he opened the country to new ideas, impressing foreign diplomats and others with his enlightened attitude and his thirst for knowledge. In 1863, he built Bangkok's first paved road, Charoen Krung ("prosperous city") or, as it was known to foreigners, New Road. This four mile (6.5 km) street running southeast from the palace walls and along the river, he lined with shophouses to be rented to Siamese merchants.

He paved dirt roads and introduced new technology to encourage commerce. He fostered improved relations with European countries, impressing them with the dynamism of Bangkok and laying the groundwork for the changes which he knew Siam must make if it was to avoid being colonized, as was occurring with alarming frequency in neighboring countries.

The foreign community was among the first to move into the areas opened by the construction of New Road. They built their homes in the region of the Oriental Hotel and along Silom and Sathorn Roads, both bucholic retreats at that time. Numerous letters to the editor of the *Bangkok Times* of 1900 complain of the writers' inability to take the evening air or ride their phaetons along Windmill Road (Silom) due to the "foul odors" wafted by the winds from the truck gardens that the Chinese farmers nourished with nightsoil.

King Mongkut's thirst for knowledge led, ironically, to his death. Using scientific instruments and charts, he predicted a total solar eclipse. To convince doubting royals and foreigners that his computations were correct, he transported a huge party to Prachaub Khiri Khan down the southern peninsula where he had predicted the eclipse would be at its fullest. To the wonderment of all, he was precise in his calculations. Unfortunately, he contracted malaria during the outing and died on his return to Bangkok.

While Rama IV played a pivotal role in setting the stage for modernization, it was his son, Chulalongkorn (1868-1910) who carried the country into the 20th century. During his reign, he abolished the last vestiges of slavery, introduced electric lighting in 1884 and opened the nation's first hospital, Siriraj, in 1886. He hired Danish engineers to build an electric tram system 10 years before Copenhagen had one.

Left, 19th-century engraving showing King Rama IV in front of the Royal Palace. Right, a formal portrait of King Rama V.

He sent his many sons to study in Europe's capitals. They came back as doctors and engineers with a sense of responsibility for moving their country forward. Chulalongkorn became the first Thai king to travel abroad, making state visits to Asian and European capitals. In another departure from tradition, he appointed a woman, his wife, as regent to rule the realm in his absence.

He changed the face of Bangkok. By 1900, the city was growing rapidly eastward. In the Dusit district on the northeastern outskirts he built a palace and constructed roads to link it with his palace. Other noble families followed, building elegant mansions. In the same area, he arranged the construction of Wat Benjamabophit, the Marble Temple, the last major Buddhist temple built in Bangkok. He encouraged the importation of automobiles about the same time they began appearing on the streets of America. Soon, Bangkok was marvelling at the new wonder that was sputtering along at hair-raising speed sending horse carriages into the ditches and history.

The winds of change: The changes during the reign of King Rama VI (King Vajiravudh, 1910-1925) were as much philosophical as physical. Students traveling to Europe were now exposed to revolutionary ideas. King Vajiravudh fostered a strong sense of nationalism and encouraged a spirit of challenging accepted ways, little knowing how his initiative would eventually be interpreted. He published a newspaper in which the issues of the day were discussed and encouraged nobles to take part in royal dramas, many of which he wrote himself.He even translated many of Shakespeare's plays into Thai.

Bangkok took the first steps away from reliance on an agricultural based economy by introducing new industries. The first manufacturing company was registered in 1912. With the new industries, Bangkok took on a new look with offices along the river banks and factories in what were formerly rice fields.

The revolutionary spirit fostered by King Vajiravudh had disastrous consequences for the Absolute Monarchy during the reign of his successor, King Prajadipok (1925-1935). Through a series of circumstances, the young man who in his youth had been low on the ladder of succession, suddenly found himself on the throne. His experience as a soldier ill-prepared him for the cataclysmic events taking place around him at an ever accelerating pace.

His predecessor had put a severe drain on

the Treasury, leaving Prajadipok with a lack of finances to run the country precisely at the time when the world and Thailand were being shaken by the Great Depression. In 1932, the Chakri dynasty celebrated its 150th anniversary and the Memorial Bridge, the city's first bridge spanning the Chao Phya River, was opened but the air reverberated with calls for change.

The King opposed the calls for democracy on the grounds that Thailand was not ready for it, an assertion the reformers challenged. The combination of revolutionary clamor and a severely damaged economy that necessitated cutting the staffs and salaries culminated on June 24 with a revolution that replaced 700 years of Absolute Monarchy with constitutional monarchy, placing civilians for the first time in the seat of power.

What began with high hopes as a democracy soon became a dictatorship as the new leaders declared a moratorium on democracy for a further 10 years. Unable to reconcile his own rule with the new leaders, King Prajadipok chose to abdicate in 1935. He was replaced by a young boy, King Ananda, who spent most of the next 11 years studying in Switzerland.

During the latter half of the 1930s, Thailand was caught in a struggle between military and civilian leaders, each succeeding the other as heads of government in seesaw but bloodless battles for power.

The military sought to impose discipline on a people adrift after the fall of the Absolute Monarchy which had governed them for centuries. These leaders were preoccupied with "modernizing" the country along Western lines, including misguided attempts to force Thais to wear shoes and hats in emulation of Westerners, a move greeted with wry derision by independent-minded Thais and soon after dropped.

In the spirit of the revolutionaries who had toppled the Absolute Monarchy, the civilian leaders were bent on transforming the nation's economy but seemed to move too quickly for the military. The military response was to brand the reformers Communist, a term with its connotations of destruction for the monarchy and religion which fill Thais with horror. It was a stick which military leaders would for the next 40 years use to beat would-be reformers both in the city and in the economically disadvantaged

A Royal Barge, photographed in 1865.

countryside, depriving of legitimacy any grassroots attempts to improve the quality of life for the ordinary Thais.

During World War II, the military government found it expedient to capitulate to the Japanese although the Thai ambassador to Washington refused to deliver Thailand's declaration of war. An active underground flourished throughout the war and at its close, Thailand was deemed by the Allies never to have declared war and was thus not regarded as a defeated enemy and punished.

In 1946, King Ananda returned to Thailand but shortly after, died under mysterious circumstances. Four years later, his brother,

Bhumibol Adulyadej, was crowned the new King of Thailand.

New perspectives: Following World War II, Bangkok began in earnest to develop its economy along the lines of European countries. During the 1950s, new industries were inaugurated and the government initiated the first of many five-year plans, streamlining its administration accordingly.

Bangkok began to change dramatically in response to the new prosperity. The last of the major canals were filled in to make roadways. The city began its big push to the east as Sukhumvit and Petchburi Roads changed from quiet residential areas to busy, business-filled thoroughfares.

More than anything, it was the arrival of American forces involved in the Indochina war that gave the city its present look. Large infusions of money resulted in a burgeoning economy, multi-storied buildings and a population that swelled in response to the new jobs offered. The Thai military, which had steadily been gaining power in Thai politics, reached its peak of influence during these years.

The 1970s saw a rekindling of the revolutionary spirit of the 1930s with students engaging in polemics and demonstrations in support of a more open form of government. The Student Uprising in 1973 that overthrew the military dictatorship expressed a popular desire for a new constitution and a more democratic government.

This period of experimentation lasted for three years until 1976, when a right-wing counterattack—by this point a popular reaction to the uncertainty and chaos that had prevailed—brought back a military-dominated government but one that was more responsive to the needs of the country.

The 1980s have seen the vertical growth of Bangkok. Its skyline has changed dramatically with the erection of 30-and 40-story buildings. Shopping malls, condominiums and office buildings have become the dominant form of architecture as Buddhist temples once were, this is a clear indication of the new imperatives in Thai life. New ring roads and expressways have also changed once-quiet streets into arterials as Bangkok has sought to cope with its worsening traffic problem.

Today, Bangkok looks less like a city created for ethereal gods than one built for the earthly gods of commerce and convenience. In a sense, its 20th century look is only a façade. Beneath it all, in quiet temple courtyards, in busy markets, in parks, in back lanes and in the streets of the old city, Bangkok is still Bangkok, a city of the senses whose allure defies simple explanation.

Left, Rama VII delivers the new constitution. Right, the present King on the day of his Coronation.

A CULTURAL FABRIC

Early morning in the courtyard of the Temple of the Emerald Buddha, drinking in its dazzling architecture, listening to the dawn breeze ringing the eaves bells, imbibing the fragrance of flowers and incense, it is impossible not to wonder about a people of infinite patience and surpassing craftsmanship who created this and scores of other monuments around Bangkok.

Who are these people who can incorporate diverse elements into a harmonious whole, whose religion is of such compelling force, whose sense of oneness and organizational ability enables it to bring together individuals into a community of action inspired by the same goals?

From many, one: The harmonious diversity seen in the temple characterizes Thailand as a whole. Since its foundation, Thailand has assimilated a wide variety of nationalities and religions, people who within their own countries were often at war with each other. Yet, within its borders, they have lived in peace, a history free of civil wars and religious persecution. In almost every instance, Thailand has reacted to adversity as a united nation, ignoring color, race and creed, embracing rather than excluding new peoples.

Bangkok is a microcosm of that harmony. The names of districts are testament to its tolerance and memorials to people of widely varying backgrounds. Ban Tanao was settled by Mons from Tenasserim in Burma. Makassan near the Indra Hotel became the new home of Muslims from the Indonesian city of Makassar.

Ban Baht, the Village of Monk's Bowl Makers near the Golden Mount was once known as Ban Kamain (Village of Cambodians). Baan Yuan (Vietnamese Village) on Samsen Road was settled by Vietnamese Catholics escaping persecution in the 1830s. Ban Tawai (Burmese Village) was named for Burmese timber merchants from the area of Tavoy.

With many of these nations Thailand fought major wars lasting centuries, yet their people were assimilated into the city's vibrant cultural fabric. Today, few traces of their former cultures remain, not because these were suppressed but because the city into which they introduced themselves adopted them without reservation.

Mysterious origins: The origin of the ethnic Thais has been hotly debated for decades. Popular tradition claims they fled here from China to escape the depredations of Kublai Khan's hordes sweeping southward out of Mongolia. The theory would explain Thai empathy with later immigrants.

Other theories suggest they originated in Thailand a millennium or two ago; those Thais found in today's China are said to have emigrated north from Thailand about 1,000 years ago. Whichever conjecture is correct, it is accepted that the Thais' first home in Thailand was in the northern hills.

As the centuries passed, they shared the country with ethnic Laos who populated the Northeast bringing with them a similar language and culture and the Mons of western Thailand. The South was the stronghold of Malay Muslims. Ultimately, members of these cultures found their way to Bangkok, drawn by the economic opportunities the city provided.

The population was augmented by Hindu and Sikh Indians who arrived as merchants, and by the Chinese who had been on the scene for centuries but large numbers of whom arrived as laborers early in this century and worked their way up into positions of prominence.

The Chinese, who number nearly five million in Thailand, and the Indians have been absorbed into Thai society, taking Thai names and nationality. Whereas the ethnic Thais sought government positions as ladders to success, the Chinese-Thais meanwhile have dominated commerce and shaped much of the country's economic development outside the traditional sphere of agriculture.

Other ingredients in the melting pot have included Japanese, Portuguese and other Europeans, many of whom intermarried and all of whom left their imprint on Thai culture and cuisine.

Three pillars of the Thai nation: To a Thai, three pillars support his country. As represented by the three colors in the Thai flag, there is the land and its people (red), the purity of religion (white), chiefly Buddhism, and the monarchy (blue) binding together the other two elements.

Of the three, the monarchy is a pivotal force. Although His Majesty King Bhumibol Adulyadej does not govern the country, he has considerable influence, serving as a beacon of high moral standards and a bellwether in times of trouble. He is regarded with almost god-like reverence as much for his unique personality as for the office he holds.

He was crowned in 1950 as the ninth monarch of the Chakri dynasty. In 1955, he made an extensive tour of the provinces, becoming the first monarch in modern history to visit the economically deprived Northeastern region. What he saw there spurred him on a quest to develop the rural areas of the country, an endeavor to which he has devoted his life. He began with projects to wean northern hilltribes away from grow-

Preceding pages: Giant leather fan puppet; dancers pay respects at the temple before performing. Left, shop selling Royal souvenirs. Right, on Chulalongkorn Day, students pay respects to the former King's statue.

ing opium by introducing vegetables and fruits, (many of which had never been cultivated in Thailand) and by initiating programs to market them.

He soon expanded his projects to include farmers in other remote parts of the country. He oversaw the development of irrigation schemes, swamp drainage, new crops, schools and health programs. He has spent up to eight months of each year in the countryside, often in inhospitable terrain.

As a young man he was a Buddhist monk, but his reverence for the religion has not caused him to ignore his role as Protector of all Religions, a duty he carries out by holding frequent discussions with Muslim and other religious group leaders. With his own funds he financed the translation into Thai of the *Koran* for the nation's Muslims.

He also personally hands out large numbers of diplomas to university graduates each year, sails, plays the saxophone and paints in addition to performing his ceremonial functions. His portrait hangs in most homes around the nation and his face is projected in cinemas before each movie with every viewer standing at attention while the royal anthem is played. It quickly becomes apparent to the visitor that this is not blind devotion to an autocratic leader but genuine respect engendered by his personality and by the works he has performed.

Forms of statecraft: Under the nation's Constitution (there have been 11 since 1932), government administration is vested in a tripartite system made up of executive, legislative and judicial branches. The legislature comprises a 260-member Senate appointed by the Cabinet and approved by the King and a 347-member Parliament elected from the nation's 73 provinces. Elections are held whenever the Prime Minister calls them, usually as the result of losing a vote of confidence in Parliament.

The Judicial branch of Thailand is comprised of 80 Courts of First Instance, a Court of Second Instance—an Appeals Court located in Bangkok—and a Supreme Court, also located in Bangkok. Civil court appointments are decided by a Judicial Council composed of sitting Supreme Court justices and retired justices subject to approval by the King. All courts operate independently of the Justice Ministry.

Executive power is wielded by a Prime Minister selected by the majority party or a coalition of parties. He formulates and executes policies through a Cabinet of 13 ministers. While the Prime Minister and the Parliament might seem far removed from the population except at election time, they are, in fact, responsive to the electorate. It is not unusual for a delegation of disgruntled citizens to rent a fleet of buses to lodge a noisy protest against an official or a decree with which they disagree.

Ministers, even the Prime Minister, talk with these delegations to remedy problems, though with the clamor generated by the local press it would be difficult for leaders to ignore their protests. In part, it reflects the sense of family which constantly appears in Thai conversations and in exhortations to stand together against common enemies. Although leaders are regarded as "fathers" and accorded the respect given to elders in Asia, they are accountable for their actions.

In large towns like Bangkok, administrative power is vested in the Municipality under the leadership of a popularly-elected governor. The long arm of the Interior Ministry reaches into the countryside to select provincial and district governors. At this point, the government's power theoretically ends and grass-roots democracy begins. *Pu Yai Baan* (village headmen or headwomen) are selected by the villagers themselves. A group of *Pu Yai Baan* elect one of their member as a *Kamnan* or commune head, the number of villages in each commune depending upon the populations of each individual villages.

It would be remiss not to mention another, very pervasive, force in Thai politics: the military, notably the army. Though not involved in politics or commerce to the extent it once was, the military has ways of making its wishes known and its influence felt. A new phalanx of officers, many of them educated abroad and responsive to social needs, has been moving up through the ranks and has been insisting that government officials be more mindful of social problems and initiate means to solve them.

The military and the monkhood—a young man's principal obligations in Thai society.

The pervasiveness of Buddhism: Down the centuries, Thailand has been dominated by a single religion: Buddhism. It is said that the Indian Emperor Asoka sent missionaries to convert the inhabitants of Thailand in the third century A.D. By the seventh century, there were Buddhist religious communities in Nakhon Pathom and Lopburi to the west and north of Bangkok; Sri Lankan monks were invited to 13th

century Sukhothai to purify the religion. Today, Buddhism is professed by 92 percent of the nation's population.

Present-day Thais practice Theravada Buddhism, also known as Hinayana or Lesser Vehicle, Buddhism. It calls for a priesthood of men who voluntarily enter the monkhood for at least 15 days once in their lives. Many enter and never leave, preferring a life of contemplation to the hurly-burly of secular life. The military must grant a soldier leave to join the monkhood should he so desire. Most Thai and foreign companies provide paid leave for monks' much the same way as Western companies give maternity leave to their employees.

The monkhood both educates a man in the tenets of the religion and allows him to make merit to atone for his sins so that when he is reincarnated, he will return as a higher being. When he becomes a monk, a Thai man makes merit not only for himself but for his mother and sisters as well. Although there are no ordained nuns, many women don white robes, shave their heads, and live in secluded parts of a monastery. There, they meditate but cannot preach nor officiate in ceremonies as monks do.

Monks are expected to live ascetically although the limits of "asceticism" have been stretched to include Volvos. Obliged to obey 227 moral precepts, they live on what they are provided by the laity. Each morning, they rise before dawn and put on their saffron robes. It is a moving sight to see these monks silently pad barefooted along the streets carrying their alms (do not insult them by calling them "begging") bowls which are filled with boiled rice and condiments by the Buddhist faithful waiting before their houses.

What's *Wat*: In addition to the famous *wats* tourists visit, there are literally hundreds of Buddhist *wats* in the city and suburbs, usually sited in serene pockets of densely-packed neighborhoods and serving as hubs for spiritual and social life. The term *wat* defines a large walled compound made up of several buildings including a *bot* or hall where new monks are ordained, and one or more *viharn* where sermons are delivered.

It may also contain a belltower, a *ho trai* (library) and *guti* or monk meditation cells as well as *stupas* (called *chedi* in Thailand) containing the ashes of wealthy donors, emulating the Buddha whose ashes and relics were placed, by his instruction, in a mound of earth. There may be a government school on the premises. If there is any open space in the grounds, it is a sure bet one will find it filled with happy children playing soccer or *takraw*.

"Sunday" for a Thai Buddhist is *wan phra,* a day of sermons each week according to the lunar calendar. At this time, the faithful take food to the monks who must eat before noon, and then sit listening to the monks chant sermons. During winter fairs, held to solicit donations to repair the *wat*, the *wat* compound becomes a carnival with rides, variety shows and the terrible din produced by loudspeakers at full volume. Fairs provide an insight into how ordinary Thais enjoy themselves. Finding the nearest one is no problem: just follow your ears.

Three Thai holidays—*Magha Puja* in February, *Visakha Puja* in May, and *Asalaha Puja* in July—occur on full moon nights and celebrate important events in the Buddha's life. Buddhists throughout Bangkok gather at their nearby *wat* shortly after dusk to hear special sermons. They then clasp their hands together before their faces, their fingers twined about flowers, incense sticks and candles, and as the full moon is rising, follow the monks in a procession three times around the *bot*. It is a magical, mystical night, made even more enjoyable for the visitor by the Thai penchant for welcoming outsiders' participation in their ceremonies, helping them with the particulars of buying candles and lighting incense.

The other Buddhism: Mahayana Buddhism is practiced by the nation's ethnic Chinese and Vietnamese. Although its doctrinal differences with Theravada Buddhism (which stresses that one who has reached enlightenment can pass directly to *nirvana*, a heaven of everlasting bliss, as opposed to Mahayana's belief that each person achieving *nirvana* has a responsibility to

Left, ceremonial blessing of a Thai airliner.

return to earth to help others reach the same goal) are minimal, the manner in which they celebrate is far removed.

Mahayana Buddhist activity takes place at temples with an outer court yard surrounding a high-ceilinged hall. The hall interior is dominated by a high altar backed by the principal Buddha images. The dimly lit interior is thick with incense smoke and the air resonates with the rattle of bamboo sticks being shaken out of cans to tell fortunes. In the court yard, houses, money and even Mercedes-Benz made of paper are burned in ovens and sent via the smoke to departed loved ones to help ease their lives in the afterworld. The atmosphere is one which Westerners associate with the mysticism of the East, which is a noisy, chaotic piety that masks a strength of belief as firm as an ancient rock.

Islam and others: Islam was introduced in southern Thailand during the 13th century when it was first brought into Malaysia by Arab traders. Today, some two million Thais, mostly in the South, profess the religion. About 99 percent of Thai Muslims are Sunni and one percent are Shi'ite. More than 100 mosques are found throughout the city. There are pockets of Muslims in the Makassan district just north of the Indra Hotel, and to the east in the Hua Mark region.

They intermingle with Thai Buddhists, and there has never been any friction. A special government fund finances the repair of mosques, government-employed Muslims are given special leave for important Muslim holidays and are required to work only half-days on Friday, which is the Islamic holy day. Like the special dispensation given to Buddhist men to enter the monkhood, Muslim men are given four months' leave with full salary to make the Haj pilgrimage to Mecca.

Christian missionaries have always been welcome to prosetelize in Thailand but have not had the success they had in some Asian countries. This is due in part to the strength and vitality of Buddhism and because Thailand lacked the Christian colonizers who occupied other Asian countries.

Today, Christians comprise less than one percent of the population and most are concentrated in Bangkok and a few major towns. Dozens of denominations exist and Roman Catholic, Anglican, Lutheran and numerous other churches are found around the city. It goes without saying that Thais enjoy any excuse for a festival and in the past few decades Christmas has become almost as popular as New Year, influenced in large part by department store promotions. Foreigners seeking to escape the interminable carols of the Christmas season are advised to avoid Bangkok.

While Bangkok's Indian population is scattered throughout the city, its four Hindu and two Sikh houses of worship are primarily in the Pahurat market area. Most religious holidays are observed privately except for the exuberantly celebrated Sri Mariamman festival in September. At the popular Hindu temple on Pan Road, a huge chariot is pulled along Silom Road in a colorful ceremony. People of all faiths join in, wrapping their hands around the heavy hawser to tug the great vehicle along and are showered with gifts of oranges.

Power of the unseen: Visitors are often baffled by the spirit houses found in front of office buildings, hotels and homes. They assume that spirit worship is somehow part of Buddhism since the spirit houses resemble Buddhist temples. As in many areas of the world, the belief in the spirits of rocks and trees to explain natural phenomena predates the advent of Buddhism. Despite the appeal of Buddha's teachings, spirits have maintained a tenacious hold on the Thai imagination.

Along highways one sees clusters of spirit houses built to pacify the tormented spirits of people who have died violent deaths in horrendous crashes at that site. One cannot build a house without performing ceremonies to ensure the spirits will feel welcome in the new house. Once it is built, a spirit house must be erected and offerings of flowers and incense placed at it every day to appease what can often be malevolent spirits. Thus, the two exist side by side, the Buddha's teachings ostensibly denying the existence of spirits. The Thais prefer to choose the safe route of double insurance, just in case.

Left, the Colonel oversees offerings at a new spirit house. Right, Thai classical musicians.

For the same reason, most Thai Buddhists wear necklaces bearing small amulets imprinted with a Buddha image. They are intended as reminders of the Buddha's precepts but are worn by many people as a talisman against harm, much in the way Catholics wear St. Christopher medals. In extreme examples, they are said to ward off bullets and knives.

Thai attitudes: Visitors are struck by the

ubiquity of Thai smiles and friendliness. Thais excel in transforming work into fun. The key concept is *sanuk*, a word which can be translated as "fun" or "enjoyable." Indeed, the quantity of *sanuk* activity contains is the gauge of whether or not it is worthwhile pursuing.

The demands of city life have changed much of the casual way of life formerly found in the countryside, but it is a rare Thai who does not enjoy getting together with his friends (the suggestion that one might go off on his own to a dinner or a holiday is decried by Thais as *mai sanuk*, "not fun"). Office life must contain a certain amount of chatting and passing around of snacks for it to avoid being *mai sanuk*, an attitude which would relieve the tedium of much of the office work found elsewhere in the world.

There is a sense of family about all Thai activities, a clustering that does not exclude outsiders. For the visitor invited to join one of these gatherings, it is a time of fun with food passed around without regard to who pays, of drinks shared with no expectation of reciprocation (and no sharing of the bill at the end of a meal; one person picks up the tab and it is never the visitor), of friendly questions, of openness seldom found elsewhere. It is not unusual for a visitor to wander into a small city lane and be invited to join a group for a meal or a drink, nothing more than his presence is required.

When a visitor encounters a tense situation, it is usually because of language difficulties. In this instance, it is best to adopt another Thai attitude, *jai yen* or "cool heart," dealing with the problem calmly to reach a solution. It is difficult to stir a Thai to real anger but touching him, shouting at him or in any way threatening his or her strong sense of independence will effect an immediate and often unpleasant response.

Closely allied with this is a concept that provides the answer to all life's vicissitudes: *mai pen rai*, a phrase that eludes precise translation but is usually rendered as "never mind." Thais would rather shrug their shoulders in the face of adversity than to escalate the situation. Any solution which contributes to re-establishing calm is welcomed. The Thais have survived intact as a sovereign nation by adopting a superb sense of compromise and not worrying about any inconsequential matters.

Time off: Half a century ago, there were 40 official holidays per year. That was the official number; how many "sick leave" days were taken to participate in other celebrations will never be known. The number of festivals on the Thai calendar (not including family celebrations like weddings and topknot cutting ceremonies) far exceeded 40. Today, official holidays have been reduced to 13 and unlike Hong Kong and Singapore, Thais work a five rather than a five-and-a half-day week.

Masked dance has been a mainstay of traditional Thai culture.

Three holidays are associated with events in Buddha's life (see page 55), four others celebrate important events in the life of the Royal Family—Chakri Day (April 6), Coronation Day (May 5), and the birthdays of His Majesty and Her Majesty (December 5 and August 12 respectively)—and are essentially private affairs. Two days are given for New Years, one for Constitution Day.

Three others are reserved for ancient festivals—Songkran, the Ploughing Ceremony and Loy Krathong—that are among the most fascinating in Asia. Then there are the smaller, unofficial festivals that brighten city life. (A complete list is found in Travel Tips.) Enough festivals are celebrated in Bangkok that it is possible to plan a vacation to coincide with at least one.

The arts: Thais have combined a lively imagination, a superb aesthetic sense and a fine hand to produce some of the most detailed and arresting visual arts found in Asia. In the performing arts, its dance dramas are among the world's most dazzling with elaborate costumes and graceful, enchanting movements.

Literature: Thais have always placed a heavy emphasis on oral tradition and it's a good thing too because most of its classical printed literature was completely destroyed by the flames of Ayutthaya's destruction which took place in 1767.

Moreover, as tropical insects have a particular relish for the palm leaf paper on which manuscripts are written, books are manifest examples of the Buddhist tenet that nothing is permanent. The classical works which exist today came from late night sessions during the reigns of Rama I and II when scholars delved into their collective memories and, on breeze-cooled palace verandas, recreated an entire literature.

At the heart of Thai literature is the *Ramakien*, the Thai version of the Indian classical tale, the *Ramayana*. This enduring story has found a home in the literature of every Southeast Asian nation. In Thailand, it forms the basis of a dance-drama tradition. Understanding it allows one to comprehend a wide variety of dramatic forms, its significance for Thailand's monarchs who have adopted the name Rama as their own, and its role as model for exemplary behavior.

The *Ramakien* is the vividly told tale of the god-king Rama and his beautiful wife, Sita, paragon of beauty and virtue and model for all wives (pre-Women's Lib) to follow. Sita is abducted by the nasty 10-headed, 20-armed demon king Tosakan, who imprisons her in his palace on the island of Longka, importuning her at every turn to divorce Rama and marry him.

With his brother Phra Lak, Rama sets off in pursuit, stymied by mammoth obstacles to test his mettle. Along the way, he is joined by the magical white monkey-god, Hanuman, a mischievous but talented general who is one of the Thais' favorite characters. Hanuman and his army of monkeys build a bridge to Longka. After a pitched battle, Tosakan is killed, Sita is rescued, and all live happily ever after (or until the sequel).

Another classical work, pure Thai in its flavor and treatment, is *Khun Chang, Khun Phaen,* a love triangle involving a beautiful young woman with two lovers, one a rich, bald widower and the other, a poor but handsome young man. This ancient soap opera provides a useful insight into Thai customs, manners and morals of the Ayutthaya era.

Written by Sunthorn Phu, the poet laureate of the early 18th century, *Phra Aphaimani* is the story of a rebellious prince who refuses to study to be king but instead plays the flute much to the disgust of his father. After numerous exciting adventures, this prodigal son returns home to don the crown and rule his father's realm. These

Left, young Thai dancers perform at Wat Rachanada. Right, a puppet play recreates popular stories.

stories or segments of them can be seen in Bangkok drama theaters or in Thai restaurants offering cultural shows.

Modern Thai writing is characterized by a social consciousness that focuses on the plight of the rural poor, on the impact of the city on the young and on those transplanted by economic necessity from the countryside of their birth, on alienation and on the struggle to make a life in a rapidly changing economy and society.

Drama: When discussing Thai theater, one cannot use the word "drama" without breathing the word "dance" immediately before it. The two are inseparable, the puppeteers danced the emotions they wanted the stiff figures to convey. It is thought that these movements evolved into an independent theatrical art.

The most popular form of dance-drama is the *Khon* performed by dancers wearing brilliantly crafted masks. An evening's entertainment comprises several episodes from the *Ramakien* (the entire *Ramakien* would take 720 hours to perform, slightly longer than even the most ardent theatergoer is prepared to endure). Only the characters of Rama, Sita and Phra Lak, appear without masks but their features are kept so stiff that they look like masks.

dancer's hands and body expressing the emotions that his silent lips do not. In effect, the actor is a mime with the story line and lyrics provided by a singer and chorus at one side of the stage. An orchestra creates not only the atmosphere but an emotive force.

It is thought that the movements of dance-drama originated in the *Nang Yai* performances of the 16th and 17th centuries. Huge buffalo hides were cut into the shapes of characters from the *Ramakien*. Against a translucent screen backlit by torches, puppeteers manipulated these figures to tell complex tales of good and evil. As they moved the hide figures across the screen, the

The expressionless masks focus the viewer's attention on the dancers' movements and here, one sees grace and control of surpassing beauty; a dismissive flick of the hand, a finger pointed in accusation, a foot stamped in anger. The favorite character is Hanuman in his white monkey mask, whose dance movements would tax even the strongest viewer.

The most graceful of the dramatic arts is the *Lakhon*. There are two forms: the *Lakhon Nai* (Inside *Lakhon*) which was once performed only inside the palace walls and only by women, and the *Lakhon Nawk* (Outside *Lakhon*) performed beyond the palace walls by men. Of the two, performances *Lakhon Nai* is the more popular.

Garbed in costumes as elaborate as their movements, the performaers glide slowly about the stage, even in the most emotional moments, their faces impassive, devoid of smiles or expression. The heavily stylized movements convey the plot and are quite enchanting, though for most foreign visitors 30 minutes is sufficient to absorb the essentials of the play. *Lakhon*'s rich repertoire includes the *Ramakien* and tales like *Inao* with romantic storylines.

The second culture: There have always been two cultures in Thailand: palace or at Lak Muang when a troupe is hired by a worshipper to give thanks for a wish granted or a lottery number that has hit. A variant often seen in markets is *Lakhon Ling*, the monkey theater where the principal roles are played, as the name suggests, by monkeys.

Bangkok's *Ngiew* or Chinese opera theaters have closed their doors forever, victims of television with its unending *kung fu* programs. Wandering in a market at night, however, one may come across a performance that has been arranged as part of the entertainment during a funeral (grief is experienced privately: what one shares with friends is happiness). They can also be seen

and village. The village arts are often parodies of the palace arts, burlesques with pratfalls and heavy-handed humor. *Likay* is the village form of *lakhon*. Broad, bawdy humor is its mainstay, played out against gaudy backdrops to an audience that walks in and out of the performance at will, eating and talking and having a good time regardless of what takes place on stage.

It is possible to glimpse *likay* at a *wat* fair at *wat* fairs during the winter.

Left, girls learn to dance with expressive finger movements at Silpakorn University while right, boys practice Ramakien monkey movements out in the courtyard.

Puppet theater has also lost most of its Bangkok audiences to TV but a few troupes remain. *Hoon Krabok* puppets similar to Punch and Judy puppets tell the story of *Phra Aphaimani*. Delicately crafted, they are charming to watch. Performances are often arranged by major hotels during the year-end holiday season.

Modern Thai drama has yet to come into its own in a major way. Leading hotels produce stage plays but they are primarily for popular entertainment; pastiches, soap operas, comedies, direct translations from plays which were popular in the West.

The village in the city: The counterparts to the grace and beauty of classical dance are the traditional dances performed in villages by farm families. Each region has its own special form.

Harvest, fingernail, candle and fishing dances are performed by groups of women in village costumes. In dances of flirtation they are joined by male dancers who attempt to weave romantic spells about their unsmiling but appreciative partners. These dances are performed at the Thai-style restaurants and at the cultural shows at the Rose Garden and other parks.

Music: Classical Thai music eludes all finely tuned ears. To the uninitiated, it sounds like a mishmash of contrasting tones without any pattern. To aficionados, it has a very distinct rhythm and plan. The key is to listen to it as one would jazz, picking out one of the instruments and following it, switching to another as the mood moves one.

Thai music is set to a scale of seven full steps but is normally played as a pentatonic scale (the scale of *Auld Lang Syne).* The rhythm is lilting and steady with speeds varying according to section. Each instrument plays the same melody but in its own way, seemingly without regard to how others are playing it (it sometimes seems as if politics has been set to music).

Seldom does an instrument rise in uninterrupted solo; it is always being challenged, cajoled by the other instruments of the orchestra. In a sense, it is the aural counterpart to Thai classical painting with every space filled and a number of separate strands woven together seemingly at random but with a distinct pattern.

A classical *Phipat* music orchestra is made up of a single reed instrument, the oboe-like *phi nai*, and a variety of percussion instruments. The pitch favors the treble with the result that the music sounds airy rather than stentorian. The pace is set by the *ching*, a tiny cymbal, aided by the drums beaten with the fingers. The melody is played by two types of *ranad,* a bamboo-bar xylophone and two sets of *gong wong,* tuned gongs arranged in a semi circle around the player. Another type of orchestra employs two violins, the *saw-oo* and the *saw-duang*. It is usually heard accompanying a Thai dance-drama.

Left, an exquisite lacquered window with figures of foreign traders. Right, a delicate-faced Buddha comes out of his cast in a foundry at Thonburi.

The *ja-kae*, a stringed instrument similar to a Japanese *koto*, sits flush with the floor and is often played as a solo instrument in the lobbies of some of Bangkok's larger hotels and restaurants. A separate type of orchestra performs at a Thai boxing match to spur the combatants to action. It is composed of four instruments: the *ching,* two double-reed oboe-like flutes and a drum. It plays a repertoire entirely its own.

Originating in the countryside but having found a permanent home in the city as well are the *klawng yao* or long drums. They are thumped along with gongs and cymbals as accompaniment to group singing. Never played solemnly, they lend an exuberant note to any occasion and for a Thai, it doesn't take much of an excuse to have an occasion. It may be a procession on the way to ordain a new monk, a bus trip up-country, or a *kathin* ceremony in the late autumn when groups board boats to travel upriver to give robes to monks at the end of the three-month lenten season.

The *klawng yao* beat an infectious rhythm, inviting one to join in a *ramwong*, a dance which, despite its simple steps and body movements, eludes most foreigners' attempts to execute. One's participation, not his skill, is important to a Thai. No one will force you; the rewards for joining are laughter and warm acceptance.

Architecture: It is odd that influences so diverse as those of India, Cambodia and China could be combined to produce an architecture that is unique, bearing little resemblance to its progenitors. Thai architecture does it brilliantly. The style of Bangkok's classical temples and palaces are the final step in a long eon of evolution that saw architecture styles change from massive to light, similar to that of how Romanesque evolved into the fragile Gothic architecture of Medieval Europe.

Like the architecture of Angkor Wat, every part of a Thai *wat* has symbolic significance. The capitals of columns are shaped either like water lilies or lotus buds, the lotus symbolizing the purity of Buddha's thoughts in that it pushes through the muck of swamps to burst forth in blooms of extraordinary beauty.

The *cho-fa* on the end of the roof represents the *garuda*, the vehicle of Vishnu; in its claws it holds two *naga*, mythical serpents that undulate down the eaves. The *garuda* is also a royal symbol and companies bearing it on their building facades operate By Royal Appointment. Every other other element on a *wat* has roots in ancient myth and legend.

Sculpture: The focal point of the *bot* and *viharn* interior is the Buddha image. The image is not considered a representation of the Buddha but is meant to serve as a reminder of his teachings. The casting in bronze or carving in wood or stone of Buddha images constitutes the bulk of Thai sculpture. Buddha images epitomize the zenith of the sculpting art and employ some of the finest artistry (and hence command some of the highest prices) of any arts. Superb examples of *bas relief* sandstone carving can be seen around the base of the *bot* of Wat Po. Delicately executed, the dozens of panels depict scenes from the Ramakien drama.

Painting: In similar manner, the inner walls of the *bot* and *viharn* are traditionally covered in paintings, usually displaying a high degree of skill. In the days before public education, a *wat* was the principal repository of knowledge for the common man. Monks were the teachers and the inner walls of the temples were illustrated lectures, cartoon strips as it were, of Buddhist lore.

The principal themes are the life of Buddha and the *Tosachat*, the last ten of 550 *chadok* (incarnations) of a single soul before he was born as the Buddha, thus ending a long cycle of lives and passing into *nirvana*. The *Tosachat* are moral tales illustrating selflessness, sacrifice and personal perfection of one's soul.

The back wall generally depicts the *Maravijaya* or Victory over Mara in which all the earthly temptations are united to break the meditating Buddha's will and prevent his achieving *nirvana*. He is guarded by the goddess *Mae Toranee* who helps him by wring-

ing out her hair, sending a torrent of water to drown the evil spirits.

The murals at Wat Buddhaisawan in the National Museum are among the finest examples of Thai painting. Others include the murals at Wat Suthat and the avant garde 19th-century paintings at Wat Bovironivet. Though restored several times with less than perfect accuracy or regard for previous artists' efforts, the *Ramakien* murals in the

Left, Royal Barge oarsmen at the Kathin ceremonies in 1987. Right, traditional lacquer hats worn by oarsmen of a second Royal Barge.

cloisters that surround Wat Phra Kaew include wonderful, whimsical scenes of village and palace life.

Royal and not-so-royal architecture: Palace architecture conveys a lightness similar to that of *wats*, employing many of the same motifs and materials. Homes for ordinary people share the same sensitive treatment as those for the exalted. Thai-style teak wood houses with their inward-sloping walls and steep roofs seldom fail to charm with their airiness and their marvellous adaptation to tropical climates.

Raised high off the ground on stilts, they are the perfect foil for floods and other intruders and allow the free flow of cool breezes. The best example is the Jim Thompson House with its superb collection of Thai art; numerous other examples line the banks of the silvery network of canals that crisscross the Thonburi suburbs.

Occupying the middle ground between the two is shophouse architecture in the Sino-Portuguese mode. Stout walls and often ornate window and roof treatments are the hallmark of a type of housing once preferred by Chinese shopkeepers. As in yesteryear, the downstairs serves as a place to market one's goods; the upstairs is the family home. Shophouses at Tha Chang boat landing to the northwest of the Grand Palace are particularly fine examples.

The minor arts: Thai classical minor arts are marked by a delicacy and sureness of execution. Among the most stunning are the lacquer and gold works that cover the window shutters of most *bot* and *viharn*. Thai artists employ the time-honored technique of covering a plank of wood with seven coats of *lac*, the black sap of the *sumac* tree. A scene is drawn on a sheet of rice paper and a pin is used to prick holes along the outlines. The paper is then laid on the lacquered wood and a bag of ashes or lime is tapped gently against the paper. When the paper is removed, lines of ash-white dots remain to indicate the pattern.

The artist then paints with the yellow sap of the *mai khwit* tree all the areas he wishes to remain black, much the same way a batik artist paints with wax those areas whose color he does not wish to change. When the paint has dried, he covers the entire surface with gold leaf. When the wood is gently washed with water, the gold over the *mai khwit* painted areas washes away, leaving the gold figures to gleam against the midnight sheen of the lacquer.

The best examples of lacquer painting can be found on walls of the Lacquer Pavilion in the Suan Pakkad Palace. It also decorates the ornate manuscript cabinets found at Suan Pakkad and in the Buddhaisawan Chapel.

Mother-of-pearl, as executed by Thai artists, differs from its Chinese counterpart both in the material and the technique used. Thai artisans use the Turban shell which secretes nacreous material along its outer rim which means that it will not peel with age as does the Chinese type.

Moreover, Thai artists cut the patterns in small bits, affix them to a wooden panel and fill the spaces between with the same black lac used in lacquer and gold artworks. Two of the finest examples are the 200-year-old doors of Wat Po with scenes from the *Ramakien* and the doors of Wat Rajabophit depicting in tiny detail the various royal decorations awarded to nobles of old.

Of teak and rosewood carving, not an art at which Thai craftsmen excelled, there are several fine examples, notably the doors of Wat Suthat carved by King Rama II. Goldworking, silversmithing, neilloware and manuscript painting (often as beautiful as the Medieval illuminated manuscripts) are other arts at which Thais are supremely skilled. Good examples can be found in the National Museum.

Lesser, but no less exacting and beautiful arts have evolved both from the palace and the village. Vegetables and fruits are carved into beautiful flowers, a palace art preserved by many of the city's major hotels. The fragrant garlands sold on street corners and at the Erawan Shrine are intricate, beautiful and incredibly inexpensive for the labor involved in making them. They seldom fail to seduce visitors into taking them to their hotels to bathe their rooms in delicate scents. Thai artisans also bring a high level of skill to basket weaving, artificial flower crafting and a host of other arts requiring extreme dexterity and patience.

Modern arts: Modern Thai painting is devoted to three principal themes: country scenes, abstract art and an exploration of Buddhist subjects. Of the three, the genre with the most artistic merit are the reinterpretations of old Buddhist themes. Country scenes, while evoking the beauty of the Thai rural areas, are usually turned out in great quantities to satisfy a desire for "something to decorate the living room wall." Although some good works exist, abstract art travels down a well-trodden road taken by Western artists some years ago.

To gain an appreciation of the types of entertainment which appeal to ordinary Thais, especially those in up-country villages, step into an air-conditioned theater. Shot on low budgets, the films are, with rare exception, made from templates rather than scripts. They consist of recycled soap opera material that runs the gamut from pathos to comedy to romance to action with a heavy dose of macho confrontation that seems at odds with the gentle people one encounters on travels through the city or countryside. Alternatively, there are the boy-meets-girl movies with the latest teenage heartthrob romancing the shy ingenue.

Right, this larger-than-life movie poster attracts instant attention.

PRINT
45
MIN.
45 Min.
Sold and serviced by
Kodak
DRUG STORE
ถ่ายรูปสี ขาวดำ
1 ชั่วโมงได้
SONY
NEC
INDRA
TAXI

tac
tac
TAXI
TAXI

PLACES

Bangkok, City of Angels, is an assault on the senses, a maelstrom of sights, sounds and scents that the traveler both absorbs and is absorbed by, drawn into a culture and held fast by its allure. On the surface it looks like an ordinary city; penetrate its mask and you discover everything you expected the exotic Orient to be.

How you break through is another matter. It is not easy to find your way around Bangkok. With a flat landscape, no discernable city center (not even a defined business district or diplomatic enclave) and a road system without logic (including schizoid streets that change their names four times along their length) it is the very antithesis of a planned city. Like much about Thailand, it just happened.

This leaves the traveler with both a dilemma and a challenge. He can depend on the wisdom of tour guides (an easy way out) or taxi drivers (assuming their English is up to it) or simply accept the challenge and head out, making his own discoveries.

For the traveler with lots of time to spare, the latter course of action is of course the most rewarding, one that allows him to see Bangkok in depth, the way it should be seen. There are surprises lurking everywhere, many of them beyond the scope of this book to incorporate and therein lies the city's charm. Bangkok is a city you unfold like a patterned silk, discovering its multi-hued, multi-layered beauty as you explore its breadth and richness.

Where to start?: By taking big areas and breaking them into small areas. Bangkok, or *Krungthepmahanakorn* as it is officially known, encompasses land west and east of the Chao Phya River. The section west of the river is called **Thonburi**. Aside from the riverside Wat Arun, Wat Rakang, the Royal Barge Museum and the myr-

iad fascinating canals that slice through the countryside, there is not much for a traveler to do, so already he has half the city under control.

Bangkok east of the river presents a bigger problem. Aside from the Golden Mount there are no prominent landmarks. The best is to start as the city itself started and work outward and eastward; that is, to begin with the area where most tourists spend their first day in Bangkok, the old Royal City called **Ratanakosin Island**. Embraced by a bend of the Chao Phya River and Klong (canal) Lawd, it contains the city's principal palaces, temples and other monuments. From there, you move off the island to an area bounded on the east by the city wall. The remaining sights are beyond the wall.

While all the attractions noted are worth certainly seeing, it is recognized that many travelers have very little time at their disposal. Thus, we have noted "must see" sights and appended comments on the relative interest of others. In some cases, we have noted only the salient points about a site, leaving it to leisurely travelers to discover the other treasures it offers.

Preceding pages: Entrance to Lumpini Park; Bangkok's notorious traffic; entrance to Wat Arun. Left, Emerald Buddha awaits offerings of the King and Queen while a crowd burns incense in the courtyard outside (right).

Getting to and around the Royal City is reasonably easy. A hotel limousine, taxi or public bus will deliver you there, and once there it is easy to find your way around. Although Bangkok is not a city for strollers—the noise and broken sidewalks defeat all but the hardiest—the Royal City presents the most promising opportunities for wandering and photographing. To minimize the effects of Bangkok's torrid heat, confine walking and temple touring to the morning, shop at midday and spend the late afternoons relaxing on the canals.

Thai command of English is not quite to the level of Hong Kong or Singapore, but Thai helpfulness in getting you where you want to go (even conducting you there) more than makes up for the linguistic deficiencies. A welcome move is the recent decision by the Bangkok Bank to post some of its staff as part-time tour guides at important tourist sites. Fluent in English and French, they make themselves available to tourists needing information.

The maps found in this section should suffice to orient you but more detailed maps sold in bookstores are listed in the Travel Tips section. Note that the words *Thanon*, *Soi* and *Trok* on street signs mean "Street (or Road), Lane and Alley" respectively. *Tha* or *Ta* means "landing" or "dock," *Klong* means "canal."

Beginning at the beginning: Between the river and Klong Lawd lies the heavenly city in which the angels of this City of Angels are said to live. It is an area rich with some of Asia's most stunning architecture, a tribute to the artistic skills of its creators and testament to the strength of belief in religion and the nation.

At its very heart is **Wat Phra Kaew**, the Temple of the Emerald Buddha, Thai Buddhism's holiest edifice. Like St. Peter's to Catholics and Mecca to Muslims, Wat Phra Kaew is a beacon, a

focal point of a Thai Buddhist's attention, a sacred site to be defended with his life. The Wat Phra Kaew/Grand Palace complex covers an area of 2.43 million square feet (218,400 square meters) and is encompassed by a crenelated brick wall 1.2 miles (1.9 km) in circumference. On entering the gate on Na Phralan Road, look left across a grassy esplanade to the glittering spires of Wat Phra Kaew.

The beauty and grandeur of the view is matched only by the one you receive on entering the temple courtyard itself. The imagination that created it was inspired not only with religious fervor but with a superb sense of fantasy. Everywhere are reminders of a world little known to outsiders, a world of mythical beasts and demons.

The 20-foot (six-meter)-tall *yaksa* (demons) who guard the portals, the demons in their sparkling uniforms who, Atlas-like, support the golden *chedi* on their hands, the ethereal gilded bronze half-bird, half-human *kinara* and *kinaree* who watch from the upper terraces, the proud *singha* (lions) that stand sentinel at the *bot* doors, the fierce, spear-bearing warriors on the *bot* doors who guard against the entry of evil spirits, all suggest imagination run rampant like a small child frightening himself with tales of imaginary beings.

Buddha reached Enlightenment on the banks of a river while facing the rising sun, so by tradition, the main buildings of all *wat* must face either east or a body of water. Hence, the central structure of Wat Phra Kaew, the **Chapel Royal**, completed in 1784 by Rama I (1782-1809), is built on an east-west axis.

Everything about the Chapel suggests the brilliance of the sun. Its outer walls are covered in gleaming leaf-shaped golden tiles. The windows are encrusted with gilded angels, the doors bear *dvarabaan* guardians, the red ceilings are a celestial vault with lotuses rendered in gold.

Entry is through the two flanking doors; the central door is reserved solely for the King. Inside, one's attention is immediately drawn to a small statue high on a pedestal in the center of the hall: the **Emerald Buddha**, the most sacred image in the realm. The30-inch (75 cm) tall, 18-inch (45 cm) wide jadeite image often disappoints visitors expecting something more grand. In fact, the image more than makes up for its small size with an event-filled history stretching back centuries.

The image first appeared in Chiang Rai in 1434. Lightning shattered an old *chedi* revealing a stucco image. For decades, it was regarded as inferior and ignored. Years later, the stucco coating crumbled away revealing a translucent green image glowing in an unearthly manner. A series of miracles confirmed its special nature. Thought to bestow fortune on the kingdom that possessed it, it became the object of great battles that saw it move across the map over the next few centuries.

The statue eventually found its way to Vientiane, Laos. In 1780, it was captured from the Laotians by the future King Rama I. It finally rested at Wat Arun until the completion of the Chapel Royal to which it was moved amid great rejoicing. There, from its lofty pedestal, it has watched over worshippers and the kingdom for 200 years. At its base, Thais place candles and incense sticks while praying for blessings and forgiveness.

The other buildings of the complex are equally impressive. To the north on a raised terrace are three structures nearly as sacred as the Emerald Buddha. Surrounded by gilded bronze *kinara* (male) and *kinaree* (female) with their graceful flowing lines, is the **Prasad Phra Thepidon** or Royal Pantheon. The original was built in 1855 but was destroyed by fire and was rebuilt in 1903. The handsome building with its tiled roof topped by a Khmer-like *prang* or spire holds statues of the first eight Chakri kings.

To its west is the **Library** built to hold the *Tripitaka*, the holy Buddhist

Preceding pages: Wat Phra Kaew at sunset. Below, drawing room of the Chakri Mahaprasad in the Royal Palace.

scriptures. The original building was also destroyed by fire, ignited by fireworks during a festival to celebrate its completion. It has an air of fragility about it; stand at its base and gaze up its thin columns that seem to go on forever into the sky. Its glory is its delicate, multi-tiered roof fashioned like the crown of a Thai king.

Perhaps the most impressive of the three is the gold-clad **Phra Si Ratana Chedi** built on a similar design of Phra Si Sanphet in Ayutthaya. The elephants at its base recall the white elephants possessed by previous Thai kings, the number of white elephants an Asian monarch owned signified the power he held. To the north of this trio is a model of the **Angkor Wat**, which is a magnificent stone city of the gods built by the Khmer empire of Kampuchea during the 12th century. Belltowers, shrines, statues and boundary markers fill the rest of the courtyard.

Enclosing the complex on four sides are cloisters whose murals tell the marvellous *Ramakien* story like one gigantic comic strip. To convey several incidents in an episode, a character or group of characters appears several times in the same background, compartmentalized by rows of trees and palace walls like comic strip frames.

If you are not familiar with the story, concentrate on the small scenes of ordinary life: fairs with shadow puppet theaters and other amusements, home life, courting and flirtation, children playing ancient games they still play today, even opium smokers and gamblers. The murals have been repainted several times over the past two centuries, but while they have lost some of their original fine detail, they retain their energy and vivacity.

The 100 baht ticket includes entry to Wat Phra Kaew, the Grand Palace and Vimarn Mek. Opening hours are 8:30 a.m. through 4 p.m. daily. A gate located in the southwest corner of the compound leads into the Grand Palace.

Until 1946 the home of kings, the **Grand Palace** is worthy of the adjective that appends its name. Its breadth of scope and design conveys regal grandeur with structures that sparkle like Thai eyes. Thais tend to build complexes piecemeal, one building at a time, one often replacing a previous structure. This gives them a chance to stand back and take a long look before moving on to the next bit of construction. Unfortunately, they tend to squeeze a lot of buildings into very small spaces so there are few unobstructed vistas from which one can fully appreciate their beauty.

The centerpiece, the magnificent **Chakri Mahaprasad**, was the last building to be constructed, completed in 1882 by King Rama V, also known as King Chulalongkorn. Chulalongkorn engaged British architects to build a grand hall where the elephant stables had formerly stood. They chose an Italian Renaissance style but traditionalists in the royal court objected to such a foreigner in their midst and asked that it be modified by crowning it with three

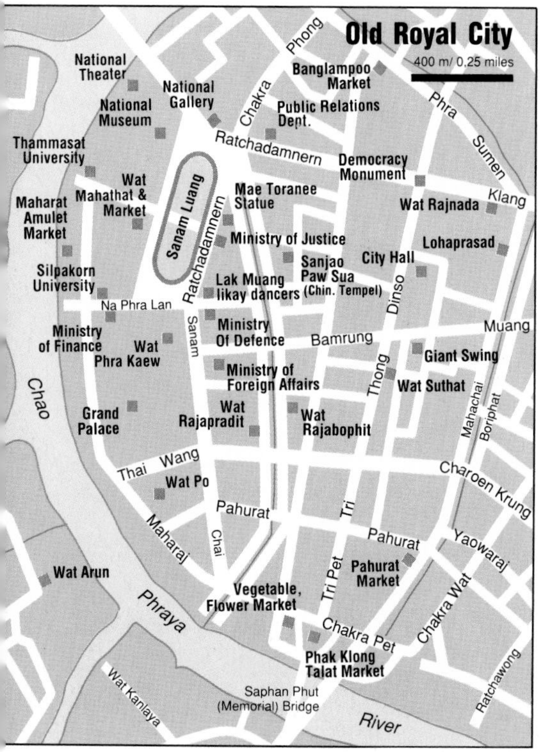

very Thai spires. The result is often referred to as "the *farang* (foreigner) wearing a *chada,*" the tiered headdress worn by Thai classical dancers.

The central spire holds a golden urn containing the ashes of past Chakri kings. The pair on either side hold the ashes of princes of royal blood. The courtyard is dotted with ornamental ebony trees cut in Chinese style like a poodle's tail. Heavy drapery, gold filigree and portraits of Chakri monarchs fill the interior.

To the left of the Chakri Mahaprasad is a door that once led to the royal harem to which no man except the king was admitted. The palace guard in this sector was composed entirely of women, a contingent of Amazons whose prowess with sword and the martial arts matched that of most men.

West of the Chakri Maha Prasad is the delightful **Dusit Maha Prasad**, built in 1789, the first brick building to replace the original flammable wooden buildings. It stands on the site of the former Amarindrabhisek, a wooden building that was struck by lightning and burned to the ground. As the flames crackled, King Rama I personally carried out the heavy teak throne.

Considered to be pure Siamese architecture, its nine-cornered *chedi* caps its steep roof; *garudas*, the vehicles of the god Rama, guard the gables. Formerly an audience hall, it is now the final resting place of deceased kings before their cremation on Sanam Luang. The furniture surrounding the throne belonged to Rama I.

East of the Chakri Maha Prasad is a building whose bricks resonate with history. Built by Rama I, the **Amarin Vinitchai Throne Hall** is the northernmost of the three-building group known as the Maha Montien. The group served as the bedchamber for Rama I and the royal residence for Rama II and III. In the early days of Bangkok it was also the royal court of justice where cases were heard and adjudicated by either the king or his ministers. And by tradition, each new king spends the first night after his coronation here.

Its exterior is rather ordinary. The elephants of visiting dignitaries and nobles were tethered at the gold-topped red poles which stand at the entrance. Inside, the throne sits atop a boat-shaped base. In former days, this was hidden by a screen of brocade curtains. At the appointed time, conch shells blared a fanfare and the curtains parted to reveal the seated king, ready to begin an audience. From this first hall, only the highest princes passed into the second two buildings, the Paisal Taksin and the Chakrabardibiman.

The inner buildings of the Grand Palace complex include the **Borompiman Hall**, a guesthouse for state visitors, and the **Sala Sahathai**, used for royal banquets; they are not open to visitors. The Grand Palace is open daily, 9 a.m. through 6 p.m.

On leaving the complex, stop at the **Coins and Royal Decorations Museum** which contains a beautiful collection of coins dating from the 11th cen-

...eft, ...aborate ...of detail ... the Dusit ...a-...prasad. ...ight, a ...ore ...mplete ...ew.

tury A.D. The hall also holds royal regalia, decorations and medals made of gold and studded with precious stones. Open daily except Sunday from 9 a.m. through 3:30 p.m. Admission fee: 20 baht per person.

North of Wat Phra Kaew is **Sanam Luang**, the field of kings. The northern half of this huge oval was once covered by the Wang Na or Palace of the Front, the home of the Second King, a Vice-King who ruled when the King was indisposed. Late in the 19th century, the eastern half of the Wang Na was dismantled leaving only the western half which is now the National Museum.

Sanam Luang is a superb site for viewing Wat Phra Kaew and other royal buildings. It is also the venue for some of Thailand's most important royal ceremonies. To begin with, it is the cremation ground for deceased kings. Enormous cremation pavilions are specially erected for the occasion and are dismantled once the body has been consumed. The Plowing Ceremony, the New Years festival, and the anointing of the Phra Buddha Sihing, considered the kingdom's second holiest Buddha image the day before Songkran, also take place here.

A parade passes Sanam Luang.

The real excitement occurs in March and April when the zephyrs waft over the field and the kite season begins. Besides ordinary kites, there are giant combatants in the war for supremacy of the skies (see Sports). In the northwest corner, *takraw* players battle it out.

West of Sanam Luang are **Thammasat University**, the **National Theater** and, sandwiched between them, the **National Museum**. One of the largest museums in Southeast Asia, the National Museum at 4 Na Phrathat Rd. (Tel. 221-2522, 234-1396) houses the nation's biggest, most comprehensive collection of Thai art as well as a large collection of Southeast Asian art.

The Thai collection spans the eons between the Neolithic and the present and includes some of Asia's most striking bronze sculpture. Of special interest are the rooms filled with palanquins and elephant howdahs, ancient weapons, dioramas of pre-historic life, boats, old photographs, textiles, costumes, puppets, flags and porcelains.

Some of the best mural paintings Thai artists have ever created cover the walls of the **Buddhaisawn Chapel** in the Museum compound. Along the lower portions of the walls are superb renditions of 28 scenes from the Buddha's life. Above the windows, five bands of *thep* (angels) kneel in silent respect to the realm's second most sacred Buddha image, the Phra Buddha Sihing in the center of the hall. The paintings, dating from between 1795 and 1797, are a joy to behold.

The museum is open daily except Mondays and Fridays from 9 a.m. to noon and 1 p.m. to 4 p.m. Adults: 20 baht; children: 10 baht. Guided tours begin at 9:30 a.m. and are free. They are offered in various languages as follows:

English: Thai Art and Culture (Tuesdays), Buddhism (Wednesdays), Pre-Thai and Thai Art (Thursdays).

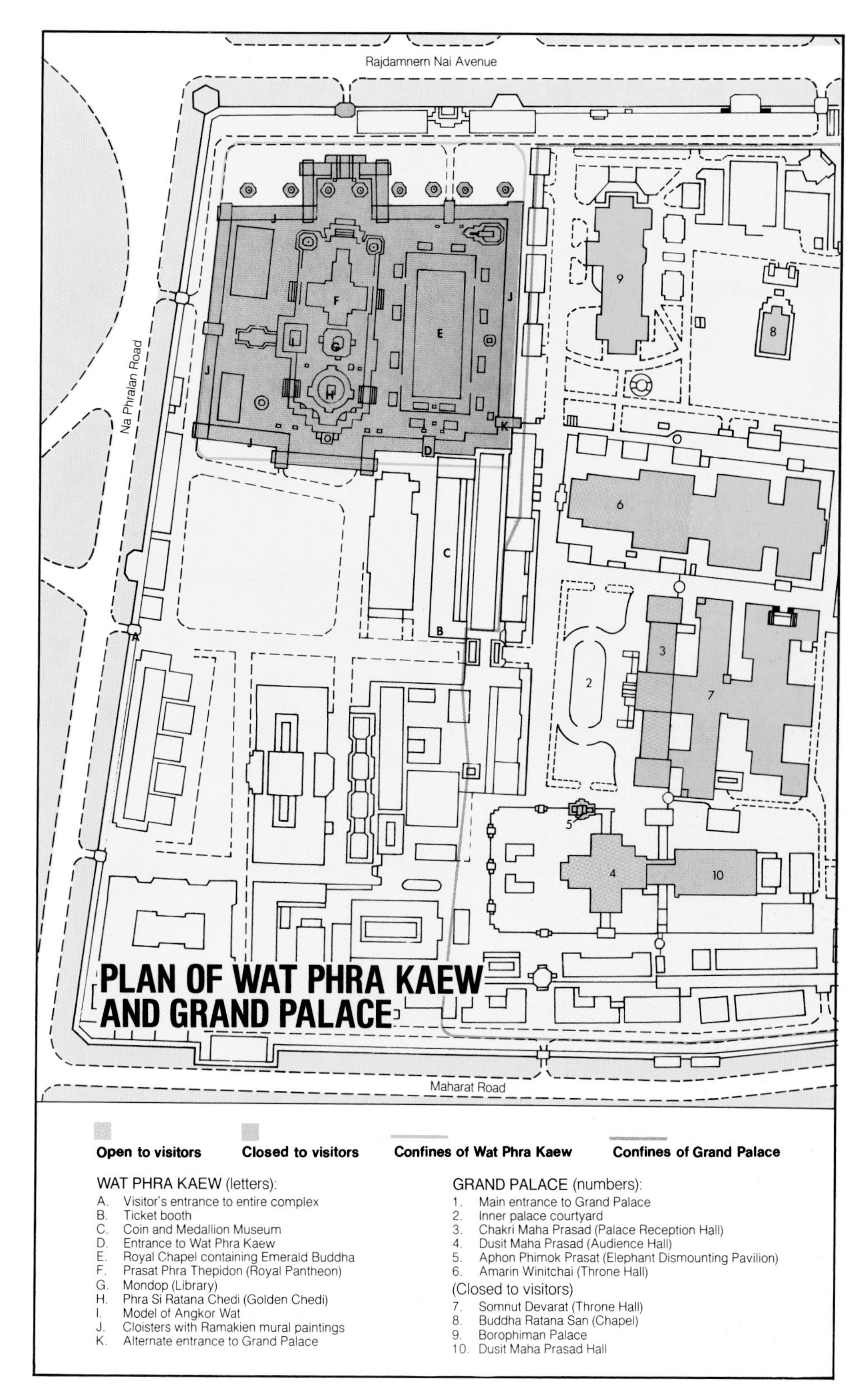
Rajdamnern Nai Avenue
Na Phralan Road
Maharat Road
PLAN OF WAT PHRA KAEW
AND GRAND PALACE
Open to visitors
Closed to visitors
Confines of Wat Phra Kaew
Confines of Grand Palace
WAT PHRA KAEW (letters):
A. Visitor's entrance to entire complex
B. Ticket booth
C. Coin and Medallion Museum
D. Entrance to Wat Phra Kaew
E. Royal Chapel containing Emerald Buddha
F. Prasat Phra Thepidon (Royal Pantheon)
G. Mondop (Library)
H. Phra Si Ratana Chedi (Golden Chedi)
I. Model of Angkor Wat
J. Cloisters with Ramakien mural paintings
K. Alternate entrance to Grand Palace
GRAND PALACE (numbers):
1. Main entrance to Grand Palace
2. Inner palace courtyard
3. Chakri Maha Prasad (Palace Reception Hall)
4. Dusit Maha Prasad (Audience Hall)
5. Aphon Phimok Prasat (Elephant Dismounting Pavilion)
6. Amarin Winitchai (Throne Hall)
(Closed to visitors)
7. Somnut Devarat (Throne Hall)
8. Buddha Ratana San (Chapel)
9. Borophiman Palace
10. Dusit Maha Prasad Hall

French: Pre-Thai and Thai Art (Wednesdays).

German: Thai Art and Culture (Thursdays).

Japanese: Thai Culture and Pottery (first two Tuesdays of the month), Buddhaisawan Chapel (third Tuesday of the month), Pre-Thai and Thai Art (fourth Tuesday of the month).

Spanish and Portuguese: Pre-Thai and Thai Art (Wednesdays).

North of Sanam Luang across the busy approach to the Phra Pinklao Bridge is the **National Gallery** at 4 Chao Fa Road (Tel 281-2224). Less interesting than the National Museum, the gallery exhibits traditional and contemporary Thai art. Open every day except Monday and Friday from 9 a.m. to noon, 1 p.m. through 4 p.m. Admission fee: 10 baht.

Off the northeast corner of Sanam Luang is the intriguing statue of **Mae Toranee**. A key figure from the Buddha's life, the statue was erected by King Chulalongkorn at the turn of the century as a public water fountain. The goddess wrings torrents of water out of her hair to wash away evil spirits threatening the meditating Buddha. It is an apt symbol in a city that each September and October submerges Atlantis-like as the Chao Phya River, swollen by monsoon rains, spills over its banks and floods Bangkok's streets.

Opposite the northeast corner of Wat Phra Kaew is **Lak Muang**, the first structure King Rama I (1782-1809) built in 1782. It swarms with Thais making wishes for success in life. Recently enlarged and re-decorated, Lak Muang is the home of the city's guardian spirit. In it is a stout *Siva lingam* honoring the powerful Hindu god Siva. It is a potent symbol of the city's strength. Next to this is a recent addition, the pillar of Thonburi over which Bangkok's governor now rules. Its main attraction is the *likay* theater performance paid for by supplicants whose wishes have been granted. Open daily 7 a.m. through 4:30 p.m. Free.

Lak Muang symbolizes the city's strength. Right, museum piece.

South of Wat Phra Kaew is **Wat Po**, site of the Reclining Buddha and one of Bangkok's most important and certainly most intriguing *wats*. Bangkok's oldest and Thailand's largest temple complex, Wat Po contains some of the kingdom's finest art. You enter by the south gate on Chetupon Road.

Built in the 16th century, it took 12 years for Rama I to restore it, beginning in 1789. Its chief attraction is the massive **Reclining Buddha** that occupies the whole of a *virhan* in the northwest corner of the complex. Measuring 152 feet (46 meters) long by 50 feet (15 meters) high and plated in gold, it depicts the dying Buddha lying on his side, the position in which he chose to enter *Nirvana*. Walk around to his feet to see the intricately-wrought designs in mother-of-pearl. The 108 symbols on his soles are the ancient signs by which a Buddha can be recognized.

Wat Po's *bot* is considered to be one of Bangkok's most beautiful. Girdling its base are sandstone panels superbly carved depicting scenes from the *Ramakien*; nearby vendors sell handsome rubbings of them. The equally-striking *bot* doors are also devoted to *Ramakien* scenes brilliantly rendered in some of the finest of mother-of-pearl work found in Asia. The cloisters surrounding it contain some of Bangkok's finest Buddha images.

Wat Po has been called Thailand's first university. Its walls were once covered in murals depicting people and places of the world, a veritable illustrated encyclopedia. Today, it houses a school of herbal medicine. In the old days, the stone *rishi* (hermits) in the courtyard were aids in diagnosing illnesses. Against the eastern wall is a hall of masseurs who employ traditional methods to squeeze fatigue and pain from travel-weary muscles. Try it for only 120 baht per hour. Open 8 a.m. through 4 p.m. daily. Wat Po is open daily from 8 a.m. through 5 p.m. Admission fee: 10 baht.

On Prachan Road, **Wat Mahathat**,

Commercial transactions at Wat Po. Right, entrance to Wat Po.

whose name translates as "the Great Relic Monastery" (there are nine Great Relic *wats* in Thailand), houses Mahachulalongkorn Buddhist University, one of the two most important monks' schools in Thailand. The original Ayutthaya-period *bot* was destroyed in 1782 by fireworks. There is little to recommend the visitor about its successor which was reconstructed in 1844 and became an important meditation center in Thailand. The largest *bot* in Bangkok, it is very plainly decorated having almost the austerity of a New England meeting hall. The *wat* is most interesting on *wan phra* Buddhist holy days, a time when it becomes an open market for, among other things, herbs and medicinal plants.

Farther west at **Maharat Landing** is an amulet market with an array of Buddhist amulets, images and occult objects including phalluses which are worn around the waist or placed at an alter to induce potency or fertility.

Of interest primarily to art lovers is **Wat Rajapradit**, a beautiful small haven of peace on Saranrom Road with its *bot* covered in gray Chinese marble. The *wat* is a study in Asian art styles with a Sinhalese *stupa* behind it; to the east, a *Traipidok* prang in Khmer style; and on the west a third in the style of the *Bayon* at *Angkor Thom* in Kampuchea. Especially interesting are the *bot* murals of the ancient Royal Ceremonies of the 12 months painted in 1864. Open daily from 9 a.m. to 6 p.m. Free.

Across the river: Within easy reach of the Grand Palace are three sites on the western bank of the Chao Phya River. Directly across the river from Tha Chang Wang Luang landing is **Wat Rakang**, one of Bangkok's prettiest *wats*. Built by Rama I, it sits back from the river and offers a lovely cross-river view of the Grand Palace.

Rakang translates as "bell" and describes the many sonorous bells rung at 8 a.m. and 6 p.m. each day. The *wat* itself is without particular artistic distinction but the library behind it has

Buddha-bedecked interior of Wat Mahathat.

superb murals, dating from 1788, of the *Ramakien* and the *Traiphum* (Three Worlds), the Buddhist cosmology. Nearby are three wooden houses once occupied by Rama I. They and their superb gold and lacquer windows were restored in 1982 by Fua Harapitak, one of Thailand's leading artists.

One of Thailand's most impressive structures, **Wat Arun** is the image most people conjure up when they think of Bangkok. Better known as the **Temple of Dawn**, Wat Arun appears in the Tourism Authority of Thailand's logo. Reach it via ferry from the Tha Tien landing, a superb vantage point for an early morning photograph.

Like other towers in Bangkok, it has undergone several incarnations in reaching its present height of 343 feet (104 meters). In the Ayutthaya period, it was only 50 feet (15 meters) tall. In 1780, King Taksin stored the Emerald Buddha in its *viharn*. Rama II began, and Rama III completed, the work of raising its base to 122 feet (37 meters) and building atop it a 221-foot (67-meter) *prang*.

The *prang* represents Mount Meru, the earthly representation of the 33 heavens; the topmost heaven is guarded by a ring of demons. At the four corners are four smaller *prangs* each with niches containing equestrian statues of *Phra Pai*, the god of the wind.

You reach the upper terrace by one of four stairways located at the four cardinal points. At the bottom of each stairway is a pavilion containing an image of Buddha at the four key events in his life: birth, meditation while sheltered by a seven-headed *naga* serpent, preaching to his first five disciples and in an attitude of death attended by his followers. At the top of each stairway is a niche containing the figure of the god Indra riding a three-headed elephant.

The climb to the terrace is rewarded by a view of the river and of the temples and city beyond. Here, also you gain a close-up view of the *prang*'s unique decoration. The surface is a field of

Monk's quarters at Wat Arun.

flowers made from pieces of broken Chinese pottery, some of it quite rare, donated by Buddhist devotees. The courtyard surrounding the *prang* is guarded by tall *yaksa* demons. A song every child sings tells how the *yaksa* of Wat Arun fight the *yaksa* of Wat Po. Open daily, 9 a.m. through 5 p.m. Five baht for admission.

The Royal Barge ceremony is a rare event so spectacular that it alone would justify a trip to Bangkok. Held in October, a fleet of 51 barges floats majestically down the Chao Phya River carrying the King to Wat Arun to present new saffron robes to the monks. The presentation ceremony, called *Kathin*, marks the end of the three-month Rains Retreat or Buddhist Lent, a period during which the monks remain in the monastery and alms are taken to them by the Buddhist laity.

The decoration of the low, narrow barges represents the epitome of woodcarving skill in the kingdom. The barges are propelled by the arms of 2,200 brilliantly-uniformed oarsmen who chant ancient hymns to count cadence. Anyone who has seen it will testify that it is one of the most moving sights and sounds Asia can offer, a ceremony so beautiful it plunges viewers into awed silence as it passes.

Unfortunately, the ceremony is only held on rare occasions—*Kathin* ceremonies in 1967 and 1987 and the Bicentennial celebrations in 1982—though there has been some clamor to make it a yearly event. It is possible to experience its visual beauty by visiting the **Royal Barge Museum** on the bank of Klong Bangkok Noi.

The museum is easily reached by boat but if traveling by car, go to 80/1 Rim Klong, Arun-Amarin Road in Thonburi (Tel. 424-0004). Here, you'll find the *Sri Suphannahongse* whose prow resembles the mythical swan for which it is named after. The 145-foot (44-meter)-long barge bears the King during the procession.

Also here is the *Anantanagaraj* with its seven-headed *naga* serpent bow and representatives of each of the other classes of barge. The lush gilded vegetation which decorates the sides of the barges is superbly carved. Open daily from 8 a.m. through 6 p.m. 10 baht admission. To see how the procession looked in the old days, see the mural paintings in the *bot* of Wat Pathumawanaram on Rama 1 Road.

Between the island and the city wall: For sheer beauty, few *wats* can rival **Wat Rajabophit** on Rajabophit Road off Atsadang Road. Built by Rama V (1868-1910) in 1870, it marks a radical departure from other *wats*. Its tall *chedi* is enclosed in a circular cloister covered in yellow tiles that seem suffused with the bright tropical sun.

Built into the northern wall is an ornate *bot* with doors covered in finely-detailed mother-of-pearl insignias of the five royal ranks, a motif repeated in the windows. Open the doors to the interior which looks like a miniature Gothic cathedral with a vaulted ceiling in brown with gold leaf on the ribbing.

A Royal Barge in full regalia on the Chao Phya. Right, majestic Wat Arun.

The *wat* is open daily from 8 a.m. through 8 p.m. Free admission.

Wat Bovornivej on Phrasumane Road was built by Rama III in 1827 and lived in by Rama IV (1851-1868) for most of the 27 years he was a monk. It is the home of the Supreme Patriarch, the "Pope" of Thai Buddhists, it has been chosen by kings including King Bhumibol for their ordinations as monks. Catholic theologian Thomas Merton died here.

Of particular merit in this otherwise drab *wat* are the superb paintings in the *bot*. The artist, Khrua In Khong, never traveled outside Thailand yet blazed new trails away from the traditional two-dimensional approach to painting by introducing three-dimensional perspective in the style of the 16th century Venetian school.

He probably saw the subjects he painted—ante-bellum Southern mansions, American race courses—only in pictures and postcards yet he brilliantly employed them in somber yet arresting fashion to illustrate Buddhist themes. At the bottom of walls dark hues indicating evil, it becomes lighter as one's eye ascends towards the ceiling where good is depicted.

The paintings on the double row of columns running from back to front of the *bot* relate the progress of man from barbarous to exalted state in accordance with Buddhist precepts. The murals are unique in the history of Thai painting. You may have to ask the monks to open the *bot*. Open daily 8:30 a.m. to 10 p.m.

Wat Suthat on Bamrungmuang Road contains Bangkok's tallest *viharn*, some splendid wood carvings and a courtyard of intriguing Chinese statuary. The *viharn* is the first building on your right. Begun during the reign of Rama I and requiring 27 years to complete, it was built to hold the 26-foot (eight-meter) tall 14th century bronze *Phra Sri Sakyamuni Buddha* moved downriver on barges from Sukhothai's Wat Mahathat, a gargantuan feat of engineering considering the times.

Wat Rajabhopit

ORGANIZED TOURS

Bangkok tour agencies combine several attractions in small packages that make easy work of sightseeing. All offer substantially the same tours for the same reasonable prices. The tours are conducted in English, French or German and guests are transported by air-conditioned coach. Many agencies maintain desks in hotels where tours can be booked. Here is a typical menu of the tours offered:

Grand Palace, **Emerald Buddha** (half-day; a.m., p.m.): Grand Palace, Wat Phra Kaew.

City and Temples (half-day; a.m., p.m.): Wat Benchamabophit, Wat Po, Wat Traimitr.

Jim Thompson House and **Suan Pakkad Palace** (half-day, a.m.).

Damnern Saduak, **Rose Garden** (full-day): Tours include; Floating Market, world's tallest *chedi* at Nakorn Pathom, lunch and cultural show at Rose Garden.

Damnern Saduak, **Elephant Show** (full-day): Floating Market, "Elephants in Thai History" show.

Rose Garden (half-day, p.m.): Gardens, cultural show.

Ayutthaya, **Bang Pa-in** (full day): *Oriental Queen* boat cruise to Thailand's former capital and the summer palace at Bang Pa-in. Buffet lunch on board. Return by bus.

River Kwai (full-day): River Kwai bridge, Allied POW cemetary, lunch cruise up river into jungle.

Vimarn Mek (half-day; a.m., p.m.): World's largest golden teak palace.

Ancient City (half-day, p.m.): Replicas of Thailand's architectural wonders in one-third size.

Crocodile Farm (half-day, p.m.): World's largest crocodile farm with 30,000 crocodiles.

Thonburi Canals (half-day, a.m.): Tourists are taken on a cruise through Thonburi's canals, visit the Wat Sai Floating Market and the Royal Barge Museum.

Prices are around 350 baht ($13.75) per day for a half day tour and 750 baht ($29.50) for a full day tour. The price includes pick-up at your hotel, all transportation, a tour guide, all admission fees and, where indicated, lunch.

The agencies also offer a variety of dinner cruises up the Chao Phya River, serving a set meal along the way. A bar serves mixed and bottled drinks which may be included in the ticket price or charged separately.

A cruise through the canals east and west of the river is usually conducted in a barge pulled by a tugboat which allows you to savor the tranquility of canal life. It gives you a chance to see the Thai countryside and eat dinner either on board stop at a small village where cultural shows are conducted.

Whatever your reservations about exploring a city in tour groups, they are a worthwhile way to see a lot of sights in a short time.

ıe feature
the
ganized
ur: the
ligatory
oup pose.

The interior walls of the *viharn* are an explosion of imagination with the retelling of the last 24 *Chadoks* or incarnations of Buddha before he was Enlightened. Dating from the reign of Rama III (1824-1851), they are vivid, imaginative portrayals of heavens and hells, angels and monsters, fantastic mythical creatures that must have delighted the artists to dream up and draw. Crisp and lively, they mark a departure from the formalism of the Buddhaisawan Chapel.

At the rear of the *viharn*, the *bot* boasts massive teak doors 18 feet (5.5 meters) high, five feet (1.5 meters) wide and six inches (15 cm) thick. They were carved in beautiful nature motifs to a depth of two inches (5.5 cm) by King Rama II.

The courtyard is a museum of statuary with stone figures of Chinese generals and scholars. They came as ballast in Thai ships returning from rice deliveries to China. Given to merchants who had no space for them, they were donated to *wats* like this, Wat Po and Wat Arun. Even more beautiful are the bronze Chinese horses with their green patina sheen. The cloisters that surround the courtyard are filled with gilded bronze Buddha images. The *wat* is open daily, 8:30 a.m. to 6 p.m. The *viharn* with its murals is open only on Saturday, Sunday and Buddhist holidays; 9 a.m. through 5 p.m.

A Frenchman passing Wat Suthat was once heard to whisper an astonished "Bangkok has a guillotine?" There is a certain resemblance but the **Giant Swing** (*Sao Ching Cha*) served less sanguine purposes. Since the 14th century, the long-haired, white robed Brahmin priests have been a permanent fixture in Thai royal life. They are in charge of conducting royal statecraft and rite of passage ceremonies including christenings, the snipping off of a child's topknot when he or she reaches puberty, coronations, royal death ceremonies and others. They have also introduced the pantheon of Hindu gods like Siva, Brahma, Indra and others who keep popping up in Thai architecture and statuary.

The Giant Swing was built for a Brahmin ceremony to honor the Hindu god *Siva*. Once held each January, a bag of gold was placed atop a 50-foot (15-meter) pole and a pair of young Brahmins, each standing on one foot, would strain to set the huge swing in motion, slowly gaining altitude until one managed to snatch the bag off the pole. Miscalculations sent many plummeting to the ground below. The ceremony was suspended in the 1940s. Today, pigeons scrabble for corn scattered by visitors around the Swing's base.

Across the street to the northwest is the **Brahmin Temple**. It is of little interest architecturally but provides a contrast with the elaborately decorated Wat Suthat. North of Wat Suthat on Dinsor Road is the City Hall and down Dinsor where it intersects with Rajdamnern Klang Avenue is the **Democracy Monument**. Erected to commemorate the nation's first

A 19th-century American sailor (left) guards the entrance of Wat Suthat (right).

constitution in 1932, it has been a rallying point for public protests.

More interesting are the shops on Bamrungmuang Road east of the Giant Swing that sell monks' robes, image stands and numerous other religious items Thai Buddhists donate to monks or purchase for the shrines and meditation rooms in their homes.

Two blocks west of the City Hall down Mahanop Road is **San Chao Paw Sua**, a Chinese Buddhist temple. As with most Chinese temples, it bustles with activity and bright color from early in the morning to late at night providing a vivid contrast with the serenity of Theravada Buddhist *wats*. If you lack time to tour Chinatown, pop in here for a few moments and let the chaos swirl around you. Although the light is dim, there are great opportunities for photos; take a tripod.

In a convenient cluster at the intersection of Rajdamnern Klang Avenue and Mahachai Road are three slightly different attractions for those with time to explore. In the forecourt of **Wat Rajnadda** behind the Chalerm Thai movie theater is an amulet market like the one at Maharat landing. Stalls upon stalls sell amulets and occult objects providing a fascinating look at a facet of life with considerable hold on Thai imaginations. Open 6 a.m. to 6 p.m.

Behind the *wat* is one of Bangkok most unusual and most beautiful structures, the **Lohaprasad**. Built by Rama III, the multi-tiered building is modelled on an ancient monastery in Sri Lanka built in 161 B.C. with 1,000 meditation cells. Like a giant pink wedding cake, it rises stairstep fashion in six tiers to a height of 111 feet (33.5 meters). Iron spires crowning its dozens of towers give its name of Loha ("metal") Prasad. A circular stairway at its core ascends to the top floor for a nice view of the Golden Mount and the neighborhood. No longer used, this thoroughly charming, unique building is normally locked and you must ask one of the monks to open the door.

A Brahmin priest celebrates the Queen's birthday. Right, looking out from the Golden Mount.

THE NATIONAL MUSEUM

Dating from 1782, the attractive main building of the National Museum was originally built as a palace. It was only in 1966 that the flanking houses were added. For an overview of Thai art history, following the evolution of the Buddha image through time may serve as a splendid introduction to the country's rich past.

The National Museum is one of the biggest in Southeast-Asia and contains countless religious artefacts.

Dvaravati-Period (6th - 11th century): The statues appear monkish, showing broad, smiling faces and curly hair. Indian influences are obvious in the stylised gowns and inclined positions of the standing Buddhas.

Rooms 32 and 33 display *Dvaravati*-statues, groups of musicans and dancers, all fashioned from terracotta

Srivijaya-Period (7th - 12th century): In Southern Thailand this specific style of artistic development is predominant. Strong Javanese influences are noticeabel. Srivijayan bronzes are exhibited in room 35.

Lopburi-Period (11th - 14th century): The statues of gods, goddesses and Buddha figurines are carved from stone and resemble those of Cambodia. They seem humanized and depict strong masculine features. (Rooms 89 und 31).

Chiang-Saen-Period (11th - 13th century): Although typical for the northern Thai art, this style also incorporates Indian influences. Most Buddhas are seated and have round faces as well as curly hair. (Room 41).

Sukhothai-Period (13th - 14th century): This style is generally considered the first genuinely Thai style. Most original are the bronze scuptures. Many Buddha statues are characterized by

The National Museum.

oval faces with eyes that are hidden under heavy round eyelids. Their bodies, however, tend to be rather stylized with flowing, slender shapes. (Rooms 42 and 43).

Don't forget to take a look at the well-known striding Buddha cast in black bronze.

Ayutthaya-Period (14th - 17th century): During this phase, various style elements were integrated but forms stayed slender and always elegant. Background decorations are plentiful, demonstrating how wealthy and powerful the kingdom of Ayuddhaya had been at that time. (Rooms 44 and 45).

Bangkok- or Ratanakosin-Period (18th century till the beginning of the 20th century): Now, round and sweet faces predominate. Garments are elaborate, carefully sculptured and ornamented. These stautes appear to be much more decorative than those of previous periods.

Unforunately, just a few of them are exhibited at the National Museum.

Across Mahachai Road to the east are the remains of the city wall including an original watchtower. Through an archway in the wall is an area that at first appears to be a slum. Treading farther into the interior, you come upon a thriving **Bird Market**. These are not ordinary birds but cooing doves that command prices of 100,000 baht and more. They repay their owners by singing sweeter than other doves at huge competitions in Bangkok, southern Thailand and Malaysia. Here, they hang high on poles to enjoy the air and sunshine in gilded cages befitting their exalted status. Shops in the compound sell elaborate bird cages, some of which are works of art.

Beyond the walls: East of the canal at the base of a tall man-made hill called the Golden Mount is **Wat Saket**, a *wat* undistinguished except for its late Ayutthayan lacquered windows and the grim role it played in Bangkok's history. The *wat* was the city's charnel-house where plague victims too numerous for funeral pyres were laid out for the vultures to eat.

An epidemic in the reign of Rama II killed 30,000 people who were taken out of the city through the *Pratu Pii* (Ghost Gate) and laid here. Soon the sky was black with vultures and the feast began. The scene was repeated with plagues in 1873, 1881, 1891 and 1900 that killed 10,000 each. At the *wat* is a *Bodhi* tree (its leaves have "tails"), the type of tree under which Buddha reached Enlightenment. This tree grew from a cutting brought from Sri Lanka in 1818 and is still thriving. Open from 8 a.m. through 6 p.m. Free admission.

At Wat Saket start the 300-step ascent to the summit of Phu Khao Thong, the **Golden Mount**, a hill that provides a superb panoramic view of the city. For years, the hill, 261 feet (79 meters) to the tip of its spire, was the highest point. Its construction is one of the engineering marvels of the 19th century.

It was begun by Rama III (1824-1851) as an immense *prang* on the banks of Klong Mahanak. It proved too heavy for the soft earth and as workers were constructing the second tier, it collapsed. Rama IV (1851-1868) started again and encountered the same problems until engineers sank 1,000 teak logs into ground and then built a mountain atop them.

Its crown is a golden *chedi* built in 1863. Relics of the Buddha brought from Nepal were placed in the *chedi* in 1897. Until World War II, it served as a watchtower with guards armed with signal flags to watch for enemy invaders. In World War II, it was used to sound howling sirens during air raids by British bombers, the Thais having sided with the Japanese. The *wat* stages a very noisy fair each November. Open from 8 a.m. to 6 p.m., free admission.

Of the many villages which once lay in the heart of the city, one remains. **Baan Baht**, down Trok Baan Baht between Boriphat Road and Worachak Road, can be identified from a distance by the tap-tapping of hammers on metal. This is the village that makes the alms bowls monks carry on their morning rounds. A true cottage industry, the villagers use charcoal fires, hand bellows and hammers to shape flat pieces of metal into bowls of surprising sophistication. Modern factories threaten the village with extinction, a living relic of antique Bangkok. The village isn't the cleanest place in the city so do not wear your best clothes or shoes.

Wat Traimitr is an ordinary temple on Traimitr Road near the city's main railway station, Hualampong. Neither is its Buddha image of any particular artistic merit but one fact sets it apart from all others in the city and for this reason is a magnet for visitors.

The 10-foot (three-meter)-tall image was once encased in stucco. In 1957, while workmen were shifting it, a sling broke and the image fell to the floor cracking its plaster skin. Puzzled by the metallic glow emanating from the crack, the workmen peeled away the outer casing and discovered a gold image weighing 5.5 tons.

Left, forging a monk's bowl and right, staircase to the King's bedroom at Vimarn Mek.

Because it was known that Ayutthaya period abbots had often covered their precious images in stucco to protect them from marauding Burmese armies, the 1957 discovery set off a treasure hunt. Around the kingdom in the deep of the night, tiny hammers could be heard tapping away but nothing of equal value was ever found. Open everyday from 9 a.m. through 5 p.m. Free admission.

Another colossal image but with considerably less value is the 106-foot (32-meter)-tall Standing Buddha at **Wat Intraviharn** on Visut Kaset Road. Like the Wat Traimitr image, it is worth visiting only for its curiosity value.

Wat Benjamabophit was the last major *wat* built in Bangkok. It is attractive as much for the activities which surround it as for its concessions to Western design. Like many temples in Bangkok, it was built on the site of a previous, smaller *wat*. Its sponsor was King Rama V who in 1900, shortly after he had moved into a palace in the vicinity, ordered that it be built.

The outer walls of the cruciform *bot* are clad in gray marble imported from Carrara, Italy, giving it its better-known name, the **Marble Wat**. Stained glass windows illuminate an interior that holds a beautiful copy of the Phra Buddha Jinnaraj, a famous image in the northern town of Phitsanuloke.

The cloisters around its back court are filled with 53 Buddha images in the major styles of South and Southeast Asia, some originals, some copies, a veritable mini-museum of Buddhist sculpture. The *wat* is most interesting in the early morning when Buddhists gather under the trees before its gates to give food to monks. When the *bot* behind it is bathed in morning sunlight it offers superb photo opportunities. It is also a popular gathering place on the three main Buddhist holidays. As the full moon is rising, Buddhists walk in candlelight procession three times around the bot. For the photographer with fast film and a tripod, it means a

ffering to nonks in ront of Wat enjama-ophit.

photo for the album. The non-photographer, can join the procession. Open daily, from 8 a.m. through 6 p.m. 10 baht admission fee.

Across the canal to the northeast is **the Chitrlada Palace**, home of Thailand's Royal Family. As the wooden mansion is cloaked in trees, there is little to see other than the guards on patrol across the moat and the cows grazing contentedly just beyond the fence, participants engaged in a royal program to improve dairy production for the rural areas.

Even when Thai monarchs sought to live informally, to let down their royal hair, they did so in grand style. A superb example is **Vimarn Mek**, (Celestial Residence) behind the old National Assembly Building. The 81-room mansion billed as "the world's largest Golden Teak structure" was built by King Chulalongkorn as a country retreat for himself and his large extended family. Today, it reflects the splendor of the Thai court and the exquisite taste with which it furnished its palaces. Open Wednesdays through Sundays, 9:30 a.m. through 4 p.m. 50 baht per person, free guided tour.

Eastern Bangkok: A royal home of a different sort is **Suan Pakkad** (Cabbage Patch) at 352 Sri Ayutthaya Rd. (tel. 245-4934). Five traditional Thai houses were brought to Bangkok during the 1920s and erected in a compound then in the middle of empty fields. The houses now contain numerous artifacts as well as antique gold and lacquer manuscript cabinets. One building contains one of the country's best collections of neolithic Ban Chiang pottery.

Its treasure is the **Lacquer Pavilion** constructed from two pavilions found near Ayutthaya. The inner walls are covered with priceless gold and lacquer scenes from the Buddha's life, enchanting scenes without parallel anywhere in Thailand. They include Frenchmen in tall plumed hats astride fat, prancing horses in 17th-century Ayutthaya. A magnificent museum presentation by any standards. Open everyday except Sundays, 9 a.m. through 4 p.m. 50 baht.

If Suan Pakkad has a rival it is the **Jim Thompson House**, 6 Soi Kasemsan 2, Rama 1 Road (Tel. 215-0122). Only two decades have passed since the ex-World War II intelligence officer who introduced the world to Thai silk disappeared one sunny afternoon in 1968 while on a stroll in Malaysia's Cameron Highlands. The charming mystery man left behind a thriving silk business and a beautiful home that is everything a Thai house is meant to be.

Several teak houses were moved from Ayutthaya and reassembled at the edge of a canal (Thai houses are built in panels attached to pillars by wooden pegs so are eminently transportable). Set in a beautiful garden they are filled with antiques from Jim Thompson's fabulous private collection. Asian artifacts, Khmer statues and other priceless works are beautifully arranged in a home anyone would want to own. Open

Left, elegant table setting at Jim Thompson's House. Right, Buddha and disciples cross the river at Suan Pakkad's Lacquer Pavilion.

daily except Sundays from 9 a.m. through 4:30 p.m. Adults: 80 baht; Children: 40 baht. Guided tour.

Only for those in the vicinity of Siam Center, **Wat Pathumawanaram** is prized for its tranquility amid the din of traffic; a great place to take five from tramping through the city. Its *bot* contains some excellent murals, the lower walls telling the story of Sithanonchai, a hero of Thai literature and the upper walls bearing a magnificent procession of Royal Barges.

To understand the importance of spirits in Thai life, spend 10 minutes at the **Erawan Shrine** at the intersection of Rajdamri and Ploenchit Roads (also called the Rajprasong intersection). In 1956 the nearby Erawan Hotel was under construction. Plagued by a series of inexplicable accidents and delays, the owners called in spirit doctors who decided that in chopping down trees to build the foundation, the workmen had deprived the tree spirits of a home.

The owners immediately erected a shrine with a statue of Brahma to house the spirits and the hotel's construction was completed without additional problems. Much like the Statue of Fatima and the grotto at Lourdes, the shrine has gained a reputation as a granter of wishes. Supplicants travel here from all over the city to light incense, leave floral garlands and make their pleas for success in school exams, marriage and the lottery.

The Thais thank the spirits by giving teak elephants or hiring a resident classical dance troupe to perform a thanksgiving dance. It is a fascinating spectacle redolent with the mystery of the East. Visitors can buy a candle, incense and garland and make their own wish. Open everyday 7 a.m. through 11 p.m. Free admission.

The **Kamthieng House** at the Siam Society at 131 Soi 21, Sukhumvit Rd. (Tel. 258-3491) is the nearest to an ethnological museum that you'll find in Bangkok. The 200-year-old Northern Thai house, moved here from Chiang

The Erawan Shrine attracts an evening crowd of worshippers.

Mai, holds fishing and agricultural implements as well as cooking utensils. Open daily except Sundays and Mondays from 9 a.m. to noon, 1 p.m. to 5 p.m. Adults: 20 baht; Children: 10 baht.

The **Bhirasri Museum of Modern Art** at 90 Soi Attakanprasit, South Sathorn Rd. (Tel. 286-8965) is Thailand's showplace for modern painting and sculpture. Check the newspapers for announcements of exhibitions. Open daily except Mondays, 10 a.m. to 6 p.m. Free.

Pockets of people from the past: Despite the seeming homogeneity of its predominantly Thai Buddhist population, Bangkok was built by a multitude of nationalities, small pockets of which are scattered throughout the city. While these neighborhoods have remained more or less intact, many of their residents have moved elsewhere, and now live side by side with their ethnic Thai neighbors with an admirable absence of racial friction.

Muslims have integrated into Bangkok's social fabric but prefer to cluster in small communities around mosques which stand like small islands in peaceful seas of Buddhists. The prayers of the muezzins are muted in deference to their neighbors, men wear white prayer caps and Muslim restaurants have small Arabic inscriptions on their windows to indicate they serve ritualistically-clean food but otherwise there is little to suggest it is anything but an ordinary Thai neighborhood.

The Burmese traders and the Khmers who dug the canals have been completely assimilated as have the Laotians. Vietnamese Catholics who fled religious persecution in the early 1800s founded a community (Baan Yuan) on Samsen Road, but few reminders of their cultural roots remain.

Indians have also blended into the community and, except for the turbans worn by some sects, are as Thai as the Thais. Many are cloth merchants operating stalls in **Pahurat** market. The most popular Hindu temple is far away

Left, Muslims at evening prayer. Right, Chinese Christians celebrate mass at the St. Rosary Church.

on Silom Road at the intersection with Pan Road. Wat Phasri Maha Umathewi, better known as **Wat Kaek** (Indian Temple), is especially interesting during the festival of Sri Mariamman in September when bystanders pitch in to pull an enormous chariot through the streets amid boisterous rejoicing.

One minority has virtually disappeared from its traditional enclave: the **Americans** and **Europeans**. Most arrived to pursue commercial, diplomatic or religious interests; but few came to settle permanently.

The Oriental Hotel area is a museum of their monuments: the hotel itself, the East Asiatic Co. next door and the **Oriental Plaza** shopping plaza between the hotel and New Road. Along the river between the Oriental and the Royal Orchid Sheraton are the superb French and Portuguese embassies and, beyond the canal to the north of the Royal Orchid, is the attractive **Wat Kalaya** (Rosary Church) which is now a Thai Catholic church.

Chinatown: By far the biggest concentration of non-ethnic Thais are Chinese and the area known as Chinatown has retained much of its cultural integrity, to the point where in some of the backstreets one hears more *Tae-chiew* (the dialect of southern China spoken by most Chinese-Thais) than Thai. Deep in these alleys, the visitor will encounter resonances of the Middle Kingdom, and pre-Mao.

Chinatown occupies the area between New Road and Songwat on the north and south, and between Chakrawat Road on the west and Krung Kasem Road on the east. The face it presents to the world is one of noisy but bland conformity to the dictates of commerce and architectural economy. Step behind its facade, however, and into a myriad of lives swirling through tiny lanes. Walk through them and recapture the flavor of a culture that despite its veneer of modernity, is little changed from 50 years ago.

There are two interesting walks which convey the essence of Chinatown. The first is along Soi Wanit through the heart of **Sampeng** where, two centuries ago, Chinese merchants set up shop after vacating the area where the Grand Palace was to be built.

Sampeng has a history that is anything but serene. It has had its exalted and not-so-exalted moments. There are few traces of its most notorious era around the turn of the century when it functioned as the city's green light (so called for the green lanterns which hung above the brothels), gambling and opium den district.

Daily newspapers headlined stories of bar brawls, gruesome gangland murders and pitched battles between warlord armies fighting to defend or acquire turf in highly lucrative illicit businesses, a precursor to Chicago of the 1920s and 30s. Today, it has settled into the complacency of commerce but the bustle and streams of goods and people that flow through its narrow alleys are unchanged.

Tour one: The walk begins at **Wat**

Left, member of Bangkok's Sikh community. Right, incense fills the air in a Chinatown temple.

莊嚴

Pathum Khongka on Traimitr Road. Also known as **Wat Sampeng**, this Thai Buddhist temple anchoring the eastern end of Sampeng predates the founding of Bangkok by nearly 100 years making it one of the oldest wats in the city. Its grisly role in history is that it was the execution ground for nobles convicted of state crimes.

Before entering Soi Wanit, walk north on Songsawat Road to **Wat Samphathawong**. Also known as **Wat Koh**, this gilded temple is surrounded by beautiful old teak houses that serve as monks' quarters. In the late afternoon sun, the rich hues of the wood blend beautifully with the saffron robes of the monks and the gold Buddha images glistening high in the temple gables.

Continue along Soi Wanit, turning right at Yaowaphanit Road and left again at Soi Sampeng to arrive at **Talat Kao**, the "Old Market." Not the cleanest of markets, it is interesting for its produce and for its chaos. Go early in the morning; no matter how early you get there the market will already have been active for several hours. It is virtually dead by 10 a.m.

Return to Soi Wanit and continue walking west. From here on, nearly every turn to the left into a small lane will be rewarded by arresting sights. Forget your map and just wander; you won't be lost for long. There are shops so small one wonders how they can survive. There are Chinese shrines (*sanjao*) with old men pottering about sweeping, reading or talking with friends, the shrine also serves as an old people's home.

In these narrow lanes, you not only peer into households, you virtually become a member of the family so open are the lives they live, a lack of privacy that most Westerners would find intolerable. You may also be repelled by the lack of cleanliness in the alleys. But this is quickly counterbalanced by the personal cleanliness of the people and their homes and by the obvious warmth and energy that the area exudes despite

Chinatown is famous for its goldsmiths.

what many would term deprivation.

Back on Soi Wanit, continue west, noting on the southeast corner of Trok Sanjao Mai the remains of a 300-year-old home now converted into a shop. A block beyond is the handsome facade of the former Gold Exchange with its imposing tiers of balconies.

Farther on, on the left, is a red sign with gold lettering denoting the entrance to **Wat Chakrapat**. The *wat* is Thai but the higgledy-piggley ecclectism of its layout and buildings is right in keeping with the chaotic turmoil of the rest of Soi Wanit.

It, too, is an Ayutthaya-period *wat*. Its principal attractions live in a pond inside on the right. They are the descendents of an old one-eyed crocodile called "Blind Old Guy" who was a fearsome beast half a century ago when unwary bathers in the canals just outside of town could suddenly find themselves on the dinner menu. The croc fell on hard times and the abbot of the *wat* took pity on him and gave him a home. He finally died, the loser in a battle royal with a younger crocodile.

To the left behind the *viharn* is a grotto with what is reputed to be the shadow of a Buddha, a supernatural phenomenon which looks like it may have had some help from a human touch-up artist. Watching over it is a fat disciple of Buddha once said to have been a handsome man forever chased by women who constantly interrupted his meditations. To put a stop to their attentions, he stuffed himself to obesity which quelled their ardent passions. This is piety of a strength alien to most men. One wonders if his beatific smile is inspired by the serenity of religious contemplation or the memory of his days gone by.

Leave by the western gate, turning right at the first corner to rejoin Soi Wanit. Turn left, cross the canal and you are on Mahachai Road. Cross it and walk into the **Pahurat** market, famed for its multitude of textiles on sale there. If you find you still have energy, con-

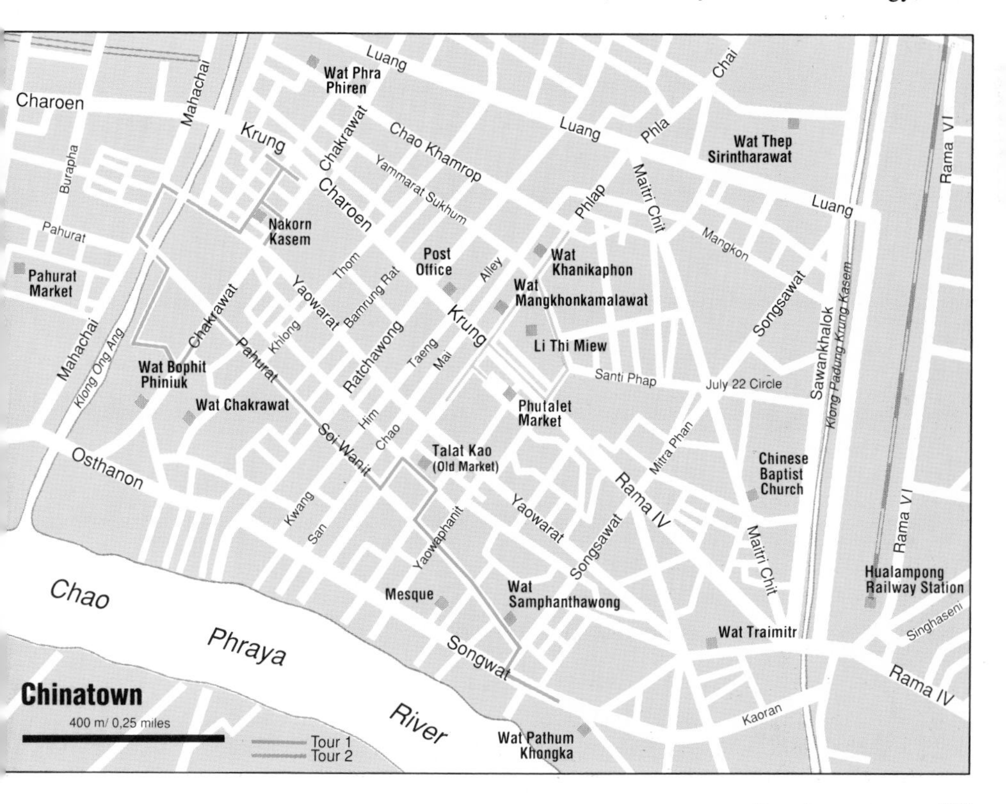

tinue north on Mahachai to the intersection, turning right onto Yaowarat Road. Cross the canal and turn left into the warren of small streets.

This area, *Nakhon Kasem*, was once known as "Thieves Market" and was the fencing district for "hot" items stolen by burglars. It has gone legitimate these days but it is still possible to find small antique shops with odds and ends. More interesting, however, are the vendors who crowd the sidewalks selling all sorts of hardware items as well as grey market electrical appliances at bargain prices.

Tour two: A second walking tour is shorter but no less interesting. It begins in the northeast corner of Chinatown at **Wat Mangkhonkamalawat** (better known as Wat Mangkhon) on New Road. The Mahayana Buddhist temple is the biggest found in Chinatown. Walk further into it to see the activity around the altar.

Back on the street, turn left and left again into the narrow lane called Soi Issaranuphap. Along it are shops selling Chinese religious items which make interesting home decorations. Paper suits and money to be burned for the dead are found here as well. Halfway down on the right is an interesting little shrine which has been restored to its detriment but which is still worth taking a look.

The lane ends at Plabplachai Road. The traveler can continue straight and turn left into **Wat Khanikaphon**. The bright orange *wat* is an anomaly in the neighborhood but then, its predecessor was a bit of an oddity. It was built by a former brothel madam named Mae Lao Faeng to atone for her sins. Its name, "Khanikaphon," means "woman who sold women." Locals know it as Wat Mae Lao Faeng.

Attached to the *wat* and just beyond it is one of Chinatown's busiest *sanjao*. If you are lucky, there will be a *kong tek* ceremony in progress. Here, luxury automobiles, houses, servants, kitchen appliances, computers, televisions and

A house, a car and money to spend accompany a Chinese in the afterlife.

a host of imaginative items all made of paper are burned to send them to relatives and loved ones thereby ease their lot in the afterlife.

Retrace your steps down Plaplachai but angle left. Look into the shops selling *kong tek* items and at the shops on the opposite side of the street selling crimson and gold shrines for Buddhist homes. Down the street on the right is **Li Thi Miew**, one of Bangkok's most charming Chinese temples. It is Taoist rather than Buddhist and its interior design is as close to the paintings of temples in ancient China as you will find anywhere. Down the street on the left are shops selling Chinese teas. Select the raw tea and watch the shopkeeper wrap it in small parcels using paper bright with calligraphy.

Plabplachai again angles right but just before it rejoins New Road, turn right into an interesting alley which takes you into Issaranuphap Lane. Turn left, and you are back at Wat Mangkhon. You can end your walk here or cross New Road and continue on the southern extension of Issaranuphap Lane. A short distance in, turn left into **Phutalet Market** which is similar to Talat Kao, the market mentioned in the first walk.

Like the rest of Asia, Chinatown shuts its doors to the outside world for several days each February for the Chinese New Year celebrations. The time to see Chinese enjoying themselves is during the **Moon Festival** on the full moon night of September. In the evening, they set up small altars to honor the moon goddess. The treats are the small mooncakes which have few rivals for tastiness.

A few weeks later in October, the Chinese once again enjoy themselves during the **Vegetarian Festival**. Mounds of vegetarian food are prepared, thousands of candles and incense sticks are burned and the air is rent by the clash of cymbals as the colorful and exciting Chinese opera programs get underway.

Offertory candles in Wat Mangkhon.

CANALS

For most travelers, a cruise along the **Chao Phya River** or through Thonburi's vast network of canals is one of the highlights of a Bangkok visit, an experience no other Asian capital can offer. A boat journey up the river passes major city landmarks including Wat Arun, Wat Po, Wat Phra Kaew and the Grand Palace and some of the city's oldest and most elegant houses.

Elsewhere in the world, buses show one the bright face of a city; railway trains the city's backside. Bangkok's riverboats, like trains, take you behind the city's mask, past markets unloading produce and flowers from up-country truck farms, old men tossing nets to catch small, silvery fish, a family having a picnic on a boat landing, a decrepit old spinster of a mansion with sagging eaves, a riverside school.

Life on the river: Trains of huge steel barges ride high on the water or, freighted with sand, barely crest the waterline, every wave threatening to swamp them. Like their cousins the metal barges, old teak rice barges have a family home perched on the stern. A gaggle of giggling kids tightrope-walk the hawser stretched between the lead barge and a tugboat straining against the current.

Proud old Chinese barges with their rounded, Rubenesque hulls and T-bar bridges are loaded at a dock. Ferry boats run at right angles to the flow of traffic, half-naked boys using the roof as a diving platform, leaping off laughing and swimming to shore. Small boats with men stripped to the waist, their heads encased in helmets connected by hissing tubes to an air compressor, dive to the river's bottom in search of treasure or trash to sell to scrap metal dealers. Water-borne vendors carry their kitchens with them, cooking and serving noodles and popcorn and spooning out ice cream, tooting their horns to alert children of their approach.

There are boats of every description: boats with steaming vats of color asking house to house for housewives wanting to dye used clothes; tugs with shark's teeth painted on their prows; long-tailed boats roaring through the water kicking up tall rooster tails; fishermen's boats; express boats; bum boats; sampans. There's never a dull moment on the Chao Phya.

The best time for a river trip is the early morning when the sun crests the rooftops and illuminates Wat Arun, or late afternoon when the sun bathes the Grand Palace, Wat Po and all the mansions and markets in a golden light.

There are several ways to cruise along the river. The most popular are the **express boats** (*rua duan*). Long and lean, these white boats with their red stripes are the commuter buses of the river, making regular journeys between Thanon Tok and Nonthaburi. They operate every 15-20 minutes between 6

Left, tiered roofs, and longtail boats: a classic image of Thonburi. Right, cleaning day on the canal.

a.m. and 6 p.m., stopping at the landings noted on the map.

A ticket is three, five or seven baht depending on the distance traveled; a real bargain. Their huge diesel engines are noisy so sit near the front. If you are traveling between tourist sites along the river, the boats are excellent ways to beat the traffic.

The express boats take you north beyond the city limits. You head out into the countryside past stilted houses, bound for the market town of Nonthaburi, a 45-minute journey. And all for seven baht.

Cruising downriver from the Oriental Hotel, you glide past old factories, warehouses and romantic old freighters moored in the river. The last stop is Thanon Tok, literally "the road drops" (into the river), the end of New Road. To vary the journey back (not recommended during the rush hour), walk back through the intersection with Rajdapisek Road to catch a No. 1 or No. 75 bus that will take you to the foot of Silom Road or the vicinity of the Oriental Hotel.

In a class by themselves are the *Oriental Queen* day-trip to Ayuttaya and Bang Pa-in, a trip to Wat Phai Lom (home of the open-billed storks), and rice barge tours described in the Day Trips section of this book.

One of the most popular destinations is the Floating Market. Although it was played out some time ago, there are tour operators who still take visitors to Wat Sai in the vicinity of Wat Arun. If you have a choice, hold firm for the more vibrant, more authentic **Floating Market** at **Damnern Saduak**. It is farther away but worth the trip.

The Floating Market is an Asian wonder unique to Thailand. In hundreds of lush lowland canals and rivers a charming scene is repeated daily. As the dawn sun is setting the water aglow with a silvery, salmony hue, women in straw peasants' hats load tiny sampans with fruits, flowers, vegetables and cooked foods and desserts and begin

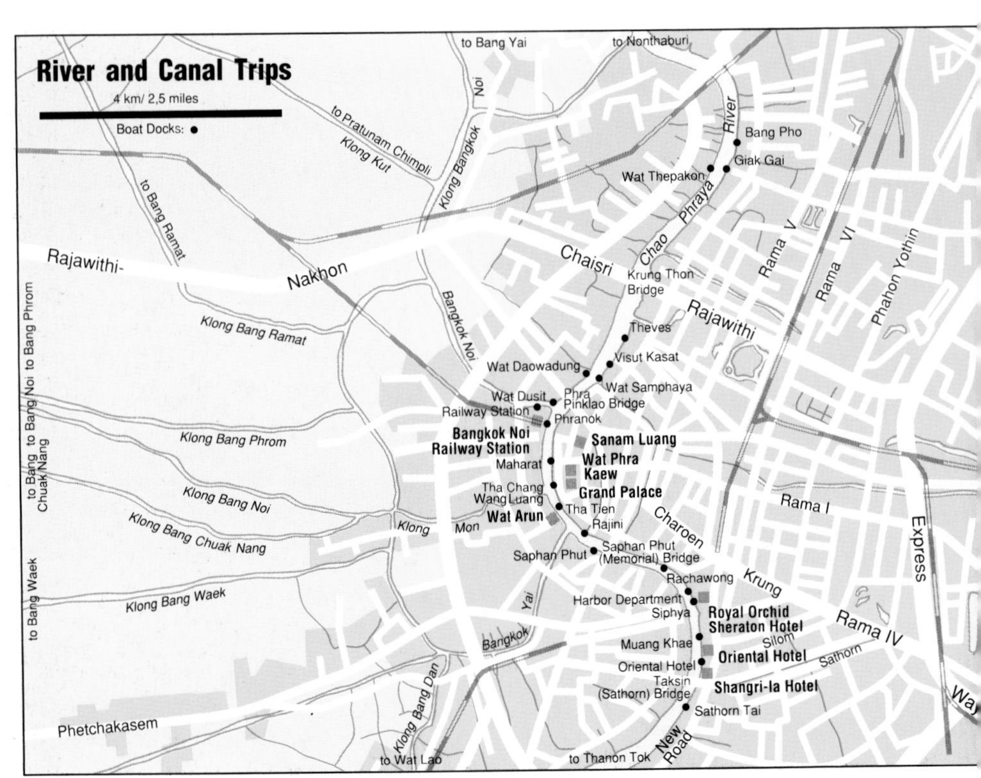

paddling silently to market. There, they trade their produce from boat to boat, shrewdly bargaining for the best prices but, more importantly, enjoying a morning chat with friends.

For photographers, the Floating Market is a feast of colors and shapes, photogenic faces and picturesque scenes. It also tempts the tongue with a dizzying array of Thai snacks and fruits. Most travel agencies make a full day of it, combining it with a stop at Nakhom Pathom, the world's tallest *chedi*, and lunch and a cultural show at the Rose Garden (See box on Organized Tours, page 93).

Explorers undaunted by public transportation can go to the Southern Bus Terminal on Charansanitwong Road on the far side of Thonburi. Buses leave for Damnern Saduak at 20-minute intervals between 6 a.m. and 5:30 p.m. Coaches leave hourly between 7 a.m. and 8:30 p.m. for the two-hour ride. The bus stops at a pier where a long-tailed boat can be hired for a trip to the market.

In the evening, enjoy the drowsy river aboard a floating restaurant. You cruise past Bangkok's most beautiful landmarks while dining sumptuously on a Thai set menu. There are also romantic dinner cruises through the canals east of Bangkok aboard a tranquil rice barge.

Cruising the klongs: Far more interesting for the intrepid traveler is a journey through the canals (*klong*, in Thai) on the Thonburi side of the river. Once past the modern housing tracts, you enter a world of thick jungles and coconut plantations, scenery straight out of *Apocalypse Now*. Perched on the riverbanks like so many top-heavy herons are houses on stilts with families bathing in the canals or cooking on their verandahs.

There are quaint old Buddhist temples peeking through a screen of coconut trees, cows grazing on lush plantation grasses, tropical birds in the palm trees that overhang the canal. It is everything one expects of a tropical

Certain areas still retain the city's traditional waterborne way of life.

jungle, a journey into the past as life was once lived and a voyage of mystery into the heart of darkness.

The Chao Phya Express Boat Company operates a tour through the canals to Klong Bangkok Noi which leaves the Royal Orchid Sheraton Hotel at 2:55 p.m. and returns at 6 p.m. Snacks, fruit and drinks are included in the 130 baht price. Tel: 465-3836, 466-4505.

Crystal Tour (Tel. 251-3758) takes guests aboard a rice barge to Klong Mon, Taling Chan and Bangkok Noi on the Thonburi side of the river between 3 p.m. and 5:30 p.m. daily. Pick up is at the Royal Orchid Sheraton Hotel; the cost is 250 baht including fruit and soft drinks.

The World Travel Service tour (Tel. 233-5900-9, Ext. World Travel Service) travels by long-tailed boat to Klong Bang Yai and transfers to a rice barge for a trip up the river to the Rama 6 Bridge, stopping at the Boonrawd Brewery pier for a coach to the guest's hotel. Daily from 2 p.m. to 6 p.m.; 310 baht per person including fruit, dessert and a soft drink.

For do-it-yourself travelers, two types of boats journey into the canals: the *rua hang yao* or **long-tailed boats** and the small boats that formerly carried supplies into the interior. Long-tailed boats are aptly named for the long shafts that connect the propeller to an onboard car engine. The long-tail is the ingenious Thai answer to the difficulty of maneuvering in the narrow, shallow canals.

The boat itself is very narrow and of very shallow draft requiring that passengers hunker down two to a seat. Passengers with long legs may find the journey somewhat uncomfortable. The sensation of speeding along inches above the water (often being drenched in mist; passengers are provided with umbrellas), and the sights to be seen make the trip well worth it.

Long-tailed boats are the buses of the canals. From terminals near the Grand Palace and the Memorial Bridge (see

Speeding up the Chao Phya.

map), they make regular journeys deep into the canals, stopping wherever passengers wish to disembark. Ride to the end of one canal and then walk for a half hour through the plantations to the end of another canal. There, catch a boat back to the starting point along the river. The fares are three to five baht depending on destination.

An excellent, very compact book called *50 Trips through Siam's Canals* by Geo.-Ch. Veran (also in French) provides detailed maps and itineraries. You can also rent a long-tailed boat for about 200 baht per hour and plan your own journey. A long-tailed variant which guarantees a hair-raising trip is the wide, flat-bottomed speedboat that whizzes over the water at breakneck speed.

More comfortable by far are the small **rice boats**. These have cushioned seats and take visitors to the Floating Market at Wat Sai. They can also be rented from private operators just off the veranda of the Oriental Hotel or in the area around Tha Maharat for 150-250 baht per hour.

Their drawback is that they are too big for some canals. The depth of canal water is affected by the tide; if the water is too low, the boats lack sufficient draft, if too high they will not fit under the bridges. Thus, they are best used only for the larger canals.

Popular rice boat routes include a two-hour journey that travels upriver to Klong Bangkok Noi for a brief stop at the Royal Barge Museum. Further on, turn left into Klong Kounsri. This canal eventually joins Klong Bangkok Yai that flows into the Chao Phya near Wat Arun. From there, it is a short journey back to your starting point.

Another possibility is to cruise south under the Bangkok Bridge (*Sapan Krung Thep*) and into Klong Dao Kanong and from there into Klong Sanam Chai. This will take you into the area known as **Suan Phak** (Vegetable Garden) an area of jungles straight out of the *African Queen*.

Loaded to the gunwales, a painted barge serves as living quarters and goods carrier.

MARKETS

Plunge into a Bangkok market and you plunge into the mainstream of Thai life. This is where the ordinary Thai does his shopping. Thais of all ages are inveterate bargain hunters so that among the poor, you'll find the rich, their chauffeured Mercedes-Benzes, BMWs and Volvos parked outside. They come seeking strange and exotic fruits and foods, plants, cheap clothes and a thousand and one other items found nowhere else.

For a visitor, a stroll through a market is a journey into the vibrant grassroots economy the energetic Thais have created. If you've spent time in other Asian countries, you'll immediately realize that Thailand is a very rich country with tremendous natural wealth and people of enormous resourcefulness.

Spend hours just browsing, marvelling at the immense variety of products, kibitzing with the vendors and other shoppers all of whom treat this not as a journey of necessity but as an outing to be enjoyed to the fullest. Buying something is not the point—although it is unlikely with the variety of items offered that you will leave empty-handed. Haggling is an essential art but pursue it in a light-hearted fashion. You'll probably end up paying more than the locals but who cares, you're still getting a bargain.

The Weekend Market that used to be at Sanam Luang in the shadow of the Emerald Buddha outgrew its home and moved several years ago to more spacious grounds on the north of the city. Hugging Paholyothin Road, the **Chatuchak Weekend Market** occupies 31 acres of land parcelled among 5,000 stallholders.

What they sell is the world, this part of it anyway. Clothes, pets (including some you wouldn't want in your house like pythons and monitor lizards), luscious fruits and vegetables, antiques, pseudo-antiques, brass utensils, plants, army surplus goods, leatherware, rice, toys, furniture, birds, tape cassettes, dinnerware, stationery and even hair coloring can be found. Some prices are fixed, others are arrived at by bargaining. The aisles are shaded by awnings but it can still be stifling so limit your shopping to the morning hours.

Pratunam Market in the city center is Chatuchak on a smaller scale and with a smaller selection. Hole-in-the-wall tailoring shops (seamstresses with sewing machines) can whip together an outfit designed from a magazine picture provided it isn't haute couture fashion. You're not likely to be interested in the skimpy sequined bikinis with "Hot" emblazoned on the rear that go-go dancers examine with the intensity of a sommelier perusing a century-old bottle of Mouton Rothschild, but buy a casual outfit for day wear. Choose your cloth at one stall and have it tailored at one just down the aisle.

Bangrak Market on New Road is

Left, flower market at Pak Klong Talad and right, the Sunday market at Chatuchak Park.

even smaller. Its specialty is floral wreaths and garlands. Ordinary flowers are transformed into stunning works of art requiring hours of painstaking work and then are sold for a pittance. Anyone who has paid a New York florist extortionist prices for a simple bouquet will appreciate the difference.

Gardeners are delighted by the wealth of plants and flowers that abound in tropical Thailand. Unfortunately, there are no botanical gardens in Bangkok. The closest are the gardens of the Hilton and Siam Inter-Continental hotels but these provide only a small sampling of the thousands of plant varieties that flourish in the city. Instead, plant lovers flock to Bangkok's many plant markets to ooh and ahh over trees, shrubs and flowers they sell.

Thewes Market located on the banks of Padung Krung Kasem canal is the favorite spot for many plant lovers. Old Bangkok houses along a leafy street reflected in one of the city's main canals provide the perfect backdrop for Thewes Market. There are Crotons and Caladiums, Dieffenbachia and Dendrobia, creepers and climbers, not to mention orchids, thousands of the more than 25,000 orchid species found worldwide. For good background knowledge, read *Gardening in Bangkok* by M.R. Pimsai Amranand, available at the Siam Society.

Another venue is **Chatuchak flower market** south of the Weekend Market across Yan Paholyothin Road. Unlike the Weekend Market, the flower market stays open seven days a week.

Pak Klong Talad at the foot of the Memorial Bridge is the city's provisioner, the point of entry for the ingredients in its cuisine. Boats laden with vegetables, fruits and flowers unburden themselves on its docks where their treasures are snapped up by restauranteurs and green grocers. Explore the market, not to buy anything but to immerse yourself in the scents and sights of life in a former era in your own country, much as Les Halles once was.

Bangkok's night markets offer everything from papaya to pop music.

It begins early in the morning (which means late the night before) and is finished by 10 a.m.

A recent phenomenon is the emergence of **night markets**. Perhaps inspired by the success of Chiang Mai's well-known night market, entrepreneurs have banded together to turn daytime empty spaces into nighttime emporia selling clothes, art objects and souvenirs in the lower price categories. Many function during the day but come to life once the sun has expired. Knowing that every shopper has limited endurance and must "take five," many stalls have set up bars where one can refresh himself.

The most extensive markets are at the railway tracks near Soi 1, Sukhumvit Road; on Gaysorn Road near the Meridian President Hotel; and on a strip of land between Patpong 1 and Patpong 2. Elsewhere, vendors crowd the sidewalks the length of Silom Road (for some reason only on the north, not the south, side of the street).

PARKS

Parks are few and far between in Bangkok. It is not that they are not appreciated—on a balmy evening, it is hard to find five square meters of grass not covered by football players or families enjoying a quiet meal and chat, oblivious of traffic rushing by. It is just that the city fathers still see open space as a commodity to be bought and sold and not to be wasted on people who only want to sit on it (very unproductive and uncapitalistic). Its handful of parks are utilized to the nth degree, providing the Bangkok visitor with an insight into how Thais spend their leisure time.

Although not strictly speaking a park, Sanam Luang attracts large numbers of Thais during the late afternoon and evening. Friends converse on park benches under Flame of the Forest trees while children kick a football in an

The city's wholesale market, Pak Klong Talad: a

impromptu game or sprawl on the grass to talk.

During March and April, it suddenly blooms as a patchwork quilt of thousands of brightly colored kites offered for sale by vendors. The crazy quilt pattern is matched by the kite-filled polka-dot sky as children of all ages (some in their 70s) pursue a pastime as old as the wind.

Lumpini Park is Bangkok's oldest park. Its western entrance is marked by a statue of King Rama IV, at whose base a colorful ceremony filled with flowers is held each November 25. Located on Rama 4 Road, (open 5 a.m. to 9 p.m.) it offers two distinct faces depending on the time of day. In the morning, it is Chinese; in the afternoon, Thai.

Wander into it as the sun is rising and see elderly Chinese limbering up with *Tai Chi Chuan* exercises, the ancient slow dance that had its origins as self-defence a la *kung fu*. Sturdy old men perform graceful maneuvers with swords. Middle-aged ladies tango to the strains of scratchy old records.

Fitness-minded joggers pound down the pavements on a 1.6-mile (2.54-km) circuit, a futile, somewhat counterproductive exercise given Bangkok's air pollution. People serenade each other with old Chinese melodies played on the accordian or snatch a bowl of noodles on their way to work. Just outside the fence on Soi Sarasin, vendors offer snake blood cocktails, slaying and skinning cobras on the spot and mixing the blood with brandy in huge tulip snifters. Not a pretty sight to behold so early in the morning.

In the afternoon, the park is filled with kite fliers, model boat enthusiasts guiding their tiny craft around the lake by remote control, soccer players, budding gymnasts turning cartwheels on the grass and astrologers helping clients plan their futures.

At two landings on the western and southern banks of the northern lake, and one on the eastern bank of the southern lake, pedalboats and rowboats can be rented for a picturesque journey through the park with the Bangkok skyline as a backdrop. The concession is open from 6 a.m. to 8 p.m. Boats rent for 20 baht per half-hour. Food kiosks at various locations around the park sell snacks and drinks. A restaurant at the northwest corner offers Thai food, ice cream, beer and other drinks.

Chatuchak Park on Paholyothin Road is Bangkok's newest park. It offers a 1.9-mile (3.1-km) jogging path and lots of natural beauty as a respite from Bangkok's closeness. Rowboats and pedalboats can be rented (20 baht/half-hour) for a cruise around the lake. It provides a relaxing break from tramping through the nearby weekend market. Small refreshment kiosks are scattered throughout the park. Open from 5 a.m. to 9 p.m.

A word of warning: when the sun leaves Lumpini and Chatuchak, follow it. Both parks are dimly lit at night and become twilight zones attacting the sorts of people who thrive in murkiness.

Dusit Zoo (*Suan Dusit or Khao Din*) is on Rama 5 Road across from Chitrlada Palace. It isn't one of the region's better zoos but contains all the animals found in Asia's jungles: Elephants, rhinos, hippos, every type of simian including an orangutan from Sumatra's jungles, binturong, bears, tigers, snakes, a large aviary, and more can be found within its confines. It is also a shady park with a childrens' playground and a big lake renting pedalboats and rowboats for 20 baht per half-hour. Open daily from 8 a.m. to 6 p.m., admission is 10 baht for adults, five baht for children.

The **Snake Farm** (also known as the Saowapha Institute and the Pasteur Institute) on Rama 4 Road opposite the Montien Hotel is the second oldest of its kind in the world. Operated by the Thai Red Cross, it was created in 1923 to produce anti-venom serum to counter the many poisonous snakes which populate the rural regions of the country. It keeps a wide variety of snakes on the premises for educational purposes

Preceding pages: On the lake in Lumpini Park. Below, doing the quickstep in Lumpini.

WHERE TO FIND SILENCE AND A GOOD VIEW

Silence is as unknown to a Bangkokian as snow to a Bedouin or social conscience to a yuppie.

The best solution is to seek out a nice quiet *wat*. The depths of Wat Po, Wat Pathumawanaram and Wat Benjamabophit are good bets. The top of the Golden Mount and even Lumpini Park in the early morning are aural oases. Don't go near the river, where the boats often outblast the cars.

Viewpoints where you just sit and soak up the scenery in relative quiet are easier to find. Again, go to the top of the Golden Mount, top floor restaurants of most hotels, restaurants on the banks of the river, a Sanam Luang park bench, the edge of the lake in Lumpini Park, Chatuchak Park or Dusit Zoo (or, better yet, a boat in the middle of the lake; you get both view and peace in one go).

and offers a daily show that never fails to fascinate visitors.

It begins with an excellent 20-minute slide lecture on the work of the Institute and on the habits of dangerous snakes. The highlight comes at 11:00 and 2:00 when the audience walks to a large covered arena where handlers bring out the Siamese Cobras to demonstrate how they are "milked" for their venom. While an announcer provides explanations in English, the handlers display the impressive King Cobra which grows to 16.5 feet (five meters), has a very nasty disposition and packs enough venom in a single bite to kill 50,000 mice. The handlers also display Banded Kraits, pythons and a variety of non-poisonous snakes.

There is also a museum and a number of display cases holding poisonous Pit Vipers and non-poisonous snakes. It is one of Bangkok's more unusual offerings and one which never fails to excite viewers. Tickets are 40 baht and are well worth the price. Two shows daily at 10:30 a.m. and 1:30 p.m. Monday through Friday; one time at 10:30 on Saturday and Sunday. A note to calm the queasy: Thailand's poisonous snakes are found primarily in the farmlands. Is it extremely unlikely you will ever encounter a snake, poisonous or non-poisonous, in Thailand.

The **Bang Poo Aquarium**, 19 miles (32 km) down Sukhumvit Road on the way to Samut Prakan was once a sanitarium to which Bangkok's aristocracy repaired to escape the city heat and take the sea air. Today, it is a privately-owned aquarium with a collection of colorful local and foreign tropical fish. Open from 8 a.m. to 5 p.m. (8 a.m. to 6 p.m. on Saturdays and Sundays), the admission fee is 20 baht.

An alternative for tropical fish enthusiasts is to visit one of the many hobbyist shops around Bangkok. One of the largest and most popular is located in the basement of the Robinson Department Store branch at the corner of Silom and Rama 4 Roads.

:arly norning Tai :hi ses- :ion.

วิชัยวิทยา

DINING IS EAST

Gertrude Stein once wrote that "Dining is West" but she obviously never traveled East. Had she gone to Bangkok she would have discovered a cuisine with flavors so overpoweringly delicious she would have gone upstairs, scratched out the line and started again.

Dining is one of life's joys for Thais. The aesthetic sense they have brought to their arts have been extended to food as well, creating one of the world's finest cuisines with an infinite variety of dishes and ways of preparing them. One chef's *Gaeng Khieo Waan Gai* (Chicken in Green Curry) is quite unlike another's, meaning you could be eating it every night for a month and not once repeat the flavor.

With an astounding variety of fresh meats, vegetables and fruits grown year-round in truck gardens in Thonburi and seafood brought daily from the Gulf of Thailand, chefs have a wealth of ingredients with which to work.

The Thai love of good food has acted as a magnet for the chefs of other lands to open restaurants in Bangkok. One of the surprises for visitors is the cornucopia of cuisines, many which cannot be found in their own towns. Lebanese, Korean, Burmese, Arab, Mexican and all the European cuisines flourish in Bangkok, not to mention the fast food outlets children love.

Then, of course, there is Thai food and, equally important, a number of intriguing venues in which to enjoy it. Thais believe that "dinner" means more than a set time of the day during which to shovel food into your mouth. It is a time to have fun, to relax and talk with friends while sampling delicious dishes. Thus, the setting is as important as the food served. And here the Thais outdo themselves in the variety of restaurants they offer.

There are seafood markets where

fresh fish and shellfish are laid out on ice for you to select. There are riverside restaurants that give the diner an ever-changing view of passing boats, one of the most beautiful and interesting facets of Bangkok life. Floating restaurants cruise the river serving Thai meals during the voyage.

There are plush restaurants equal in opulence to those found anywhere in the world and rooftop restaurants (including a revolving restaurant) with spectacular views of the city. Outdoor restaurants so large the waiters are on roller skates contrast with Thai restaurants with a Thai orchestra and programs of Thai classical and folk culture. There are no-hands restaurants where a hostess personally serves her male guest every tasty morsel.

There are restaurants in the middle of bustling markets. There are small boats which paddle up to canal-side diners to serve noodle dishes and small noodle restaurants along the street; you can pull up a chair at a folding table and feast like a king until dawn. Finally, there are the noodle vendors with an entire restaurant on their three-wheeled bicycles; you don't go to lunch, lunch comes to you.

Restaurants conform to high government health standards and it is rare that one experiences an upset stomach over anything more than overindulgence (go easy on the raw oysters, however). The drinking water and ice at the larger restaurants is bottled under Health Department supervision. The water at shophouse restaurants and lower grades may not be so clean. It is best to stick to bottled soft drinks or hot tea.

Bangkok has the soft drink brands found anywhere in the world but they may be a bit on the sweet side for some palates. All major brands of American, European, Japanese and Australian liquors and wines are freely available. There is virtually no diluting or substituting; what you order is what you get.

The local beer is **Singha** or, more popular with visitors, **Kloster**. Both are

Preceding pages: Alfresco dining in Lumpini Park; Thai nights at the Siam Inter-Continental Hotel.

excellent though some people claim that Singha can leave you with a more fearsome hangover. The local cane whiskey is called **Mekhong** and packs a wallop for the unsuspecting. A bit sweet, it is drunk neat or, more popularly, mixed with club soda and lime, the traditional drink of the tropics. All major hotels prepare exotic mixed drinks utilizing coconuts and other tropical fruits to create punches that carry a punch.

For ages, coffee drinkers had a hard time of it with only Nescafe and a few local brands to choose from. Suddenly, coffee bars serving Kilamanjaro, French Roast and other gourmet varieties are springing up everywhere, even in department stores, a welcome change indeed. Most restaurants serve a variety of coffees but usually a single brand of tea. Only the largest restaurants and those in hotels understand what de-caffinated coffee is and are now beginning to recognize that strange American term "Sanka," translating it as de-caf rather than as a particular brand name.

Thais have their own special coffee, mixed with a thick black melange of coffee, chicory and god knows what else which ranks as the amyl nitrate of coffees, nitroglycerin brewed from a bean, strong enough to set a dead man's heart beating. Forgot your pacemaker? Have a cup of Thai coffee. In the markets, Thais fill the bottom of the glass two fingers high with sweetened condensed milk and pour the coffee over it. Ask for it black (Thais call the iced version *oliang*) to gain the full flavor of this exotic mixture.

Tea time: In Bangkok, tea drinking seems to be associated with nostalgia since its tea rooms all feature decor from another era. The Oriental Hotel's **Author's Lounge** is an unabashed throwback to the days of Joseph Conrad. This is not to say it isn't authentic; it was the courtyard of the original hotel and one can easily imagine a 19th-century gentleman and his lady enjoy-

.eft and ›elow, ›oadside neals are a ;ommon ight.

How To Savor Thai Flavors

Over the past several years, Thai food has become so popular in the West that many people who have never been anywhere near Asia "eat Thai" regularly. Thai food sold in Western restaurants is often excellent, and in some respects (the quality of the meat, for example) even surpasses that generally found in Thailand.

But, of course, the best Thai food in the world is served in Thailand, and visitors to Bangkok who have grown to love this great and ancient cuisine abroad will find every day filled with culinary revelations.

Fashionability breeds misconceptions, and the exoticism of Thai cuisine, with its pungent and unfamiliar ingredients, has certainly helped in the accumulation of misinformation. One apparently indestructible myth is that all Thai food is formidably hot and spicy.

While it is true that there are regional dishes—certain Southern Thai curries, for example—that are so paralyzingly hot that it is doubtful that anyone without some experience in spicy food could possibly get them down, the fact is that most Thai food is not hot at all. In fact, many Thais are just as chili-shy as the Westerner who keeps the Tabasco bottle at arm's length.

Generally, an authentic Thai meal will include at least one very spicy dish, a few that are less hot, and some that are bland, flavored with only garlic or herbs. Usually, purely Siamese creations will take their place alongside adapted Chinese recipes and dishes whose Indian influences are easy to spot. Traditionally, all entrees are served family style, set in the center of the table with a steaming plate of white rice for each diner.

Each person helps himself to a spoonful or so of one dish, placing it over the rice on his plate. When this has been eaten, he may try a spoonful of something else, gradually tasting all of the dishes served.

For seasonings, a small bowl of fish sauce with pieces of hot chili is usually included on the table. These peppers, called *phrik khii nuu* or "mouse dropping chilies" are the hottest in the world, and should be approached with caution.

Thai food is not eaten with chopsticks but with a fork and spoon. The spoon is held in the right hand and the fork is used to push food into it. Although this may feel strange at first, it looks odd in Thailand to see someone setting the spoon to one side and attempting to use the fork Western-style. The time spent mastering the more efficient Thai method is time well spent.

Chopsticks do come in handy, however, for the many Chinese-influenced noodle dishes which most Thais eat, particularly for a quick lunch. Noodles fall into two basic types, *Kuay Tiew*, or rice noodles, and *Ba Mii*, made from wheat flour. Both can be prepared in infinite ways, both as crowded, ingredient-packed, soup-style dishes, and "dry," like spaghetti, with various sauces and toppings.

Thais cultivate their noodle palates to astonishing degrees of refinement and it is not unusual for a carful of friends to drive for an entire Sunday morning to reach some shop which serves, say, a lunch of duck noodles of legendary excellence.

Anyone who has friends living in Bangkok is at an advantage when it comes to eating. Thais are passionate eaters and everyone has a mental list of favorite restaurants where marvels are served. Anyone going it alone, however, will find waiters and hotel personnel more than willing to recommend both restaurants and specific dishes.

For starters, the following menu is one possibility:

Thawt Man Kung. Shrimp are pounded together with coriander and other spices, formed into patties and deep-fried. This is served with a sweet sauce for dipping.

Tom Yam Kung. The most famous of Thai soups is made from shrimp, lime juice, mushrooms, lemon grass, hot chilies and a variety of other aromatic herbs. The spiciness of this soup varies from restaurant to restaurant, and those with a low tolerance for hot food should ask the waiter to have it made with a minimum of chili.

Gaeng Khiao Waan Gai. A creamy and spicy chicken curry, full of chicken meat, coconut cream, small, round, green eggplants and many fragrant herbs. This can be quite hot, but its aggressiveness can be tamed by spooning a little bit of it over a lot of rice.

Tom Kha Gai. Meaty bits of boned chicken in a tantalizing soup of rich coconut cream and lemon grass. Often served as an appetizer but delicious when poured over rice.

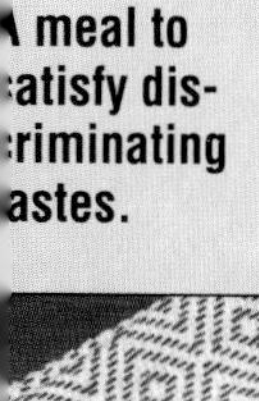
meal to atisfy dis- riminating astes.

Plaa Krapong Thawd Krathiem Prik Thai. A local salt-water fish fried until crisp with garlic and black pepper. This is served with an electrifying condiment made of fish sauce, lime juice, garlic and hot chilies. A similar dish is made with squid.

Gaeng Jued Woon Sen Sai Muu Sab. A bland soup with clear vermicelli noodles, minced pork, mixed with garlic (in quantity), crunchy mouse-ear mushrooms and various vegetables and herbs. Provides relief from more assaultive dishes.

Phak Khanna Pha Nam Man Hoi Sai Hed Hawm. A crunchy, broccoli-like vegetable fried with oyster sauce and black Chinese mushrooms. There is nothing spicy or peppery about this dish, but it has a very distinctive and delicious flavor.

Thais normally end meals with a big platter heaped with fruit like pineapple, watermelon and papaya which have already been peeled and cut into bite-sized pieces. It is set in the middle of the table and guests use toothpicks or small forks to pop pieces straight into their mouths. Alternatively, guests may be served one of the sweets described on Pages 144, 145.

ing the air while sipping piping hot Darjeeling or Earl Grey.

Today, the air is chilled by air-conditioning and the open sky is shut out by a fiberglass canopy but the atmosphere is unchanged. Tall, slender bamboo trees reach high up white-washed stucco walls that are covered in photographs of Thai royalty at the turn of the century. Guests sit on wicker sofas to sip a variety of teas and filter coffees and snack on tiny pastries under the shade of brightly-colored parasols. The very pinnacle of gentility.

Library 1918, in the **Dusit Thani Hotel**, offers similar fare as one sits in high-backed Regency chairs to enjoy the view of the gardens and the waterfall that tumbles down through them.

The Regent of Bangkok was originally the Peninsula Hotel and its lobby was modelled on that of the Peninsula Hotel in Hong Kong, one of the grand old dames of the Orient. The present management has maintained the traditional tea hours of its predecessor and provided a string orchestra in the balcony to shower soft melodies down on the imbibers.

For an evening drink: Daytime Bangkok is hard on the nerves and by rush hour (whatever that means in a city where inertia is the order of the day), all anyone wants to do is escape, preferably to sip a tall drink while looking at less stressful scenery or to get high above the streets and look down at the poor souls who have to struggle home through the horrific traffic.

The riverside terraces of major hotels are the best places to watch the sun go down. In the cool of the evening, order a colorful tropical drink or a tall glass of beer, sit back and watch the drama taking place on the liquid stage before you. At this hour, ferries move commuters between the banks, tugboats cruise up and downstream, and sampans are paddled homeward in the glow of the setting sun. The terraces of five hotels offer superb views of river life: the Menam, the Shangri-la, the Orien-

Folk dancers entertain a Tumnaktha Restaurant

tal, the Sheraton Royal Orchid and the Royal River.

The best place for an aerial view of the city as the sun is setting, is the Tiara Room of the Dusit Thani Hotel that looks down on Silom Road and Lumpini Park. Few restrooms in the world enjoy such a splendid view as those of the Tiara Room.

During the monsoon season, step in out of the rain for a late afternoon drink at the Oriental Hotel's lobby which rings with strings early each evening as an ensemble serenades patrons with baroque melodies.

Restaurants: Thais tend to dine early and most restaurants accommodate them by opening early and closing equally early which puts a crimp on those suffering from late evening hunger pangs. Most restaurants close by 10 p.m. and most hotel coffee shops are shut by midnight.

After that, it means driving in hopes of finding a quality restaurant. The alternative is to "white light" it, cruising the streets in a taxi, keeping your eyes peeled for clusters of florescent tubes popular with proprietors of late-night shophouse restaurants, market stalls and roadside noodle vendors, all of which stay open until everybody else is getting up to start a new day.

Just as there is no business district in Bangkok, there is no restaurant row. European restaurants are tucked into back lanes off Sukhumvit Road, Indian restaurants are off New Road between Silom and Suriwong, Japanese are on Thaniya Road, Middle Eastern are on Soi 3 and Soi 4 of Sukhumvit Road, while fast food chains are at Rajprasong near the Erawan Shrine and at the head of Silom Road near the Dusit Thani Hotel but everything else—Thai, Chinese, and other Asian—are scattered all over the city.

A wide array of restaurants is listed in the Travel Tips section but it is necessary to make some broad comments as a general guide to types of cuisine available in Bangkok.

Choosing the catch of the day at the supermarket-style Seafood Restaurant.

A Calendar Of Fruits

Bangkok is especially fortunate to have a wide variety of fruits coming in and out of season throughout the year so that just as one gets tired of a particular taste, another appears in the markets. Restaurants serve standard fruits like watermelon, pineapple and papaya so go to the markets to discover new taste sensations.

The flavors are as varied as the shapes and colors of the fruits that contain them. The luscious sweetness of a mango contrasts with the tartness of the Langsard, the tangy sweetness of the mangosteen with the rich flavors of the durian. If Thai fruits share one thing in common it is that they are generally sweeter than those found in temperate countries.

Some fruits found all year round:

Banana (*Gluay*). Nature has outdone herself in devising permutations on the basic banana design. Sample a different type every day and it will take you three months to run the gamut; there are more than 100 varieties. Thais eat them fried in batter, boiled and wrapped in a blanket of sticky rice, roasted and flattened with a paddle, in a sauce of sweet coconut milk, sliced thin and deep-fried like potato chips and then coated in a frosting, and just peeled and popped in the mouth. Markets and sidewalk vendors are great places to sample all the things that can be done with this amazing fruit.

Orange (*Som*). Small, very juicy, and with flavors ranging from very sweet to slightly tangy, a glass of fresh orange juice is an ideal way to start the day. Most hotels serve it freshly squeezed but if in doubt, ask for *Nam Som Kan* (squeezed orange juice).

Pomelo (*Som-O*). It is easy to mistake a *Som-O* for a grapefruit and imagine sour juice and sections that defy extrication from the rind. The Thai pomelo is heavensent refreshment on a hot afternoon: little capsules of flavor that burst as they are crushed by the teeth; rich, sweet juices that soothe as they go down.

Watermelon (*Daeng Mo*). A perennial summer favorite everywhere in the world. Since it is perennially summer in Bangkok, it enjoys special favor. Smaller than its cousins in temperate countries, it makes up in juiciness and sweetness what it lacks in size. Good things do come in small packages. A calendar of fruits follows:

January-February

Strawberries. This is an immigrant that has taken well to the cool climate of Thailand's northern hills. Smaller and tarter than temperate varieties, when slathered with whipped cream, they are as delicious as their counterparts.

March-June

Papaya (*Malagaw*). Papayas grow year-round but are especially tasty after the advent of the hot season. Sliced lengthwise and their seeds removed,

eft, early ruit stand. ight, fresh urians eady to be evoured.

their soft, pulpy dark orange meat is spooned out and eaten. Thais like to squeeze lime juice on them to add a bit of tang. Shredded papaya is the main ingredient in *som tam*, a fiery salad popular in Northeastern Thailand.

March-July

Sapodilla (*Lamood*). A surprisingly sweet, soft pulp fruit eaten peeled or halved and its sampled with a spoon. Beware of the big black seeds.

April-May

Lichee (*Linchee*). Only a decade ago, this small fruit with its thin, hard shell was regarded as sour and not tasty. A succession of green thumb miracles has created a fruit nearly twice its former size and extremely sweet. Resembling, the Rambutan, the whitish flesh conceals a big black seed.

April-June

Mango (*Mamuang*). Mangoes are the gods' gifts to humankind. Their lush yellow flesh is sweet, often bordering on tart. Hotels outdo themselves in dreaming up new ways of serving them but the old standard *Khao Niew Mamuang* (Mango and sticky rice) reigns supreme. The mangoes enjoy a strange relationship with the durian: if it is a good year for mangoes, the durian crop will be bad and vice-versa.

Durian. Not everybody's cup of tea, the durian is either hated or loved but succeeds in making converts of those who on initial contact despised it. The most expensive of Thai fruits, the durian is recognized by its hedgehog skin, the heavenly aroma (or disgusting stench to some) of its flesh, and by the rather mushy consistency of its meat. Most people are repelled by the sight of it on first encounter. Adventurous but wary diners sneak up on it by sampling it in a coconut milk sauce on sticky rice. The durian has a reputation for producing gas, for heating up the one's innards. It is a small price to pay. Persevere and you will be rewarded.

April-July

Pineapple (*Saparot*). Thailand is a top exporter of tinned pineapple and for good reason: its pineapples are sweet, with little of the sharp acidity found in pineapples from other realms. Thais eat it sliced and garnished with salt and ground chilis which, odd as it sounds, enhances its natural sweetness.

Rose Apple (*Chompoo*). One of the most refreshing of Thai fruits, the pink and green-skinned *chompoo* is pried apart with the fingers to reveal a crispy white meat with the texture of a pear.

May-August

Custard Apple (*Noi-na*). This light green hand-grenade with its knobby surface, can also be pulled apart by hand. The pulp is soft, often mushy, very sweet and very tasty. The pulpy fruit conceals long black seeds.

July-August

Longan (*Lamyai*). A relative of the Lichee and Rambutan, it resembles the Langsard with its thin yellow skin but has the Lichee's sweetness.

July-September

Rambutan (*Ngor*). Similar to the Lichee, its skin is covered in thick red hairs. There is a technique to squeezing it open to avoid squirting oneself with its juices; any Thai can demonstrate. The flesh is translucent and sweet, though the woody pit is somewhat of a nuisance because it tends to break up as one is trying to chew the flesh off it.

August-September

Jackfruit (*Khanoon*). Dividing this enormous fruit into its myriad sections is a major chore that is best left to the experts. The rich yellow sections resemble buttercup blossoms, are waxy-textured, semi-sweet and very tasty on a warm day.

August-October

Langsard. Not one of the tastier members of the fruit family, the Langsard's brownish-yellow skin conceals a fruit that is somewhat bitter and breaks into sections like a garlic cloves. It provides a nice contrast to all the sweetness of the other Thai fruits. Perhaps someday, brilliant botanists will develop a sweet variety as they have with the Lichee.

Mangosteen (*Mangkut*). One of the delightful denizens of the Thai fruit world, its hard deep red shell conceals soft pulpy sections that ooze with sweetness. A favorite Thai game is to ask visitors to guess the number of sections it contains without breaking it open (hint: count the number of "petals" in the woody flower on the bottom of the fruit).

October-February

Green Plum (*Putsa*). Shaped like a plum, the *Putsa* resembles a green apple, both in the color of its skin and in the texture of its pulp. It is eaten skin and all but be sure to gnaw around the long, very hard seeds.

Tropical Thai fruits, presented au naturel (left) and more elegantly (right).

Thai: Most of the dishes found in Bangkok are from the Central Plains (see box). Northeastern (*E-sarn*) food is quite hot and features such items as chicken roasted as only the *E-sarn* people know how; minced meat dishes under the heading of *larb*; *som-tam*, a fiery salad made from shredded raw papaya, dried shrimp and chilies; and strips of beef jerky.

E-sarn chicken is the specialty of a group of restaurants behind the Rajdamnern Boxing Stadium. A number of Northeastern restaurants are to be found in the lanes behind Paesano Italian restaurant on Soi Lang Suan. Northern cuisine with its cold rice in water (*khao chae*) is often served by restaurants offering Thai classical dancing performances. Southern food is virtually unheard of in Bangkok.

Chinese: With a country and culture as diverse as that of China it is not surprising that its chefs would have created an enormous variety of dishes. Most Thai Chinese are of *Tae-chiew* (*Chiu Chow* to a Hong Kong Chinese) descent, so the typical Thai Chinese restaurant serves *Tae-chiew* dishes with a distinct Cantonese flavor. *Tae-chiew* is famed for dishes such as thick shark's fin soup, goose doused in soy sauce, and dried blood recipes that are not to everyone's taste.

For this reason, the more widely acceptable Cantonese influence is apparent in Thai Chinese cooking. Fruits and teas are integral parts of every meal. Birds, pork and seafood are essentials and the variety of fungi and mushrooms is enough to make the senses reel. Cantonese cooking emphasizes the fast approach to bring dishes to the peak of their natural taste and color.

Other Chinese cuisines are well represented in Thailand. Shanghainese food is typified by dishes that are fried in sesame or soy sauce for a long time making them sweeter and oilier than other cuisines. Although not as varied as their southern cousins, Pekinese dishes such as Peking Duck, Mongolian Hot Pot, and wheat dumplings justify their world renown. Pekinese dishes have been enriched by the wealth of Thailand's vegetables although the Peking Duck available here takes on the guise of a goose. This should not affect one's enjoyment of the dish, however, as it is the skin that is important.

Bangkok has numerous Chinese restaurants offering a wide range of regional cuisines. Party bookings are widely accepted and special banquet menus may be ordered provided sufficient notice is given.

Indian: The cuisine is of the northern half of the sub-Continent and runs strongly to *tandoori*, *korma*, and *masala* served with rice, *chapatis* or *nan* with *lassi* to wash it down. Madrasi and southern Indian food is served at only one or two restaurants (like Amber on Soi 4), a shame because despite its extreme spiciness it is delicious.

Middle Eastern: This is a tricky category because aside from the very decidedly Arabian restaurants along

A reason to smile. Right, lunch wagon—Bangkok style.

ก.ค.๒๙

Soi 3 and Soi 4 on Sukhumvit which cater almost exclusively to Arab visitors and the Lebanese food served by The Cedars, it is difficult to know from the restaurant's name the type of food on its menu, moreso because it often serves a mix of several cuisines, for example, Indian and Arabic.

Restaurants are often denoted as "Muslim" which means they do not serve pork. Neither is their food strictly Middle Eastern nor is it Thai and its patrons are normally Thai Muslims or Indian and Pakistani Muslims.

Continental: At the top restaurants, the dishes are near carbon copies of those you would find at home. If the meats and seasonings available in the local market do not meet high hotel standards, they will be imported. Not to be ignored are the gourmet restaurants, European and Thai, in the large hotels which serve excellent meals complemented by equally high quality wines.

In restaurants whose menus are dominated by Thai food, Continental dishes tends to be approximations rather than replicas of the original. Thus, a Cordon Bleu (or Blue or Blew, as it appears on some menus) is an anemic slab of pork stuffed with slices of processed cheese. It is a Thai conviction voiced repeatedly that Western food is *jute* (bland) and seemingly a cook's conviction that he should make it as bland as possible. If dining or having breakfast in anything other than a restaurant specializing in a particular European cuisine, be prepared for some surprises. Most of the surprises will amuse you.

Vegetarian: It's slim pickings for vegetarians in Bangkok because nearly every Thai dish contains meat, strange in a land of Buddhists. There is only one restaurant devoted solely to the preparation of vegetarian dishes: **Whole Earth** on Lang Suan. There are two excellent make-it-yourself salad bars at the Hilton and the Siam Inter-Continental. Seeing their popularity, other hotels are in the process of setting up their

Night market at Pratunam.

own. For low-end salads, there are several Pizza Hut outlets. The mayor of Bangkok operates a vegetarian restaurant serving weekend lunches next to the bus terminus just west of the Chatuchak Weekend Market.

Buffets and food festivals: Many hotels serve table-bending yet economical lunchtime buffets that include Thai and European dishes. They also stage month-long festivals featuring the cuisine of a particular country, usually flying in a chef to prepare it. Keep an eye on local newspapers for announcements.

Outdoor restaurants: Bangkok's balmy evenings and tropical setting invite one to sit down to a dinner under the stars. Most outdoor restaurants are along the Ratchapisek Highway beyond the Asoke-Din Daeng intersection. They take full advantage of their rural setting, erecting Thai-style pavilions around ponds and artificial waterfalls. The largest, **Tum Nak Thai**, features the foods of all of Thailand's regions. It seats 2,000 patrons who are served by waitresses on roller skates.

Restaurants by the river: Thai entrepreneurs have finally discovered that food lovers enjoy dining by the edge of the river and in recent years have begun building riverbank restaurants. Most major riverside hotels have terraces serving Continental food. **Lord Jim's** in the Oriental Hotel lets you survey the river while enjoying seafood lunches and dinners. The Oriental's **Rim Nam Restaurant** across the river, the Shangri-La's **Salathip**, and the Dusit Thani's **Dusit Rimtam Seafood Restaurant**, have Thai-style decor and dishes.

There are also restaurants built on floating platforms moored by the riverbank. They are reached by gangways and set gently swaying by each passing wave making it difficult to know when you've had too much to drink. Most of them serve only Thai meals. **Ruan Panya** across from the Shangri-la Hotel and several on Phra Athit Road near the

All set for a sumptuous riverside. meal

Heaven-Sent Sweets

Thai chefs who boast that they can prepare a different curry for every day of the year must certainly have their counterparts among cooks who specialize in Thai sweets or *khanom*.

In Bangkok, desserts come in a bewildering but hugely tempting variety of styles, shapes and colors, ranging from light concoctions of shaved ice, coconut cream and diced melon through custards, ice creams and cakes to specialities unlike anything found in the West. Candied dried shrimp, powdered fish in syrup over coconut-cream rice, and an entire category of confections based on egg yolks cooked in flower-scented syrups are ready to satisfy the cultivated sweet tooth in any marketplace.

Bananas and coconuts grow everywhere in Thailand and their dessert possibilities have scarcely been overlooked. In fact, if these two fruits were to be removed from the list of ingredients available to the *khanom* cook, the entire edifice of Thai dessert cookery would come crashing down.

The heavier Thai confections are rarely eaten after a big meal. Desserts, served in small bowls after the rice and those dishes eaten with it have been cleared from the table, are generally light and elegant. *Kluay Buat Chii*, a popular after-dinner sweet, consists of banana chunks stewed in sweetened and slightly salted, scented coconut cream and served warm.

Another favorite, *Thap Thim Krawb*, is made from small balls of tapioca flour, dyed red and shaped around tiny pieces of crisp water chestnut. These are served in a mixture of sweetened, fragrant coconut cream and ice. The name translates as "crispy pomegranate seeds" because of the resemblance.

Anyone walking through a big Bangkok market is bound to encounter a

An array of Thai sweets— many are Portuguese origin.

sweets vendor with his pushcart. The wares displayed on his cart run the gamut from candied fruits to million-calorie custards made from coconut cream, eggs and palm sugar. These sweet temptations are generally sold in the form of three-inch squares which the vendor will wrap in banana leaves for the buyer to take home.

Many of these sweets are made startlingly inventive, putting familiar ingredients in surprising surroundings. One may completely finish off a rich pudding, for example, before realizing that its tantalizing flavor came from crisp-fried onions.

Excellent *khanom* of various types can also be bought by the bagful from roadside vendors who prepare them fresh on portable griddles. One such sweet is the *Khanom Beuang* or "roof-tile cookie" which consists in one version of an extremely thin crispy shell folded over taco-style and filled with sweet coconut, strands of egg yolk cooked in syrup, spiced and sweetened dried shrimp, fresh coriander and a sugary cream. The concoction may sound bizarre but few can set the bag down after eating just one.

In buying Thai sweets, picking what looks good is usually pretty disappointment-proof. Here are a few real masterpieces that can be asked for by name:

Sangkhya Maphrao Awn. A magnificent custard made from thick coconut cream, palm sugar and eggs, then steamed inside a young coconut. Another version is cooked inside a small pumpkin. Forget everything the nutritionists have been telling you before ordering this one.

Khao Laam. Glutinous rice mixed with coconut cream, sugar and, optionally, black beans or other goodies and cooked in bamboo segments. The bamboo is slit open and the rice eaten.

Taeng Thai Nam Kati. A canteloupe-like Thai melon cut into small cubes and mixed with ice and sweetened, flavored coconut cream.

Khanom Maw Gaeng. Another custard-like sweet, again made with coconut cream and eggs, but this time with soybean flour mixed in to thicken it. It is baked in square metal tins.

Kluay Khaek. A protein-rich local species of banana sliced lengthwise, dipped in coconut cream and flour and deep fried until the coating is crisp.

The counters of many foodshops are covered in fishbowls filled with all sorts of tempting bits, some recognizable, some not. Kernels of corn, water chestnuts, lotus seeds and black beans share space with squiggly pink and green tapioca flour "worms," the translucent fruit of the *Dtan* palm and half a dozen others.

Select as many items as will fit in a dish. The vendor then runs a block of ice across a device like an upside-down carpenter's plane to shave tiny bits of ice into the dish. He pours over the entire lot a sweet syrup.

If you sample nothing else, top off a meal with a dish of *katit*, coconut ice cream that is rich and heavenly.

isap- aring art: ar dies in cy pes.

Phra Pinklao Bridge are popular with both Thais and travelers.

Dinner cruises: If diners like the river so much, why not seat them on it rather than by it? That bright revelation has spawned a dozen or so boats which cruise up and down the river past the cityscape while serving a set menu Thai dinner. The **Tassaneya Nava** was the first to float the idea and is still one of the best.

Restaurants with views: You would think that with all of Bangkok's tall buildings there would be more rooftop restaurants. Alas, such is not the case. The **Tiara** restaurant in the Dusit Thani Hotel offers a large buffet luncheon and a formal dinner with orchestra and show. The Narai Hotel's **Rotunda Restaurant** takes you for a spin, completing a full 360 degree circuit in the hour it takes you to complete your meal. The tallest, **Sky Lounge** is 43 stories up the Baiyoke Tower. The **Normandie Grill** atop the Oriental is a gourmet French restaurant with a superb view of the river.

No-hands: For novelty value only and probably not while a spouse is within a 50-mile radius, the **No-hands Restaurant** in the **Galaxy** restaurant complex at 19 Rama 4 Road, stresses service to the *ninth* degree with a waitress armed with chopsticks gently serving you Chinese tidbits in your own private room. The owners say there is no hanky-panky but they always say that, even in massage parlors.

Markets: Having attracted an increasingly sophisticated clientele, market restaurants have moved up-market, even to the point of encasing their premises in glass and air-conditioning them. This has not detracted from the high quality of their food, only inflated your bill a tad. **Pratunam** market has become very popular for its fresh seafood. You choose your items and they are prepared in one of a hundred delicious ways, usually Chinese style though they can be spiced up to suit your taste.

Most of the restaurants in Pratunam are still open-air, creating an atmosphere of relaxed conviviality that, as much as their food, has been responsible for their popularity. **Bangrak** Market off New Road between Silom and Sathorn Roads is somewhat downscale. There is nothing fancy here, just good food as eaten by ordinary Thais on an evening out.

Seafood markets: The seafood market concept has become so popular here that it has been copied elsewhere. Hong Kong's first seafood market was opened in mid-1987 after its owners had made many trips to Bangkok to study how it was done. In most, like the **Seafood Market Restaurant** on Sukhumvit Road across from Soi 21, the diner pushes a shopping cart along freezer counters laden with an array of seafood. His purchases are totted up at a cash register and then taken away to be cooked according to his instructions. A cooking fee is charged at the same time the drinks bill is added up. Lots of fun but it can be expensive.

Thai cuisine offers astounding variety. Right, a display of fruit and vegetable carving skill.

Noontime noodles: When the clock strikes 12, Bangkok offices empty and employees stream towards their favorite shophouse restaurants. There, they peruse pans of food behind glass, choosing one or two items which are spooned onto a plate of steaming rice. There are also slices of duck (*khao mun pet*), chicken (*khao mun gai*) or pork (*khao moo daeng*) atop rice which are equally delicious.

The alternative lunchtime treat is noodles (*kuay tiew*) in a variety of shapes and forms. They may be wide and starchy, they may be hair-like and yellow. With slices of pork or fishballs, they are eaten wet like soup or dry; for both types you use chopsticks. A fun variation is *kuay tiew rua* sold near the Victory Monument. These are essentially the same noodle dishes found elsewhere but are cooked on small sampans on the canal and served to diners seated at tables on the canal bank.

Thais wash down their lunches with glasses of sweetened black tea or a black coffee whose ingredients have probably never been properly analyzed because no one really wants to know. Suffice it to say that it is thick and, with a large amount of sweetened condensed milk poured in, is enough to set your heart racing and get you through the afternoon. A lunch, complete with tea, will cost no more than 12 baht ($.50).

Dinner and cultural shows: Sample Thai cuisine and culture in the same sitting. Diners are seated in a Thai-style house either on cushions or chairs around a table on which are placed numerous dishes of Thai food. This is a good opportunity to sample several tastes of Thailand and then settle back to experience the elegance of Thai classical dancing. **Baan Thai**, **Pimarn**, the **Maneeya Room**, **Sala Norasingh** and **Sala Rim Nam** all offer excellent introductions to Thailand and should be considered for your first night in town. The Siam Inter-Continental has a Thai Night each Monday

Ready for business at this mobile counter.

and Thursday in its garden with a buffet of Thai food and a cultural show.

Late, late night: Markets and roadside restaurants are the salvation for the traveler whose biological clock is askew and who awakens at 2 a.m. starving to death. **Pratunam** market, **Bangrak** Market, vendors and tables at the entrance to Soi 38 on Sukhumvit stay open most of the night, serving basic Thai dishes like noodles and fried rice. If you just want to snack, **Foodland** supermarket on Patpong 2 stays open 24 hours.

Short cooking courses: Most visitors fall in love with Thai cuisine and want to continue enjoying it when they return home. Many major Western cities now have stores stocking all the spices and exotic ingredients required in Thai recipes. The only thing that is missing is mastery of the preparation techniques.

Thai food is not difficult to cook and it doesn't require hours of preparation. The pounding and mixing of the spices and the order in which the ingredients are to be added can be learned from a book. Most people prefer a little first-hand experience under the tutelage of a master before venturing out on their own. Bangkok now meets that need.

There are now three cooking schools, two of them associated with a well-known hotel and restaurant. Each offers courses of five and 10 days (see Travel Tips for details) at very reasonable prices. The emphasis is on main dishes rather than desserts and generally does not include the preparation of spices. By the end of the course, the student should be able to prepare a full menu of Thai traditional dishes.

The **Rim Nam Cooking School** is operated by the Oriental Hotel which now offers a Thai cuisine vacation wherein the student stays at the hotel and divides his days between classes and leisure activities.

The **Bussaracum Restaurant** and the **YMCA** (with the city's oldest cooking school) also offer short courses.

Drool school: cooking class at the Oriental.

HOTELS

Unlike many capital cities, Bangkok seems to have been built with the traveler in mind because it offers myriad rooms and at any price level one could want. And in any style: riverside, jungled, modern, venerable, luxurious, cheap, Bangkok has them all.

What sets Bangkok hotels apart from the rest and wins them international awards year after year can be summed up in one word: service. Thailand is renowned for its gracious hospitality and hotels have capitalized on this reputation, creating one of the highest staff-to-guest ratios in the world. Add to this the fact that top-class hotels have some of the city's best shopping arcades and sports and dining facilities right on the premises.

To a greater extent than in most Western capitals, hotels are hubs of the city's social life with weddings, exhibitions, awards dinners and other festivities celebrated there daily. Thais and resident foreigners entertain local and out-of-town guests at hotel restaurants, cocktail lounges and bars.

Some of the town's best discotheques and nightclubs are found in hotels. Many lobbies have Thai classical musicians, Baroque string quartets or Thai women demonstrating ancient arts like floral garland making. In short, the hotels are little islands unto themselves, oases in which you never feel stranded as you might in other cities. If you never leave your hotel you could still have a good time in Bangkok.

Neither will you hear complaints about boring hotel food in Bangkok. In a city known for its fine food, hotels have some of Bangkok's top restaurants with superb chefs from faraway lands (Bangkok is a prized assignment among hoteliers). Most hotels have several top-class restaurants serving Thai, Continental and Chinese cuisine as well as coffee shops with a wide range of good solid meals. Many hotels have their own bakeries and chocolate kitchens. Some of the best buffets are offered at breakfast and lunch time.

Left, new hotels join the Oriental on the banks of the Chao Phya.

All hotels, except bottom-rung budget inns, have swimming pools and air-conditioning. Top hotels offer meeting rooms, limousine services and business centers with secretarial services, telex, FAX and other facilities. Some have conference centers and health clubs (see Travel Tips for complete listing). Prices begin below those for comparable lodging elsewhere in the world. They rise for luxury accommodation to as much as one wants to pay, the top level being 41,000 baht ($1,600) for a suite. Rooms at top hotels have in-house video movies, 24-hour room service and refrigerators filled with drinks and snacks.

Topping the list of luxury hotels are those along the river and those set in their own tropical gardens. For years, the roll has been headed by the fabled **Oriental Hotel**. The hotel of Somerset Maugham and Joseph Conrad who featured it in their books, the old wing of the Oriental seems a leftover from the colonial era. Its Author's Lounge is a must for indulging in afternoon of tea *a la* planters of old, a mode and pace of existence which has been steamrolled into extinction by the bustle of late-20th century life.

That is not to say there aren't other hotels of equal distinction; they just haven't been discovered or touted to the same degree as the Oriental. Just downriver is the **Shangri-la Hotel** with a broad, palm-shaded terrace overlooking the busy river. Its tall lobby windows look down on an equally beautiful view making it an excellent place to cool your feet and enjoy an afternoon drink.

The lobby of **The Regent of Bangkok Hotel** is another reminder of yesteryear with its high ceilings painted in old Thai mandala and a small orchestra in a high alcove providing background music for day-long teas and snacks below. The spacious atrium with its fish pond is an oasis from city heat. Old-world elegance at its best.

The **Siam Inter-Continental** is set in a spacious tropical garden. Twenty-six acres (10.4 hectares) of old royal land in the heart of town give a country-side feel to one of Bangkok's better-known hotels. An outdoor gym and streams winding under picturesque bridges and into duck-filled ponds enhance the jungle atmosphere.

The **Hilton** is quite unlike anything one expects of a hotel chain member. Its rooms are built around an indoor garden that is rivaled only by its large outdoor garden laid out around lotus-filled ponds and a big swimming pool. Glass walls provide a splendid garden vista for diners in its coffee shop and French restaurant.

The **Dusit Thani**, one of Bangkok's first major hotels, continues to enjoy a well-deserved reputation for combining amenities every businessman appreciates with an air of graciousness. Everywhere you turn there is a reminder of Thailand and its culture. Its rooftop restaurant provides one of the most envied aerial views of the city. It is also prized for its close proximity to Lumpini Park, business establishments and the city's famed nightlife district.

The **Central Plaza Hotel** may be on the northern end of town but the expressway puts it within minutes of the city center and at the same time offers busy travelers a quick getaway to the airport. Huge conference halls make it a favorite venue for conventions yet it offers the warm ambience of a family hotel. Across the street is the famous Chatuchak Weekend Market and adjacent is one of the city's largest shopping centers.

The **Meridien President** (formerly the "President") combines modern decor with some fine old Thai art in a pleasing blend of styles. The Meridien President is a place to relax, it has a piano bar, a large shopping arcade and several fine restaurants. A major plus is its location in the very center of the

Exotic suite at the Oriental.

shopping district. Across the street is the Erawan Shrine.

The **Montien Hotel** is about as close to the entertainment district as one can get in Bangkok. It offers much more than that, however: a variety of restaurants, good location for business appointments and its own entertainment complex. The latter includes a lobby lounge with live music, a dance floor with a band and a cocktail lounge.

The **Landmark Hotel** is Bangkok's newest hotel. Just up Sukhumvit Road, it is the answer to a traveler's all-in-one accommodation. Range of restaurants, a gym, business center, discotheque and nightclub means that one need leave the premises only if he wishes; everything else is at his fingertips.

Aside from a few other first-class establishments, hotels range downwards from this point to surprisingly comfortable, well-appointed rooms for around 600 baht ($23.50) per night. Below that are the hotels with clean and simple rooms costing between 200 and 500 baht per night ($7.90 to $19.60).

For longer stays, try the clean, comfortable guesthouses with city center locations. Budget travelers head for hotels on Ngam Du Plee Road in the vicinity of the Malaysia Hotel or to the very economical guesthouses along Khaosan Road.

Up-country, there are first class hotels in Pattaya, Chiang Mai, Hua Hin, Cha-am and Phuket and other major towns. Next, come what are called "Chinese" hotels equipped only with the bare essentials like fans and showers. At Khao Yai and River Kwai, the emphasis is on rustic comfort although they have Western-style bathrooms.

Remember that during the off-season from mid-April to mid-November, hotels generally reduce their rates by as much as 40 percent or will give you a special discount if you request it when booking or checking in. You may even get a discount during high season if the hotel is underbooked or is in hot competition with a rival. It pays to ask.

Understated elegance at the Siam Inter-Continental.

TAKING PHOTOS

Few cities offer so many opportunities to take superb photographs. Bangkok is rich with colors and patterns and you can find shots in the least expected places. Allow yourself at least one roll of film per day or end up kicking yourself later for opportunities missed.

Temples and palaces are the perennial favorites among the city's many photo subjects. More interesting for the traveler are the numerous street scenes that will capture your eye. Vegetable and flower markets are good places to wander, camera in hand. The Weekend market at Chatuchak is the obvious choice but those at Phak Klong Talat and Pratunam are also obvious choices.

Rites and rituals also offers good photo opportunities. The dances and offerings at the Erawan Shrine and Lak Muang provide a variety of subjects. Early risers can catch the Buddhist monks in their orange robes as they pad silently through the streets receiving alms from Buddhist householders. On Wan Phra walk through a neighborhood temple early in the morning to observe the monks chanting sermons.

Lumpini Park is one of the best picture spots in the city. In the morning, it offers Chinese pursuing ancient tai chi exercises and rituals involving swords. In the afternoon, you'll find takraw players, boaters, children, and, during the hot season, kite sellers and flyers. Thai astrologers also display intriguing posters and banners bearing occult symbols and advertising their services.

The canals provide a glimpse of home life up close. While the long-tailed boats will speed you through the canal, they often move too quickly to allow you to compose and capture a scene. Their low roof and many struts also manage to get included in a shot. Much better are the larger, slower canal boats which afford you more time to

The Royal Palace makes the perfect background for a portrait in this old fashioned studio.

spot a shot and to compose it as you want to. Often, just standing on a bridge and shooting down on houses or boats will give you the atmosphere of a canal scene that captures the essence of Thai life in a single shot.

A big plus is that Thailand is one of the world's easiest countries in which to take photographs. Unlike other parts of the world, you can photograph the interiors of temples and religious festivals and ceremonies without objections.

Neither are there restrictions on photographing women. Thais of both sexes have no objection to being photographed, even repeatedly performing an action (for example, stringing a floral garland, crafting a lacquer plate or lighting incense at a spirit house) until you are satisfied with the shot. He won't look like he is posing and, best of all, there is no request for payment.

Bangkok's midday tropical light tends to bleach out colors. For best results, shoot between dawn and 9 a.m. and 3:30 p.m. to dusk when the light is warmer and richer. For midday shooting, an ultraviolet or skylight filter is a must; it wouldn't hurt to add a light brown filter like an 81A. If you have to shoot at midday, a polarizing filter will deepen the colors, especially the blue of the sky. Most people stay in the shade during the day so a flash is handy, especially in markets.

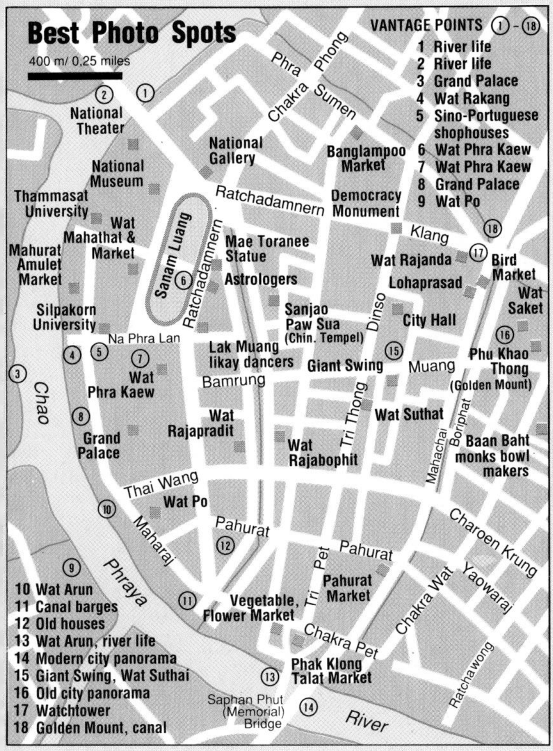

Kodak, Fuji, Agfa and Konica films in 35 mm, 120 mm and disk form are easily obtained in Bangkok. If shooting slides, choose a "warm" film like Kodachrome, Fuji, or Ektachrome Professional rather than normal Ektachrome which enhances the blues in the shadows. Avoid buying film stored in shop windows exposed to the hot sun; check the emulsion date on the box to make sure the film is good.

Bangkok now has numerous shops offering 45-minute developing and printing but the quality is what you would expect from a rush job. Seagull Sevices, Ground Floor of the Maneeya Bldg. on Ploenchit Road (next to Kentucky Fried Chicken; Tel: 251-7899) offer 24-hour processing print films and for Kodak and other slide films like Fujichrome are developed in E-6.

Photo shows: The Thai culture show at the Rose Garden (Km. 32, Petchkasem Road; Bangkok office: 253-2276) provides a superb opportunity to capture the most glittering features of Thai traditional life on film. Thai classical dancing, Thai boxing, a wedding ceremony, harvest dances and other aspects of village life are presented during a special show each day at 3 p.m.

Video cameras: More visitors are now arriving with video cameras. Most brands are represented in Bangkok so finding batteries and repair facilities is not a problem; check the telephone directory. Blank VHS and video 8 cassettes are sold in most department stores. The suggestions for subjects is the same as for still cameras with the addition of action subjects which would include takraw games, canal boats, tuk-tuks, and market scenes.

SHOPPING

The artistry that 19th-century craftsmen poured into temples, 20th-century artisans now employ in creating a wealth of beautiful products that have made shopping one of Bangkok's prime attractions for visitors. Clothes, jewelry, home decor items, handicrafts and art objects all find new homes abroad, taken there by shoppers who know a bargain when they see one.

Shopping in Bangkok is more than pushing a cart through a store. It is an adventure with surprises everywhere, items you didn't know Thailand produced and a few you didn't even know existed. Part of the adventure is in arriving at a price. Prices in department stores are fixed but those in markets and most souvenir and art shops are determined by bargaining, even when the price is stamped on the item.

Bargaining is supposed to be fun, not a clash of wills and it is generally accompanied by casual bantering. If the price does not suit you, smile and walk away. Chances are you will be accosted to return and your price will be agreed to. If not, you may find the price you want just down the block. Remember that when making several purchases at the same shop, bargain down the price for each item, and then try to bargain down the total; you can usually knock a little extra off the overall price.

Thailand's most famous product is **Thai silk**. For decades, it languished in the remote regions of the country, shunned by the Thai aristocracy who preferred imported cloths. It was a dying art when it was discovered by American entrepreneur Jim Thompson who promoted it abroad where it quickly gained wide reception for its nubbly texture and shimmering iridescence. Within a few years it became a major Thai industry.

A farang tries her hand at the fine art of bargaining.

Thai silk is thicker and stiffer than Chinese and European silks but it holds its own when transformed into a suit. It looks better on women than men and can be turned into a superb evening gown or woman's business suit by one of Bangkok's tailors. It is sold by the yard in a rainbow of colors.

It is also printed in subtle scenes and patterns and turned into pillow slips, scarves, ties, photo frames, clutch bags, lipstick holders and tissue boxes. Shops abound but among those who specialize in Thai silk are Jim Thompson Thai Silk at 9 Suriwongse Rd. and T. Shinawatr Thai Silk at 94 Soi 23, Sukhumvit Road.

Mudmee, a Northeastern silk, is a form of tie-dye wherein the threads are dyed before they are placed in the loom. It is characterized by a very subtle pattern of zigzag lines and tends to somber hues like dark blue, maroon and deep yellow. It makes a very elegant woman's dress or suit or a handsome, Nehru-necked *rajaprathan* favored by Thai officials.

Thai cotton in plain colors and prints is made into dresses and most of the items into which Thai silk is rendered. Other cotton items are tablecloths, placemats and napkins. A surprising number of visitors arrive with measurements for sofas and windows and have shops tailor and ship upholstery and curtains.

A half-dozen different hilltribes populate the northern hills and each has its own distinctive patchwork and embroidery designs mainly in bright blues, magentas and yellows. The embroidery is either appliqued on clothes or sold in short lengths for table dressings. They find their way into formal evening wear, purses and others, turning ordinary clothes and accessories into eye-catching items.

Although it is a major textile producer, Thailand imports a large amount of Chinese and Japanese silk, Chinese satin, denim, linen, poplin, wool (surprising for tropical Thailand), polyesters and polyester blends, and a dozen others can be found. Look for them in Pahurat market (Pahurat Road), Sampeng Lane, Pratunam Market, Chatuchak Weekend Market and major department stores.

The hard, very practical triangular pillows found in Thai homes serve as backrests while sitting on the floor or a sofa. They are covered in red, blue and yellow striped cloth accented by embroidery. A cousin is the small square pillow, a soft "opium pillow" just high enough to raise your head off a horizontal surface.

Bangkok has taken over men's **tailoring** from Hong Kong which simply priced itself out of the market. Select from a wide range of imported or local cloth to make three-piece suits, pants, shirts and the popular safari suits. Supply your own design or leaf through the latest *GQ* or other magazine the tailor keeps on hand.

Some shops can complete the suit in 24 hours but if you have sufficient time it is best to go back for one or two fittings before the final stitches are put in place. Among the best known men's high class tailors are Art's Tailor at 62/15-16 Thaniya Road and Perry's at 60/2 Silom Road.

Similarly, women's fashions can be crafted from cloth bought elsewhere or selected in the shop. Generally, men are more successful at getting the fit they want than are women but there are several shops such as **Noriko** and **Nusra** which are adept at creating what madame wants.

Bangkok abounds in **ready-made clothes**, a new development over the past decade. Available are brand names (not designer labels, most of which are fakes; see below) made under license to overseas companies but sold for far less. Finding large sizes is difficult (for men, American size 34 pants is the biggest) but for those blessed with small bodies, it is a shopper's heaven.

Clothes stalls at Chatuchak Market, the lower end of Sukhumvit and the length of Silom Road sell very cheap but well-made shirts (usually with fake Pierre Cardin and Ralph Lauren labels).

Up-to-date Bangkok fashions.

The dyes tend to fade after a dozen washings but at $5 per shirt who's to complain?

Leather **shoes** are made for the middle range of the market. The tanning isn't the best and the fit isn't always perfect even when specially cut for the customer. For casual wear, they are acceptable. Among the more exotic products are boots made of cobra or crocodile skin.

Thai **leatherware** is generally well tanned and durable. Leather briefcases and handbags, often made as replicas of famed European brands complete with fake trademarks, are generally of good quality. Beware of the "brass" fittings which are often a plated metal which quickly tarnishes.

Crocodiles are no longer the hunters, they are the prey. Crocodile and, to a lesser extent, cobra, skin is a highly popular material for wallets, purses, shoes, belts, and even briefcases. Prices are very reasonable.

The very moderate pricetags on **gems and jewelry** have made them another appealing shopping item. Thailand mines its own rubies and sapphires and is one of the world's leading cutters of colored gems. Rubies range from pale to deep red (including the famous "pigeon's blood" red) and sapphires come in blue, green and yellow as well as one associated with Thailand, the Star Sapphire. Many zircons have been heat treated to change them from red to colorless, enhancing their beauty but lowering their value.

Thai craftsmen turn gold, white gold and silver into handsome jewelry settings. Local designs tend towards tradition patterns so modern designs are imported from abroad and crafted here. Workmanship is generally good.

A word of warning, however. While the stones are generally of the quality and weight advertised, some shopkeepers are less than scrupulous in ensuring that the gold content of settings is of the karat number stated. Shops offer guarantees of the authenticity of each piece but these cannot always be believed. Once you have paid, it is difficult to get refunds or restitution. It is best to shop at a larger store or one recommended by friends who have shopped in Bangkok before.

Thailand's **costume jewelry** boasts attractive design and good workmanship. Because prices are very reasonable, costume jewelry pieces are good, lightweight gifts to carry home. Thailand's reputation as an orchid center has led it to capitalize on the beauty of these lovely blooms by preserving them as costume jewelry. Live blossoms are plated in gold by a special process that allows them to retain their original shape and some of their natural color. They are transformed into brooches and pendants.

Thailand is a center for **jade** by merit of its having Burma as a next-door neighbor. Most of it is smuggled across the western border. The very valuable pieces are shipped abroad; the lesser grades are cut and sold in Thailand. Rare is the nephrite or "mutton white"

Bolts of Thai silk fill the window of Jim Thompson's shop.

jade prized by the Chinese. Most common is jadeite, the bright green jade familiar to European buyers, and the less expensive pieces in a rainbow of earth colors. The jade is carved into rings, bracelets and pendants. Beware of other stones such as jasper that are often passed off as jade.

Heavily-guarded farms off the southern island of Phuket produce fine cultured **pearls** including what is reputed to be the largest pearl ever created. Pearl necklaces, earrings and other fashion accessories are offered in many Bangkok jewelry shops. Imported Mikimoto pearls are also sold in the city.

Gold pieces of the gold content advertised can be found in the shops along Chinatown's artery, Yaowarat Road. The shops are easily recognized because they seem stamped out of the same mold: glass fronts, upswept ceilings, vermillion lacquer surfaces, acres of display cases and a policeman on guard out front. Rings, earrings, bracelets, anklets and other items are sold with plain surfaces, etched with designs, set with precious and semi-precious stones and or linked chains.

Chiang Mai makes attractive **silver** necklaces, bracelets and other accessories which are sold in Bangkok shops. There is also exquisite **antique silver** including pieces worn by Thai princesses of old. In addition, there are purses, boxes, betelnut sets, teapots and much more made by Khmer, Lao, Shan, Burmese, Chinese and Straits Chinese (Malacca) masters. Specializing in antique silver is Moradok in Room 302 of the River City Complex.

Thai **hilltribe** women are known for the elaborate and very detailed jewelry they wear. The pieces are similar to American Indian jewelry with lots of small parts intricately linked together and flat pieces etched with tribal patterns. The silver content is a few percentage points shy of 100 but their raw beauty compensates for their lack of high value.

Antique hilltribe textiles are available in Bangkok.

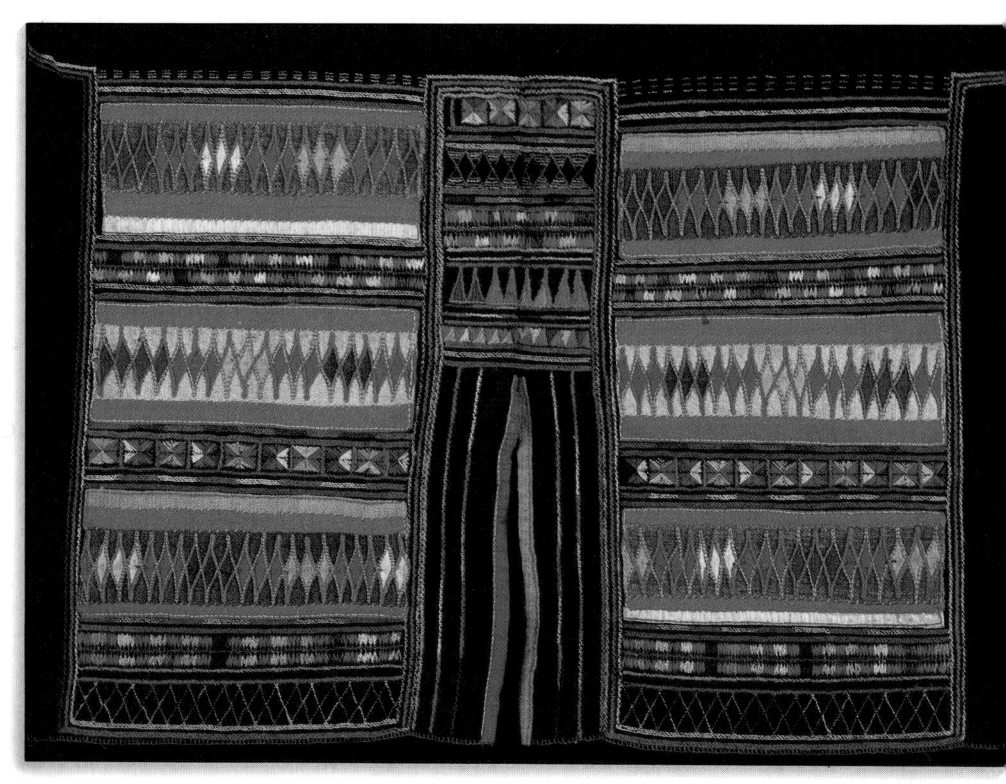

Northern silversmiths pound out a variety of bowls which they coat with an extract of tamarind to make them shine. They also weave stout silver strands into baskets. Among the more intriguing items are Cambodian silver animals. Charming elephants, chickens, horses and others are, in fact, shells which can be pulled apart and small items stored inside. Most items are replicas of antiques but their quaint beauty makes them very popular.

Thailand is one of the world's leading producers of tin, the prime constituent in **pewterware**. This gray metal makes handsome vases, plates, mugs, and other practical items with a burnished silver sheen.

The 4,000-year-old bronze utensils and jewelry found in the burial mounds of Ban Chieng attest to a high degree of skill and a lively imagination as do the 13th century bronze Buddha images. Thai artisans have carried that skill, if not the whole of that imagination, to the present day. **Bronze** religious figures cannot be taken out of the country but there are statues of classic drama figures that make handsome decorations.

Most modern bronze pieces are designed to decorate a living room. Subjects range from recumbent deer from the *Ramakien* to modern figures of flowing grace. The bronze pieces generally annealed with a brass skin to make them gleam. There are also bronze dinner sets and table implements coated in brass and usually sold in velvet or felt-lined teak cases. Small bronze temple bells can be hung in the house eaves to tinkle in the wind. Expensive and rare are the Laotian frog drums (also called rain drums) which are often covered with sheets of glass and used as tables.

Bronzeware's cousin, **brassware**, includes items as elegant as the large noodle cabinets that vendors sling on bamboo poles and carry on their shoulders as they trudge through the back lanes. There are also brass lanterns and small knick-knack cabinets. Brass

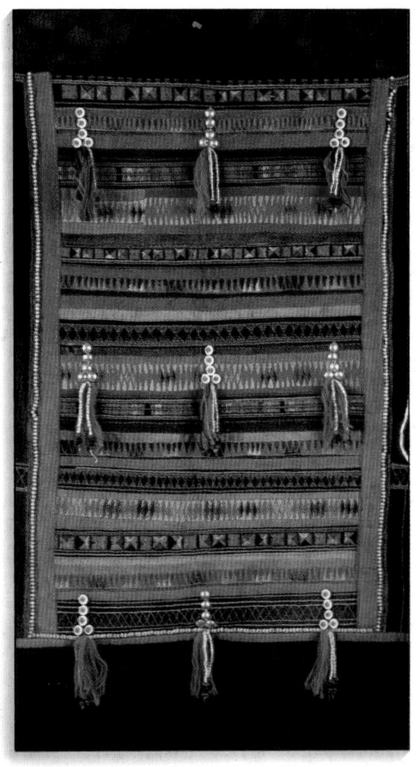

items and bronzeware with brass coatings are generally protected by a silicon layer to preserve their sheen.

Thai and Burmese **antiques** are among the finest in Asia. Most of the good Thai pieces were long ago snapped up by collectors but it is still possible to discover a treasure. It is a rare dealer who does not know the value of the pieces he sells so forget trying to find a real bargain. Dealers usually keep the best pieces upstairs so after a look downstairs, serious collectors should ask to see what else he has.

For years, up-country wooden temples and their art objects have been disappearing with alarming rapidity, sold by abbots tired of battling leaky roofs and termites. The abbots are content to tear down the old structures and with the proceeds from selling antiques, erect fireproof, insect-proof concrete temples. As a result some fine decorative pieces including the carvings found on temple gables and the *naga* (serpent) heads on eaves are readily available in the marketplace and can be exported legally.

The Thai Fine Arts Department maintains fairly strict control over the export of antiques; they've seen too many sacred relics turned into ashtrays or lampstands to trust foreigners to treat these objects with the reverence they deserve. Thus, Thai Buddha images are allowed out of the country only in very special circumstances.

Though the law specifies only Buddha images, disciples and spirit houses, the authorities are concerned enough that they insist on export permits even for the clay amulets and art pieces that have nothing to do with religion. Antique dealers can clear the buyer's purchases through the Fine Arts Department and ship them abroad. The buyer can also handle it on his own though the process is lengthy and time-consuming (see Travel Tips).

As a result of government pressure, most antique shops now deal almost exclusively in Burmese Buddha images which are not covered by the law. With the Burmese economy in shambles, antiques are very saleable items and Burmese are only too eager to spirit pieces across the border for sale in Chiang Mai and Bangkok. In addition to Buddha images, there are spirit houses, praying disciples and mythical figures. There are also Chinese ceramic pieces and some Khmer stone figures.

European antiques like the hanging Dutch lamps, old brass fans (and recent replicas) and photographs left over from the 19th century can be found in antique shops and in Chatuchak Market.

Thai shopowners have been quick to recognize that while many people are interested in antiques they are reluctant to pay large sums of money for them. Instead, they want "antique-looking" pieces as home decor items. As a result, an entirely new industry has grown up to produce them. Centered in Chiang Mai and Ayutthaya, craftsmen turn out wooden pieces such as deer, celestial beings and others, most of them modelled on Burmese pieces. Ayutthayan cabinetmakers produce wooden cabinets with glass doors and old-style grandfather clocks which are a complement to any home.

The craftsmanship of these fakes is of a surprisingly high caliber although the painting and other methods used to give the pieces an antique look are sometimes less than satisfactory. To their credit, dealers will not try to pass off the pieces as true antiques. Prices are very attractive, enabling one to give his home an Asian outlook for a very low investment.

Demand for modern Thai **painting** has been so small over the past few decades that world-class works by serious modern artists are few and far between. There are a few galleries like Visual Dhamma which sell modern paintings but most galleries find a more receptive audience for paintings of Buddhist subjects and traditional or rural scenes. This genre falls more under the heading of decorative art and includes oils, water colors, acrylics,

Right, antique Buddhas are increasingly rare. This one can be found in the National Museum.

and oil paintings over hardened sand or leaves, and, on the lower end of the art scale, on black velvet.

Art which does find a ready audience are **old manuscripts** (or copies of them) painted either on canvas or on thick *koi* paper made from the bark of a tree. There are also Burmese religious texts painted on lacquer as well as Chinese art. Thais are very skilled at framing works attractively in a wide number of designs to suit any home.

Thais are masters at producing a wide range of handicrafts. The base was laid down by centuries of court craftsmen who created works of beauty for royal patrons. The techniques have been passed down to present-day artisans. While it is possible to find high art, what is generally available is of lesser quality and should be chosen for its appeal rather than its resale value. For the methods used by Thai craftsmen, see the Cultural Fabric chapter.

Thai craftsmen are supremely skilled at setting oyster shells aglow in black lacquer backgrounds to create scenes of enchanting beauty. Because Thai **mother-of-pearl** is made from the Turban shell, it does not separate and flake as the Chinese varieties do. Check to ensure that the lacquer is really lacquer and not black paint as is sometimes used. The difference is in the sheen; if it shines, it is lacquer, if it is dull, it is paint.

If the shopkeeper tells you that lacquer normally cracks with age, point him in the direction of Wat Po who's doors have stood exposed to the weather for 200 years and not even begun to crack. Mother-of-pearl items include portraits, bowls, and utensils.

Thais also excel at **lacquerware**, the art of overlaying wooden or bamboo items with glossy black lacquer and on this black "canvas" painting scenes in gold leaf. Items include depictions of classical themes and characters, vases, cigarette boxes, elephants and other animals and bowls. As with mother-of-pearl, ensure that the item is, in fact,

Bangkok is an art lover's paradise.

coated in lacquer and not black paint.

Many shops carry Burmese lacquerware which is made by applying a matte red lacquer over bamboo or wicker items. Simple designs are painted on this with black lacquer. Handsome, often very large, baskets and trays are the main items sold.

One of Thailand's lesser known arts is **nielloware** which involves applying an amalgam of black metals to etched portions of silver or, to a much lesser extent, gold pieces. Items include trays, receptacles, betelnut boxes, teapots, cigarette cases and vases.

Glass objects are created with a blowtorch rather than a blowpipe. Bits of glass are beaded to form animals and mythical beasts. Very popular are replicas, often 20 inches (50 cm) long and set in glass cases, of a Royal Barge or of a chariot carrying the god-king Rama. The pieces appeal more for their novelty value than their aesthetics because the craftsmanship is generally not of a very high level.

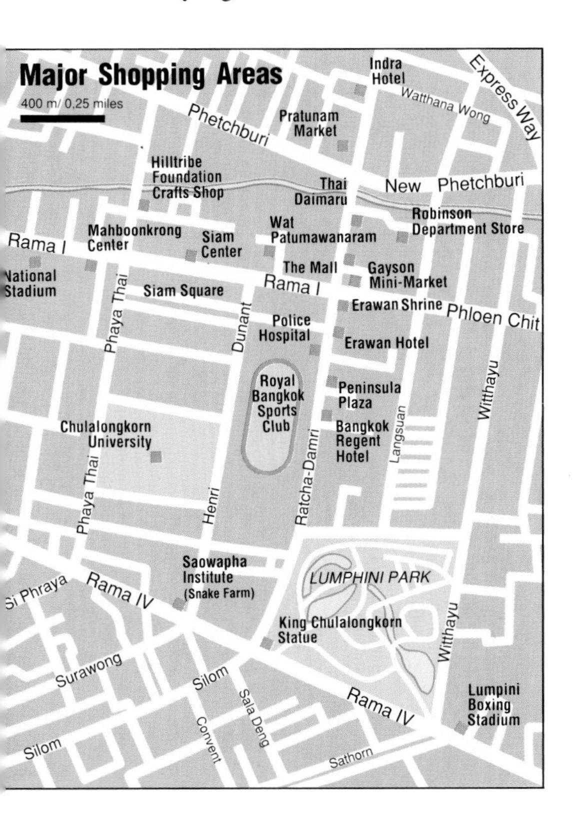

If archaeological evidence is correct, Thais have been throwing pots for 5,000 years with a considerable degree of skill. Said to date from 3600 B.C., the red whorl **pots** of Ban Chieng, the prehistorical site in the Northeast, are considered historical artifacts and export is prohibited. Copies abound, however, and can be taken out of the country.

Other historical items are the tan Sangkhaloke ceramic plates with their distinctive twin fish (resembling the Pisces sign) from kilns near Thailand's 13th century capital at Sukhothai. Originally produced for export to China, they keep turning up in shipwrecks discovered in the Gulf of Siam. Few are now available on the open market but there are numerous copies.

Various ceramic pieces are claimed to have been brought up by divers from the river that flows around Ayutthaya. Dealers insist that the pieces were dropped overboard from ships moored outside the city walls between the 14th and 18th centuries. Either the sailors were an extremely careless lot or were the originators of the throw-away economy because judging from the number of pieces offered for sale, there seems to have been more pottery than water under the ship's hulls. Treat with a large degree of skepticism any claims to the contrary.

Among the most beautiful stoneware items are those with a light jade green or dark brown glaze called **Celadon**. Said to have originated in China and been recreated in northern Thailand in the 13th century, Celadon glaze, created from wood ash (no dyes added), is characterized by a highly polished surface overlaying fine crazing. Pieces include dinnerware, lamps, serving platters, statuary and others. As its name suggests, Celadon House on Silom Road specializes in celadon ware.

Bencharong is a style of ceramics unique to Thailand. Its name describes its look: *Bencha* is Sanskrit for "five" and *rong* means "color." The five colors—red, blue, yellow, green and white—appear on somewhat delicate porcelain bowls, containers, ashtrays and decorative items. There are a few, but not many, antique Bencharong pieces.

Although it originated in China, **Blue and White porcelain** has been produced extensively in Thailand since ancient times. There aren't many antique pieces around but craftsmen are prolific in turning out a wide range of items whose quality ranges from superior to barely passable. A close look at the artistry employed in painting the scenes will reveal which is which. Plates, teapots (including the popular elephant teapots with the trunk as a spout), classical cylindrical and hexagonal teapots with brass handles, vases, ashtrays, cigarette boxes and others are found in most shops.

There must be millions of elephants wandering around Thailand's jungles minus their tusks if the number of "**ivory**" items in shop windows are any indication. More than likely, the ivory is either ivory dust glued together, bone or a plastic compound. The workmanship of true ivory is superb with patterns and designs carved in intricate, painstaking detail. Long trains of elephants, classical Chinese scenes, Chinese boxes of globes within globes, snuff bottles, letter openers and others can be found.

Thai **musical instruments** are popular gift items as much for their aesthetic beauty as for their sounds. The oldest, most respected shop is Duriyaphand at 151 Tanao Road. Especially appealing is the *kaan*, a large pan pipe sounding a bit like a bagpipe and an integral instrument in Northeastern and Laotian music. There are similar pipes made of gourds and reeds and played by the hilltribes of the North. Reed or bamboo flutes are found in many gift shops or in markets stalls.

Most **wood** products made of teak or other woods have been crafted in Chiang Mai. Products range from practical items like breadboards, serving and cutting boards, dinnersets and salad bowls to decorative items like trivets and headboards. There are also statues of mythical gods, angels and elephants some standing a meter high. Teak is an extremely heavy wood; *mai daeng*, substantially inferior to teak and lacking the beautiful grain, is cheaper and lighter.

Bamboo, **rattan**, **reeds**, **grasses**, and **palm fronds** grow wild in the jungle and have been used for centuries to make fish traps, baskets, matting and a hundred and one practical household items. Modern baskets and antique baskets (most, from Chiang Mai) are light, practical and very beautiful. They can be employed as carry-alls, turned into attractive lamps or hung on walls. Palm frond fans, placemats and colorful fish mobiles are also popular.

The very thin Yan Lipao grasses are woven into beautiful purses and handbags. Her Majesty's SUPPORT Foundation has revived this dying southern Thailand art and offers some superb clutch bags and purses trimmed with

Finely crafted models of traditional Thai dancers.

brass for formal occasions. Find them at the royal Chitrlada shops in the Oriental Plaza and elsewhere.

Bangkok is a **doll** collector's heaven with everything from dolls dressed in classical dance or hilltribe costumes to rag dolls in contemporary clothes. Bangkok Dolls makes a large range.

Tukata chao wong, the tiny painted clay dolls played with by royal daughters in former days, are generally sold as sets depicting charming scenes from everyday life. The SUPPORT Foundation has been active in reviving this art as well. There are also small clay kitchen utensils which little girls enjoy, an ideal gift for a young girl back home.

In addition to the embroidered cloth noted above, hilltribes make silver jewelry, reed pipes and toys. There is a good selection at the Hilltribe Foundation shop in the Srapatoom Palace behind Siam Center (enter from Phya Thai Road).

Under the heading of **Souvenirs** come a wide variety of items, most of them inexpensive and lightweight, that friends back home will appreciate. The shadow puppets cut from sheets of water buffalo hide (and sometimes plastic) are popular as wall hangings as are wooden and papier maché birds and other beasts clad in gold leaf and multicolored glass mosaics. Many **papier maché animals** found in stores and on sidewalks are too large and too delicate to carry long distances but if you are determined to have them, they make wonderful gifts. Close relatives are the *kangkarn* lacquer animals whose features are etched and painted in pastels.

Burmese puppets and *kalagas* (bas relief cloth wall hangings) have gained a wide acceptance in the past few years to the point that whereas five years ago they were rarely seen, today, you cannot walk into a shop without tripping over them. Nearly all are copies of antique pieces.

Thailand excels in making **artificial flowers** of such quality that the country is now a major exporter. Hand painted

ows of ainted eads await ssembly at ne Bangok Dolls actory.

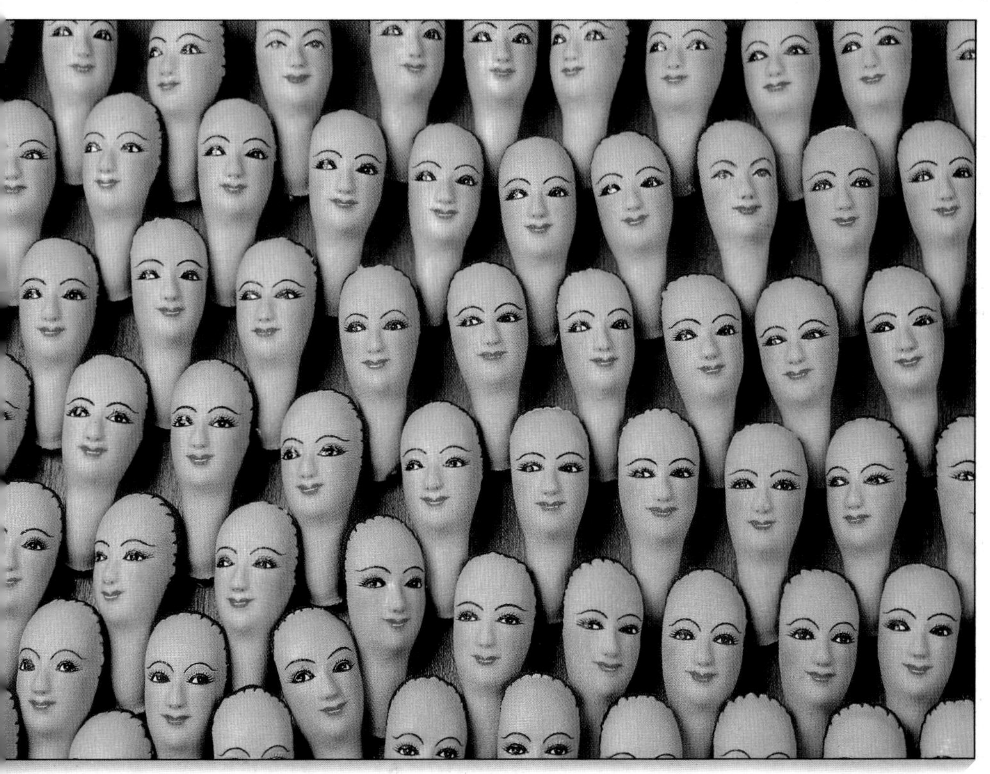

and hand assembled, they are nearly indistinguishable from nature's blooms. They are offered in a bouquet of blossoms both from tropics and from temperate climate gardens plus a number of very attractive blossoms that grew out of the fertile imaginations of very talented designers.

The intricate Chiang Mai **umbrellas** with their bamboo struts and strings are engineering works of sheer genius. They are sold in sizes ranging from parasols to large beach umbrellas, and have flowers and scenes painted on them.

The **masks** used in *Khon* masked dramas are crafted full sized and in miniature and are intriguing gift items. Lepidopterists will treasure the framed selections of **butterflies** from Thailand's jungles. A real souvenir of a Bangkok visit is a miniature version of a *tuk-tuk*, the three-wheeled motorized **trishaws** that cruise through the city streets.

Bangkok has an unfortunate reputation as a center for copying world famous brand products. It would be remiss not to mention them because they appear on every streetcorner in the city. Fake Rolex watches virtually indistinguishable from the real thing are offered by touts on Patpong and elsewhere. They are more decorative than functional but do seem to work with some accuracy.

Gucci, Pierre Cardin, Lanvin and other big names can be seen on bags, briefcases and purses which are generally of high quality but which may differ from the original enough to cause you problems with Customs officials when you return to your own country. Similarly, Lacoste and Benetton shirts are offered openly and at a fraction of the cost of an original. Use your own judgement about purchasing them.

Where to buy it: Most visitors are content to cruise and browse with no particular object in mind. If you are looking for a specific item, check the listings in the Travel Tips section. If you do not find it there, get a free copy of the Tourism Authority of Thailand's *Official Shopping Guide*. Its listings are impartially determined and are generally reliable. Its criteria for selecting a shop is based not only on the quality of goods carried but on the willingness to put the customer's interests, if not first, at least high on the list. Shops recommended by the Tourism Authority of Thailand display a sticker on their doors or windows depicting a female vendor seated by a pair of baskets.

After an initial browse through the markets, many people prefer to do their serious shopping in shopping malls and here Bangkok does not disappoint. The prices are higher than in the market but are fixed and the comfort of air-conditioning is a welcome trade-off on a hot afternoon.

Among the shopping centers with a large number of shops and types of goods are **Mahboonkrong Center** (containing Tokyu Department Store) on Phya Thai Road, **Siam Center** on Rama 1 Road, **Central Plaza** next to

Left, these umbrellas are bought for their decorative value. Right, toy tuk-tuk.

the **Central Plaza Hotel**, **Amarin Plaza**, **Suparkarn Shopping Centre** by the Taksin Bridge**, River City** (specializing in antiques) next to the Royal Orchid Sheraton Hotel, **Oriental Plaza** near Oriental Hotel. On Rajdamri Road are **Peninsula Plaza** (luxury goods), **The Mall** and **Rajdamri Arcade**, home to **Thai Daimaru**.

Arcades composed of numerous air-conditioned shops include **Siam Square** on Rama 1 Road and the picturesque **Silom Village** at 286 Silom Road. Department stores with Thai products departments include the many branches of **Central** and **Robinson**.

For a wide selection of Thai handicrafts, try the government-operated **Narayana Phand** in The Mall at 127 Rajdamri Road and the **Hilltribes Foundation** shop in Srapatoom Palace behind Siam Center (the entrance is on Phya Thai Road).

Shops ship goods by air or sea. The packing is good, the cost reasonable and the service reliable.

Duty-Free shopping: You can now do your duty-free shopping the moment you step off the plane. A new 24-hour Duty-Free shop has been opened in the new arrival lounge of Don Muang Airport for shopper convenience. It is operated by Thai International and carries an extensive selection of items.

Thai International's in-town offices offer a wide range of liquors, tobacco products, cameras, electronic goods, watches and jewelry at fixed prices. Goods are packed for pick-up at the airport on your departure. The biggest of the three downtown offices is at 485 Silom Rd (Tel. 235-4360 and is open 9 a.m. to 6 p.m. (closed Sundays). The Asia Hotel shop is on the ground floor (Tel. 215-2023) and is open from 7 a.m. to 9 p.m. daily. The duty-free shop in the departure lounge at Don Muang Airport is open 24 hours a day.

Handicraft workshops to visit: As much fun as buying objects is seeing how they are made. Most handicrafts

Amarin Plaza shopping center.

are made in home workshops or cottage industries rather than in large factories. Thus, a visit is more than an insight into the methods by which beautiful arts are made, it is an introduction to an interesting element of Thai life. For all of the workshops listed below the visitor must find his own transportation.

Thai silk is woven on upright looms at which the weaver sits to throw a flying shuttle across a warp and then press a foot treadle to firm the warp threads into the woof. T. Shinawatr conducts daily tours between 9 a.m. and 6 p.m. at its workshop at 54 Soi 107, Sukhumvit Rd. Telephone the workshop at 393-0326 or its Soi 23 showroom at 258-4073. Jagtar Thai Silk at 137/3 Sukhumvit Rd. has daily tours between 9:30 a.m. and 7 p.m., Monday through Saturday. Telephone 252-3854.

Thai bronze objects are cast by the "lost wax" process wherein molten bronze is poured into baked clay molds. Treasure Siam has a factory at 38/89 Soi 47, Lardprao Road. Open daily 8 a.m. to 5 p.m. Telephone its Siam Center showroom at 251-3597, 251-2993 to arrange a visit. Supoj Thai Bronze Trading has a workshop at 302 Moo 8, Soi 8, Suksawad Rd. Open between 8:30 and 5 p.m. Telephone 427-6471 or 427-2595.

Gem cutting is a meticulous art requiring great skill and patience. Associated Lapidary gemcutters work every day except Sunday between 9:30 a.m. and 6:00 p.m. Its factory is on the 5th fl. at 1 Patpong Rd. Telephone 233-9691, 233-9692 for an appointment. The Supermarket of Gems factory is in Bang-na and is open daily except Sundays from 9:30 to 6:30. Telephone their 987 Silom Rd. office at 233-8388 or 233-8389 to arrange a visit.

Bangkok Dolls at 85 Soi Rajatapan offers visits between 8 a.m. and 5 p.m. Telephone them at 245-3008. Thai Classic Co. Ltd. at 50/3 Soi Sriwieng, is open from 8:00 to 4:30 p.m. Tel. 234-9029, 236-3818.

Below, Siam Square and right, Robinson Department Store.

SPORTS

With Bangkok's heat and humidity it seems strange that anyone would have any desire to pursue sports, but Thais are avid athletes. If you are a sports lover, there are ample opportunities to see not only traditional Western sports but Thai sports which are impressive for skill and energy displayed. There are international-standard facilities for the active sportsman to pursue his favorite sport or even learn a new one.

Watching others play: Thai athletes play basketball and rugby but excel at football (soccer), badminton, swimming, boxing and marksmanship. International tournaments draw huge crowds to cheer their favorites. The principal venues are the National Stadium on Rama I Road just west of Mahboonkrong Shopping Center, the Asoke-Din Daeng Sports Complex off Asoke-Din Daeng Road near the northern entrance to the Expressway and the Hua Mark Stadium on Ramkamhaeng Road. Check English-language newspapers for schedules. Ticket prices are very reasonable; except for major events, it is not necessary to buy tickets in advance.

Bangkok also plays sports of its own creation. **Thai Boxing** is one of the fiercest sports ever invented and reveals a side of Thais that will give pause for thought. It grew up as a martial art on ancient battlefields and was later refined into a sport. It differs from Marquis of Queensbury rules in employing not only fists but elbows, feet, knees and nearly every other part of the body to pummel an opponent into submission. It is a tough, exciting sport with grace and grit in abundance. If you'd thought from the shy smiles that Thais were pushovers, spend an evening at a Thai boxing stadium.

A bout comprises five three-minute rounds on a 10-fight card. As interest-

Preceding pages: Kite flying takes off in March, when gusts blow across the city's open spaces. Below an upside-down version of Thai boxing—the loser gets a ducking.

ing as the ring action is, the exuberance displayed in the bleachers where punters, clutching fistfuls of money, expend as much energy and emotion as the boxers themselves.

Each bout is preceded by an elaborate stylized dance both boxers perform to honor their teachers and to invoke magic to intimidate their opponent. A high-pitched orchestra wails accompaniment to spur the combatants to action. A good introduction to the sport is *Thai Boxing* by Hardy Stockmann.

Rajdamnern Stadium on Rajdamnern Nok Avenue next to the TAT, offers bouts on Mondays, Wednesdays, and Thursdays at 6 p.m. and on Sundays at 4:30 and 8:30 p.m. Tickets are between 500 and 1,000 baht for ringside seats (depending on the quality of the card), running downwards to 100 baht. Weekend matinees are the cheapest.

Feet can be lethal weapons in traditional Thai boxing.

Lumpini Boxing Stadium on Rama 4 Road, 300 yards east of the Wireless intersection holds bouts on Tuesdays and Fridays at 6:30 p.m. and on Saturdays at 1 p.m. and 6:30 p.m. Ticket prices are the same as at Rajdamnern.

Thai boxing fans spend Saturday and Sunday afternoons glued to their television sets. For many visitors this will be sufficient introduction. What they will miss is the atmosphere of ringside. The Rose Garden offers demonstrations of Thai boxing but these are pale imitations of the real thing.

In **Takraw**, a hollow rattan ball is propelled with any part of the body except the hands. Two versions are played. In one, a team of three players faces its opponents across a head-high net on a court slightly smaller than a badminton court. Tremendously demanding, the sport requires great agility from the team members to keep the ball in the air; it is not unusual for a player to turn a complete somersault to spike a ball across the net!

In the second version, six players are spaced in a wide ring around a basketball-like net suspended high in the air. The players use their heads, feet, knees

and elbows to keep the ball airborne and, hopefully, put it into the net. A team has a set time period in which to score as many points as it can after which it is the opposing team's turn to see if it can top the total.

Unfortunately, there are few regular venues for the sport. Tournaments are held at the Din-Daeng Youth Center (Tel. 465-5325 for dates and times) four times a year and admission is free. The principal courts are at the hundreds of temples in the Bangkok area. During the winter when the weather is cool, teams practice in the late afternoons after work or school. Competitions are often held as entertainment during Thai Buddhist funerals. Tournaments are also played in the northwest corner of Sanam Luang during March and April. Free admission.

Kite fighting season is March and April when the west wind begin to waft across Sanam Luang. Thais pursue the sport with a passion, joining teams sponsored by major companies.

Two teams compete against each other. One flies a giant star-shaped male *Chula* kite nearly six feet (two meters) high. The other (there may be more than one opposing team) flies the diminutive diamond-shaped female *Pakpao* kites.

One team tries to snare the other's kite and drag it back across a dividing line. Although the contest seems one-sided, the *Pakpao* stands a good chance of downing a big *Chula*. The teamwork employed and the energy expended makes for exciting viewing. Several hours of competition start at 2 p.m.

Horseracing is not unique to Thailand but it is pursued with a particularly Thai flavor. Fanaticism seems too mild a word to describe the fans' enthusiasm. The horses are a bit smaller than the thoroughbreds raced in Europe but the sport is no less exciting. Betting is similar to the Western system with Win, Place and Show but without the various permutations of Quinella or Trifecta. Bets begin at 50 baht and run

Race day at the Royal Bangkok Sports Club.

as high as 200,000 baht. The city's two racecourses offer races on alternate Sundays. Check the newspapers for dates and tipsheets.

The Royal Turf Club at 183 Phitsanuloke Rd. in a beautiful sylvan setting across from Chitralada Palace (Tel. 282-3770) sells tickets for 50, 70 and 100 baht. Post time for the first 10 races is 12:15 p.m.; the last race is at 6 p.m.

The Royal Bangkok Sports Club at No. 1 Henri Dunant Rd. (282-3770, 282-2008) is the city's most exclusive private club but on racedays it is open to the general public. Ticket prices and post times are the same as for the RTC.

Play it yourself: Although Bangkok sports facilities are not as numerous as in other major cities, they are well developed; some are even world class. It is not difficult to get into pick-up games as Thais are always generous in welcoming newcomers.

Swimming is a cinch for visitors because every hotel has a pool filled with clean, warm water. Public pools are few as are lakes or ponds. For salt-water swimming, head for Pattaya or Hua Hin.

Tennis is popular and courts are found throughout the city but it is wise to reserve beforehand. Court rental for daytime games range from 30 to 60 baht per hour; for night games it rises to 70 to 90 baht per hour. Unless otherwise noted, you must supply your own racket and balls. Instructors are available at most courts.

Central Tennis Court at 13/1 Soi Attakarnprasit, S. Sathorn Rd., (Tel. 286-7202) is open 7 a.m. to midnight. Sawasdee Courts, (between Sois 27 and 29, deep in Soi 31 from Sukhumvit Rd.) (Tel. 258-4502) are open daily 6 a.m. to 11 p.m.

Golden Golf & Tennis, 7 Soi Soonvijai 1, New Petchburi Rd. (Tel. 318-1651) opens 6 a.m., closes 10 p.m. Racket rental: 20 baht per hour. A.U.A., 179 Rajdamri Rd. (Tel. 252-8953) is open daily 6 a.m. to 9 p.m.

Several hotels have their own courts. The Ambassador Hotel (Tel. 251-0404) is open from 9 a.m. to 9 p.m. The Siam Inter-Continental Hotel (Tel. 253-0355) is open 7 a.m. to 10 p.m. Rackets rent for 30 baht per hour, balls for 150 baht for three, tennis shoes for 20 baht per hour.

Hilton Hotel courts (Tel. 253-0123) are open for non-guests from 10 a.m to 4 p.m. at 100 baht per hour. Racket rental: 20 baht per hour. Shangri-la Hotel and Oriental Hotel courts are open only to guests.

Squash courts are found exclusively at hotels. The courts at Rama Gardens, Dusit Thani (or members of Fitness International gyms), Hilton (or members of Clark Hatch gyms) are open only to guests. The Oriental courts are also open to Royal Orchid Sheraton Hotel guests.

Courts open to non-guests are at the Shangri-la and Imperial hotels. The Shangri-la courts (Tel. 236-7777) are open from 7 a.m. to 9 a.m. Open air courts are 50 baht per hour. for guests (100 baht per hour for non-guests).

The Rose Garden Golf Course is up to par.

Air-conditioned courts are 75 baht per hour for guests, 150 baht per hour for non-guests). The Imperial Hotel courts (Tel. 254-0111) are open 8 a.m. to 8 p.m. at 100 baht per 45 minutes. Changing room is by the swimming pool.

Golf facilities and fees are so attractive that planeloads of Japanese golfers now fly into Bangkok for a weekend of golf rather than wait in long lines and pay the exorbitant greens fees in Tokyo. Greens fees in Bangkok range from 100 to 300 baht per round on weekdays and 250 to 750 baht on weekends. Caddy fees run from 90 to 150 baht per round.

At the top of the Bangkok's list is the world-class Navathanee Golf Course (22 M.1, Sukhapibal 2 Rd.; Tel. 374-7077) designed by Robert Trent Jones Jr. It is open from 6 a.m. to 6 p.m. Army Golf Course at 459 Ram Intra Road (Tel. 521-1530) is open from 5 a.m. to 9:30 p.m.

The Railway Training Center Golf Course (Tel. 271-0130) on Paholyothin Road west of the Central Plaza Hotel opens at 6 a.m., closes at 8 p.m. The Krungthep Sports Golf Course, 516 Krungthep Sports Rd. (Tel. 374-6063) opens 5 a.m., closes 5 p.m.

Driving ranges to hone your swing are found at the Siam Inter-Continental Hotel (Tel. 253-0355, ext. 7636). The fee from 7 a.m. to 5 p.m. is 90 baht per hour; 5 p.m. to 10 p.m.: 140 baht per hour. The Army Golf Course, Ram Intra Rd. (Tel. 521-1530) is open 6 a.m. to 9 p.m. The cost is 10 baht per tray of balls. Golden Golf & Tennis, 7 Soi Soonvijai 1, New Petchburi Rd. (Tel. 318-1651) opens 6 a.m., closes 10 p.m.. The fee is 20 baht/tray of balls. The Railway Training Center Golf Course (Tel. 271-0130) on Paholyothin Rd. west of the Central Plaza Hotel, is open 6 a.m. to 8 p.m.. The fee is 20 baht per tray of balls.

Oddly, Bangkok lacks mini-golf courses but there is a putting green. It is at the Siam Inter-Continental Hotel and is open 7 a.m. to 10 p.m. The fee from 7 a.m. to 5 p.m. is 30 baht per 30 minutes. From 5 p.m. to closing: 50 baht per 30 minutes. Shoes and clubs can be rented.

Petanque, the ancient Roman pastime similar to English bowls, has found a following among Thais over the past year or so. Two hotels have installed outdoor lanes: the Siam Inter-Continental and the Rama Gardens.

You can risk your life **jogging** through the streets of Bangkok but given the erratic driving and the potholes your run will likely turn into a steeplechase or a sprint through an obstacle course. If you are really determined, run in the mornings. With the air pollution, evening jogging for health purposes is a counter-productive venture. The best runs are had in Lumpini Park (5 a.m. to 9 p.m.) and Chatuchak Park (5 a.m. to 9 p.m.) with their 1.6-mile (2.54 km) and 2.3-mile (3.7 km) courses respectively. The Siam Inter-Continental, Rama Gardens and Ambassador hotels have jogging paths for guests only.

Bangkok has a chapter of the famous **Hash House Harriers**, the cross-country running fraternity that originated in Malaysia. Its members gather each Saturday at 4:30 p.m., Monday evenings at 5:15 p.m. and Wednesdays at 5 p.m. at a site announced in the sports sections of the Saturday edition of the *Bangkok Post*.

The idea is to follow a paper trail laid down through rice plantations and coconut orchards by the "hare." There are plenty of false clues and opportunities to run through muddy fields and across canals to regain the trail. The pack is kept from getting hopelessly lost by a bugle-blowing leader who shouts "On, on" when the trail has been found. The real objective of the exercise is to reach a large supply of cold beer at the trail's end, thereby negating any efforts to lose weight along the route. Everybody is welcome. Good, not-so-clean fun.

Fishing: Many restaurants let you pick your main course from a fish tank; a few let you catch it yourself. Koongten Ram Indra, 56/19 Ram Indra Rd. (Tel. 510-2636) is open daily from

Right, takraw can be a heady experience

10 a.m. to 11 p.m. Order the extras, pick up a rod and catch the main course. You pay by the weight of the fish plus a fee to have the restaurant cook it for you. Take your own rod and tackle. Catfish and Snake's-Head fish are the prey.

Koongten Fishing Hut at 113/1 Thessasamphan Rd. (Tel. 581-6689, 581-5379) offers fishing for 25 baht an hour. It will then clean and cook the fish and serve any other course you desire. Hours are 7 a.m. to 10 p.m. (Weekdays), 7 a.m. to midnight (Weekends). It goes one step farther by offering three bungalows (600-800 baht/night), two rafts (400-500 baht) and five houses at the water's edge (300 baht) so you can make a fishing holiday of it. You provide your own rod (available in most sporting goods stores in Bangkok).

For **deep-sea fishing**, head for Bang Saray south of Pattaya. Marlin, king mackerel, cobia, yellow jack, barracuda, bonito, giant groupers, red snapper, rays and black tip sharks lurk among submerged rocks. Boats, tackle and guides are available for very reasonable fees. There are small hotels in Bang Saray but most fishermen spend the night in Pattaya and head out early in the morning. Fishing trips can be arranged by telephoning Bang Saray Fishing Lodge at its Bangkok office (Tel. 233-7719, 234-3094).

Two international **fitness clubs** have branches in Bangkok. Clark Hatch (Tel. 253-0123) is at the Hilton Hotel (open weekdays, 7 a.m. to 9:30 p.m.; weekends, 8 a.m. to 8 p.m.) Fitness International (Tel. 233-1130) is at the Dusit Thani (weekdays, 6 a.m. to 9 p.m.; Sundays 9 a.m. to 9 p.m.) Both have weight rooms, aerobic exercise sessions, saunas, tennis courts, squash courts and access to the hotel pool. Both are also open to non-members.

The Ambassador Hotel gym (Tel. 251-0404) is open daily from 9 a.m. to 9 p.m. for 200 baht per session. The Menam Hotel (Tel. 289-0352) fitness center is open daily for men from noon to 10 p.m. and for women from 9 a.m. to 9 p.m. 350 baht/session. The Siam Inter-Continental Hotel has an outdoor gym for guests only.

Bangkok is the last place in the world one would think to look for an **ice skating** rink but Ice Skate occupies the second floor of The Mall Shopping Center, 1911 Ramkamhaeng Rd. (Tel. 318-1001) in the eastern suburbs. Admission are 55 baht for two hours including skate rental. Hours are: Mondays to Thursdays: noon to 10 p.m.; Fridays: noon to midnight; Saturdays: 10 a.m. to midnight; Sundays: 10 a.m. to 10 p.m.

There is also a **roller skating** rink, The Skate, on the ground floor of Central Department Store, Lard Prao branch (adjoining Central Plaza Hotel) on Paholyothin Rd. (Tel. 541-1020, ext: The Skate). Open daily from noon to 5 p.m. Tickets prices, including skate rental are: Weekdays: 20 baht; weekends: 30 baht (including one soft drink).

Gun and archery enthusiasts will find ranges and equipment only at the beach resort of Pattaya.

Keeping the kids amused: Bangkok does not offer a lot of things for children (its own or those of foreigners) to do. Department stores like the Chidlom branch of Central Department store, Thai Daimaru and Mahboonkrong reserve their top floors for electronic games arcades and miniature carnival rides like bumper cars.

Children enjoy the unusual animals of Dusit Zoo or paddling a boat in its lake or in Lumpini or Chatuchak Park. Magic Land at 72 Paholyothin Rd. near the Central Plaza Hotel is an amusement park with a ghost house, bumper cars and carnival rides. On weekdays, the 70 baht ticket covers an unlimited number of rides. On weekends, it is limited to two hours. Open 10 a.m. to 5:30 p.m. (weekdays), 9:30 a.m. to 7 p.m. (weekends).

East of town at 101 Sukhapiban 2 Rd., **Siam Park** is a theme park with water slides and flumes. It is open 10 a.m. to 6 p.m. weekdays; and 9 a.m. to 7 p.m. weekends. Adults: 80 baht, children: 50 baht. A word of warning: the park prohibits the wearing of T-shirts in the swimming areas so take plenty of suntan oil for tender young skins.

Neilson-Hayes Library at 195 Suriwong Rd. has a story hour in English for children on Saturday mornings. Children: 40 baht; parents: free. It normally begins at 10 a.m. but may vary; check the *Bangkok Post* for times.

For pre-teens and teens, the outlook is bleak. If they are content to tag along with you on tours, fine but when they have had their fill there is little to do other than cruise the shopping arcades or use the hotel sports facilities.

Odds and ends: Travelers seeking more than a cursory glimpse of Thai culture can take advantage of free lectures, music and cultural presentations. Every Saturday and Sunday from 10 a.m. to 4:30 p.m., the Public Relations Department at Rajdamnern Avenue (north of the Royal Hotel) presents old movies and lectures at its auditorium. Tel. 281-8821 or 281-8840 for details. Thai-language commentary.

The National Theater offers Thai classical dancing and music programs on Saturdays and Sundays at 10 a.m. and 2 p.m. and on the last Friday of each month at 5:30 p.m. Tickets are 30, 40 and 50 baht for adults, half price for children. Thai-language commentary.

The **Bangkok Bank**'s Pan Fah branch (at 101 Rajdamnern Klang Av. where it crosses Klong Ong Ang) presents superb concerts of Thai classical and folk music every Friday from 5:30 p.m. to 7:30 p.m. Some of the country's finest performers entertain and educate audiences made up primarily of students. Check the announcement board out front or phone 282-7487 for more program details.

The Siam Society is the oldest English-language scholarly organization pursuing Thai subjects. Some of the nation's pre-eminent Thai and foreign scholars are frequent speakers and its publications are recognized worldwide for their thorough research. Located at 131 Soi Asoke, Sukhumvit Rd., it offers

Marathons are gaining popularity, despite the heat.

lectures each Tuesday evening at 8 p.m. on a wide variety of subjects. Check English-language newspapers or telephone 258-3491, 258-3494 for lecture topics. The Society also has excellent guided tours to archaeological or cultural sites and welcomes non-members on a space available basis.

Meditation. Evening classes in the Buddhist form of meditation are offered free at the World Fellowship of Buddhist headquarters at 33 Sukhumvit Rd. between Sois 1 and 3. Each Wednesday, from 7 p.m. to 8 p.m.

Astrology. Thailand takes its astrology seriously. The starting time for nearly every major event since the official declaration of Bangkok's founding (April 6, 1782 at 6:42 a.m.) has been determined by astrologers. It is said that no major government or business decision is made without first checking to ensure the most propitious conditions.

Ordinary Thais seek the aid of astrologers (*Maw Do* = Doctors who See) to determine the proper dates for weddings, predict the success of a business venture or a prospective marriage partner, and the best time at which to begin building a house. The number of astrologers advertising their services and the daily newspapers carrying astrology columns, the Dear Abby's who predict marriage success based on a fiancee's birthdate, and magazines devoted entirely to the subject suggest that astrology is far from a dead science in Thailand.

Most Thai astrologers are numerologists, perusing thick emphemeris tomes to confirm past events and predict the future. There are also palmists and phrenologists. English-speaking astrologers are found at major hotels. The half-dozen astrologers regularly employed at the Montien Hotel charge 200 baht to read one's palm, tell fortunes by birthdate and numerology, or read character by Chinese phrenology (*Ngaow Heng*) wherein the doctor examines facial features and head. Find them on the mezzanine from 11 a.m. to 6 p.m.

Sanam Luang on a Sunday afternoon.

every day. Call 234-8060 for an appointment with the stars.

The astrologer at the Siam Inter-Continental Hotel has a desk in the convention annex in front of the ballroom from 10 a.m. to 2 p.m. daily except Sundays. He reads palms or uses the *Ngaow Heng* methodand charges 300 baht per session. Tel. 253-0335 for an appointment.

For the really desperate, there is an English-speaking foot reader (a sole doctor?) on the outskirts of town. Located at 99/13 Ngamwongwan Rd., he charges 250 baht and is open daily from 8 a.m. to 5 p.m. Tel. 589-8812 or 589-5000 for an appointment.

Astrologers can also be found sitting on the sidewalk along Rajdamnern Nai Avenue in front of the Justice Ministry. Only a few speak English and should be consulted only for fun. They use the methods mentioned above plus a few unorthodox ones like letting a bird walk across an array of cards, the card it pulls out being the one that predicts your future. See if you can figure out how he knows which one to pick. Turbaned Sikh astrologers will accost you on city streets but many are charlatans.

Massages: If you are tired after a long day of tramping through temples, have a traditional Thai massage. The technique calls for the masseur to dig deeply with his fingers into the muscles and joints. It can be painful. The reward comes later after all the tension and fatigue has been miraculously expelled from your body.

The most popular place for massages is Wat Po. In a pavilion near the eastern wall of the temple, licensed practitioners ply their ancient skills. The price is 120 baht an hour. Opening hours are from 8 a.m. to 4 p.m.

Thai traditional massage is distinct from the hanky panky that goes on in massage parlors in the entertainment belt. If you truly need a massage, look for a parlor advertising "traditional" or "ancient" massages. They are quite easily found in all corners of the city.

Astrologers waiting for customers at the Golden Mount Fair.

NIGHTLIFE

Bangkok has been characterized as a man's town. It refers, of course, not to the daytime entertainment but to the evening pastimes. There are plenty of distractions and enticements for males but for couples and even more for single women, it is very slim pickings. For children, it is a desert except for movies, night markets or hotel videos. Teenagers fare little better with discos that open only to those 20 years old and above.

As noted, there are dinner cruises and dinner/cultural shows but once dessert has been consumed and the bill paid, one wants to go out on the town. Here, the problem begins. Although a woman is safe on the streets until late in the night, there isn't a lot for her to do.

If she is of a liberal (or libertine) bent, she can attach herself to a group of males and be one of the boys (and probably learn a great deal about male behavior in the process). Two women can enjoy a drink or two in Patpong and streets of similar ilk but most women don't get quite the same thrill out of watching scantily clad go-go dancers that men do.

In a sense, the same problem holds for men who are not enticed by the bar scene. Hollywood has filled male minds with the image of virile hunks being seduced by Oriental vamps (long cigarette holders hanging from their mouths) but, like much of Hollywood, it is a myth. Unless the Thai woman has been educated abroad, the idea of being picked up in a nightclub after a bit of chit-chat is about as alien as flying to the moon.

It it not impossible for a man to meet his Thai dream girl but it is more likely to happen if (a) he has foreign friends in Bangkok or (b) is invited by Thai friends (Thais like to go places in groups) to go on a daytime or nighttime outing. It is not likely to be a one-on-one encounter. That's why it helps to have friends in Bangkok to set you up. So if you're looking for romance with a proper Thai lady, get out your address book. Otherwise, it will be a checkbook romance, as described farther on.

Preceding pages: It's all go-go in Patpong. Left, party animals.

Nightspots: While, strictly speaking, there is not a club scene nor singles' bars, there has been a new breed of nightery emerging in the late 80s that caters to a more sophisticated crowd. The first type draws foreigners and a smattering of foreign-educated, English-speaking Thais.

Napoleon is a long-time Patpong Road habitue and for years was the only nightery where one could escape go-go dancers. It is a daytime restaurant that in the evening is transformed into a jazz hall. The jazz is middle-of-the-road stuff but is well played.

Kangaroo, on the north end of Patpong Road, is an Australian-run watering spot for males, females and couples in their 20s and 30s, a very convivial lot. Unlike its neighbors, it is a clean, well-lighted place.

Bobby's Arms on the first floor of the Patpong 2 carpark is a restaurant-cum-piano bar that draws a broader age group of both sexes to drink beer, swap stories and sing-along. **Italian Connection** on Patpong 2 to the north of Foodland and **Crown Royal** to the south are cozy little bars with a pianist, videotapes and a relaxed atmosphere. They are also good places to get out of the afternoon heat.

Uptown, there is **Check Inn** on Sukhumvit Road between Sois 5 and 7 across from the Regal Landmark Hotel. Two establishments on Soi Lang Suan are both restaurants and bars. **Vinotek** at 61/2 Soi Lang Suan is a wine bar under European management and **Bolero**, around the corner at 60 Soi 2 off Lang Suan, is owned by Austrians and serves quality European food.

Recently, a number of small nightclubs have sprung up along Soi Sarasin next to Lumpini Park. These have filled a yawning gap in Bangkok's nighttime scene. It began with **Brown Sugar** and now embraces a half-dozen similar establishments. Brown Sugar offers simple meals, a jazz/folk group, drinks and a very convivial atmosphere. It is the type of place city professionals of both sexes in their 20s and 30s anywhere in the world gather. The dress is casual, the mix is Thai and foreign, and the emphasis is on having a good time in an informal way.

Music: Aside from concerts by Thai rock musicians and the occasional big name from abroad, live music means a guitarist or pianist providing background music in a restaurant or jazz. **Napoleon** stages jam sessions each Sunday afternoon (40 baht cover charge). A more subdued, New York atmosphere is found nightly at the **Bamboo Bar** in the Oriental Hotel.

Bogarts on the 13th floor of the C.C.T. Building on Suriwongse Road offers light jazz on Tuesday and Friday evenings. The coffee shop of the **Tawana Ramada Hotel** becomes a riverboat each Friday and Saturday night as a Dixieland band roars to life. On Sunday evenings, **Bobby's Arms** presents light jazz and Dixieland performed by some of the best musicians in the city.

Nearly every hotel has a lobby lounge with singers and small combos. Nightclubs with imported acts cater mainly to a Chinese clientele. **Galaxy** on Rama 4 Road is one such establishment. The Dusit Thani's **Tiara Room** frequently books stars and singers of yesteryear as well as groups of American beauty queens who enjoy a big following among Thai males.

Dancing means discos or videotheques. Hotels like the **Tawana Ramada** and the **Ambassador** have dimly-lit dance floors with live bands for romantic dancing.

The magnet for most people, however, is flashing lights, frenzied bodies and ear-pounding rock. Bangkok has some superb discos with sound and lighting systems on par with the best in the world. They tend to attract the Thai teenyboppers but also draw large num-

Left, discoing in a popular hotel is slightly more sedate. Right, Mardi Gras in Silom Road.

bers of Asians and Westerners. Bangkok not being a late-night city, they close at 2 a.m.

The **Palace Disco** on the Vipavadee Rangsit Highway is one of the most popular in the city. Its principal patrons are the sons and daughters of the scions of business and they tend to be a bit cliquish. If you had previously thought of Thailand as a poor country, the numbers of Mercedes-Benzes in the parking lot may convince you to the contrary.

The flashiest disco is the new **NASA Spaceadrome**, a multi-million dollar dance emporium in the middle of a rice paddy. With a dance floor capacity of 500 and the rest of the interior capable of holding 2,000 on a full-house night, one gets a hint of what it must be like to live in a sardine tin. Just past midnight, a huge spacecraft leaves its docking bay, moves along the ceiling and, amid smoke, sound and flashing lights, descends to the floor. For sheer circus spectacle, few places can compare. Find it by turning left off New Petchburi Road onto Ramkamhaeng Road; it is 330 feet (100 meters) further on, just past the railroad tracks.

Videotheques: Smaller, more intimate, but just as frenetic are videotheques where music is provided by the latest rock videos. They are as sleek and sophisticated as any in the West. For several years, **Diana**'s in the Oriental Plaza has been drawing a nice mix of Thais and upper-income foreigners, Asian and otherwise. **Bubbles** in the Dusit Thani Hotel also has a longstanding reputation for top-class dancing. A newcomer is **Freak Out** in the Silom Plaza just south of Patpong on Silom Road.

Combining disco with a late nightery and catering to a clientele slightly older than normal disco habitués is the **Rome Bar**. The very up-market (some of the most fashionably-dressed post-teens can be found here) bar is one of those strange amalgams found only in Bangkok. It sits in the heart of Patpong Soi 3 which is unabashedly a gay enclave.

The Rome itself is a favorite hangout for gays but its superb sound and lighting system attracts single women and couples as well. The gays seem to have retreated to the second-floor balconies but are found on the dance floor in singles and couples as well. It is all very baffling even in anything-goes Bangkok, but highly entertaining as well.

Young travelers (including those who have just shucked their backpacks) flock to the **Sugar Shack** on Patpong 2 for an evening of dancing. They compete for dance space with the go-go girls but the atmosphere is amiable and appeals to visitors from the higher-priced hotels as well.

Escorts: The newspapers are full of ads for escort services. They are aimed at the single man who wants a date for the evening but finds picking up bargirls tawdry. Ostensibly, they provide a companion for an evening of drinks and dinner. What happens after that is up to the man and the lady and is not included in the basic price.

The man visits the agency to pick his date from a book much like the albums found in modeling agencies. If he is shy or tight for time, the agency will ask him his preferences and a rendezvous will be arranged at his hotel or a neutral spot. It is a bit of a grabbag, a blind date who could turn out to be extremely charming or one barely speaking English. Seldom do the women speak other European languages.

The agencies are quick to respond if a single Western woman telephones for an escort but, because such requests are so rare, very few agencies maintain male escorts on the books or the premises. More often than not there will be a scramble among the owner and his cronies for who gets the privilege of escorting the lady. For the woman with a sense of humor, it can be an entertaining evening.

Films: Bangkok has a wealth of cinemas but, as elsewhere, the advent of VCRs has made a rather large dent in their audiences. The offerings tend towards the violent, syrupy or inane in keeping with Thai audience preferences. Nearly all originate in the U.S. and are shown in English with Thai subtitles. The foreign cultural institutes—**Alliance Francaise**, the **Goethe Institute**, **British Council** and **A.U.A.**—have regular film showings. The newspapers list titles and times.

There are numerous bars where the sole entertainment is videotapes. Many hotel lounges offer videotapes and drinks. Or, you can simply stay in your room. Most major hotels have in-house movies or you can watch one of the four Thai television channels. The fare is mainly Thai dramas and an endless succession of Chinese *kung-fu* programs that the Thai viewers lap up avidly. There are a few American programs dubbed in Thai. As anywhere, one can gain an interesting insight into the culture of Thailand by spending a few hours watching the commercials and the programs which separate them.

Patpong and her sisters: Sooner or later, you will succumb to the lure of Bangkok's infamous nightlife and go to have a look for yourself. It will be a worthwhile trip. Bangkok's nightlife is quite unlike that found anywhere.

At the center of it all are the bargirls but these are not the hardened pros of the Reeperbahn or 42nd Street. They like to have fun and appreciate foreigners, male and female, who share that sense of fun. Whatever one's feelings about the legitimacy of what is in truth an industry that exploits young women, one cannot escape the fact that what should be a very dreary place is, in fact, very entertaining.

The name of the street is Patpong. You've seen it before, dressed up as Saigon's Tu Do Street in the movie *The Deerhunter*. It is a three-block-long street that has brought untold wealth to its owners and spawned ten thousand tales, many of them tall.

By day, Patpong is a respectable street that gives little hint of what goes on there when the sun goes down. Office girls who wouldn't be caught dead

Just another night on Patpong Road.

there at night eat lunch at its many restaurants or shop at its stores. At night, all that changes. In truth, Patpong's reputation is somewhat wilder than its reality. One difference with similar districts worldwide is that there is a virtual absence of brawling; everybody has got his mind on other things or is too busy having fun.

It is useless to list the bars on Patpong because (a) they wax and wane as quickly as the moon and fold faster than a nervous poker player, (b) they are almost all alike and (c) the street is so short that within 10 minutes you will know every establishment it holds.

The usual formula is to have a long bar running down the center or one side of the room. There are platforms behind the bar and/or along the wall with mirrors, a firemen's pole, and scantily-dressed go-go dancers holding on to them. There are usually booths along the wall and girls more than willing to sit in them with you.

On entering, you will find a warm welcome, an invitation to seat you and, within minutes, a request that you buy one of the women a drink for which she receives a small commission. You can politely refuse on the grounds that you are looking for your friend or will be leaving in a moment or two. If you persist in refusing, you will find yourself sitting alone. It is best to sit at the bar so you have more freedom of movement. A sense of fun is essential as the women prefer to be with someone who can make them laugh. Dispensing laughs can often reduce the amount of cash you must dispense.

If you decide you would like the girl to join you elsewhere for the evening, you will have to pay a fee to the bar for taking her out before closing time. What you pay the woman is between you and her. Note that most first-class hotels frown on taking bargirls upstairs and no matter how well she is dressed she will be spotted immediately for what she is and asked to leave. Ask her for suggestions on where to go. Re-

Riding high in Soi Cowboy.

member that AIDS is the word on everyone's lips, so be prudent and take appropriate precautions.

Foreign women are welcome at any bar and should not feel threatened. Quite the contrary; in the small bars, they will probably be the center of attention and therefore might feel more comfortable going with a male or female friend. Women seem to feel most comfortable in the well-lit **Limelight** and **Peppermint Bistro** bars. At the Suriwong end of Patpong 2 are open air bars where you can chat, watch a video and enjoy the evening air.

While the activities downstairs are relatively tame, what goes on upstairs is a whole other story. The stories you've heard about the sex shows are all true and have to be seen to be believed. It is not a place for the squeamish or those with feminist leanings.

As you walk down the street, you will be accosted by touts brandishing menus of a dozen permutations of the things that go on upstairs. They will conduct you to clipjoints so smile and walk past them; there is so much going on along Patpong that you do not need their help to find it.

In Patpong and scattered throughout the city are **massage parlors**. Those which offer legitimate massages have signs advertising "Ancient Massage" or "Traditional Massage" and are worth calling at if you have been walking all day. The prices range from 120 to 150 baht per hour.

The massage parlors most people know, however, employ pretty women who sit behind one-way mirrors while the patron looks them over. When he has made his selection, she escorts him upstairs to a room with a bed and a bathtub.

You start with a bath, move to a massage and whatever happens after that is between the two of you and is not included in the basic price. There are also "B-course" and "Tora, Tora" massages; ask the manager to explain them to you.

Verbal enticements along Patpong.

There is an active gay scene in Bangkok, though with AIDS in evidence it has tapered off a bit. Gay bars are concentrated on Patpong 3, which must be entered from Silom Road opposite Convent Road.

After Patpong, **Soi Cowboy**, just off Sukhumvit Road between Sois 21 and 23, is the next best known nightlife area. It is not as sophisticated as Patpong but is preferred by some patrons for that very reason. The **Nana Entertainment Complex** off Soi 4 just in from Sukhumvit Road is quickly developing into another Soi Cowboy.

Late, late night: By law, bars must close by 1 a.m. on weeknights and 2 a.m. on weekends. Some establishments on Patpong are now obtaining licenses to operate as restaurants so they can stay open all night. **Peppermint Bistro** and **King's Corner** on Patpong 1 are two such bars.

That leaves late nighters with few options. People who still have the energy go to the coffee shop of the **Grace Hotel** on Soi 3, Sukhumvit Road or to the **Thermae** on Sukhumvit between Sois 13 and 15. A bit on the rough side, they are noisy and filled with free-lance bargirls. Many Western males just sit, sip a beer, talk with their friends and watch everything that is going on around them. Western women are infrequent visitors but are welcomed. Most, however, find it uninteresting. If you are turned off by Patpong and its antics, you'll like this even less.

To find out what is happening in Bangkok, check the Friday morning edition of the *Bangkok Post* for nightclub news. In Saturday's *Post*, one of the city's more popular columnists, Bernard Trink, offers tips and commentary on the bar scene. The *Nation* newspaper publishes the weekly *Saen Sanuk* which lists clubs and bars and special events. Numerous publications available at hotel reception desks list restaurants and nightclubs, although their critiques are generally tempered by the advertising they publish.

The real thing.

UP-COUNTRY

Bangkok is the starting point for numerous day trips to history and nature sites. Getting there is half the fun. Transportation facilities and roads are so well developed that you can put yourself in the hands of a tour agent, sit back and relax, or you can simply venture out on your own using local transport and be confident of a reasonably smooth trip. Many of the sites mentioned are no more than three hours from Bangkok.

If you are not already ruined, templed-out or suffering from historia, rent a car, buy a bus ticket, or take a train from Hualampong Station for a 75-minute journey north to the former capital of **Ayutthaya,** sacked and burned by the Burmese in 1767. Once you arrive, travel around the ruins on foot or hire a minibus or a *samlor*, the three-wheeled pedicab. Most of the temples and palaces are concentrated in one area but with transportation you can visit some superb temples beyond the river.

Even in ruins Ayutthaya is an impressive city. Shattered temples—their interiors gutted, their spires collapsed, their brick walls stripped of their stucco coats—still evoke a sense of the city's greatness and the awe that moved 17th century travelers to effusive praise in their letters back home.

If you are on limited time, wander in the area of Wat Mahathat, looking at Wat Rajaburana, Wat Si Sanphet with its three handsome *chedis*, and Viharn Phra Mongkon Bopit with its wing-like roofs sheltering an enormous seated Buddha. Buses leave Bangkok regularly from the Northern Bus Terminal on Paholyothin Road across from Chatuchak Park.

An hour north of Bangkok, the former summer palace of **Bang Pa-in** founded in the 17th century contains a number of intriguing mid-19th century additions. In the middle of a pond is its centerpiece, a small pavilion considered to be the epitome of classical Thai architecture.

The other buildings reflect an eclectic interest in world architecture with the Italian-style Varophat Phiman hall, compound walls with neo-classical doorways, a bridge with semi-draped Greek goddesses, Victorian buildings and the Chinese-style Vehat Chamroon palace with its lovely furniture. Bang Pa-in can be reached by buses leaving regularly from the Northern Bus Terminal across from Chatuchak Weekend Market on Paholyothin Road. Open daily except Monday and Friday 8:30 a.m. to noon and 1 p.m. to 3 p.m. Admission fee: 10 baht.

See both sites with the bonus of a comfortable journey up the river aboard an air-conditioned cruiser. The *Oriental Queen* leaves the Oriental Hotel at 8 a.m. and returns at 6 p.m. The 770-baht ticket includes a sumptuous buffet lunch, transportation around Ayutthaya and a tour guide. You have a choice of going by boat and returning by air-conditioned coach or the other way around. The advantages of returning by river are the splendid sunset views of the Grand Palace. Reserve by telephoning World Travel Service at 233-5900 or 236-0400 Ext. World.

You can also travel upriver by express boat each Sunday to Bang Pa-in and **Bang Sai** , where Queen Sirikit has established a small village where farmers can preserve ancient crafts. There is also a special demonstration of cloth weaving, basket weaving, doll making and leatherworking and a shop selling the finished goods.

On the way back, the boat stops at **Wat Phai Lom**, one of the last sanctuaries for the rare Open-billed Storks. These stately, white birds migrate from Bangladesh each December, roosting until June in trees they have nearly denuded by their own form of highly acidic pollution. The boat leaves Tha Maharat boat dock (see river map) at 8

Preceding pages: Parasailing in Pattaya, Wat Phra Si Sanphet, Ayutthaya. Below, Canal in Ayutthaya.

a.m., arriving back in Bangkok at 5:30 p.m. Cost: 140 baht per person. Telephone the Supatra Co. at 411-0305 for reservations.

Thanks to Hollywood, the **River Kwai** is now a legend and rightfully so. The Death Railway constructed along its banks and the bridge built to span it at the cost of thousands of POW and Asian lives during World War II is a testament to cruelty and courage. The State Railways offers a day trip every Saturday and Sunday.

The train leaves Hualampong Station at 6:35 a.m. and travels westward along the original track. It stops at the bridge (a rather pedestrian trestle affair) and the manicured but moving Allied Cemetery. To relieve the gloom, you are then transported to Sai Yok Noi Waterfall for a swim or a walk in the jungle. There are restaurants serving Thai food at various places along the route. The train arrives in Bangkok at 7:35 p.m. The cost is 75 baht, lunch not included.

Khao Yai National Park is one of Thailand's largest wildlife refuges and is within reach of Bangkok via a one-day excursion arranged by the State Railway of Thailand. The train leaves Hualampong Station at 6 a.m. and travels along the southern edge of the park en route to the Kampuchean border. It stops at Prachinburi where passengers transfer to buses for the trip into the park.

Herds of wild elephants and other beasts roam the 834 sq miles (2,085 sq. km) rain forest but on a short stay it is unlikely that you will see anything more than gibbons and jungle birds. Trails skirt streams and pass waterfalls where you can observe orchids and other wild flowers. The return train arrives in Bangkok at 6:45 p.m. The 140-baht ticket includes lunch. Call State Railways at 223-7010, 223-7020 for reservations.

As with all the day trips offered by the SRT, the train used definitely is not in the "Bullet" class. What it offers,

The Oriental Queen offers cruising comfort.

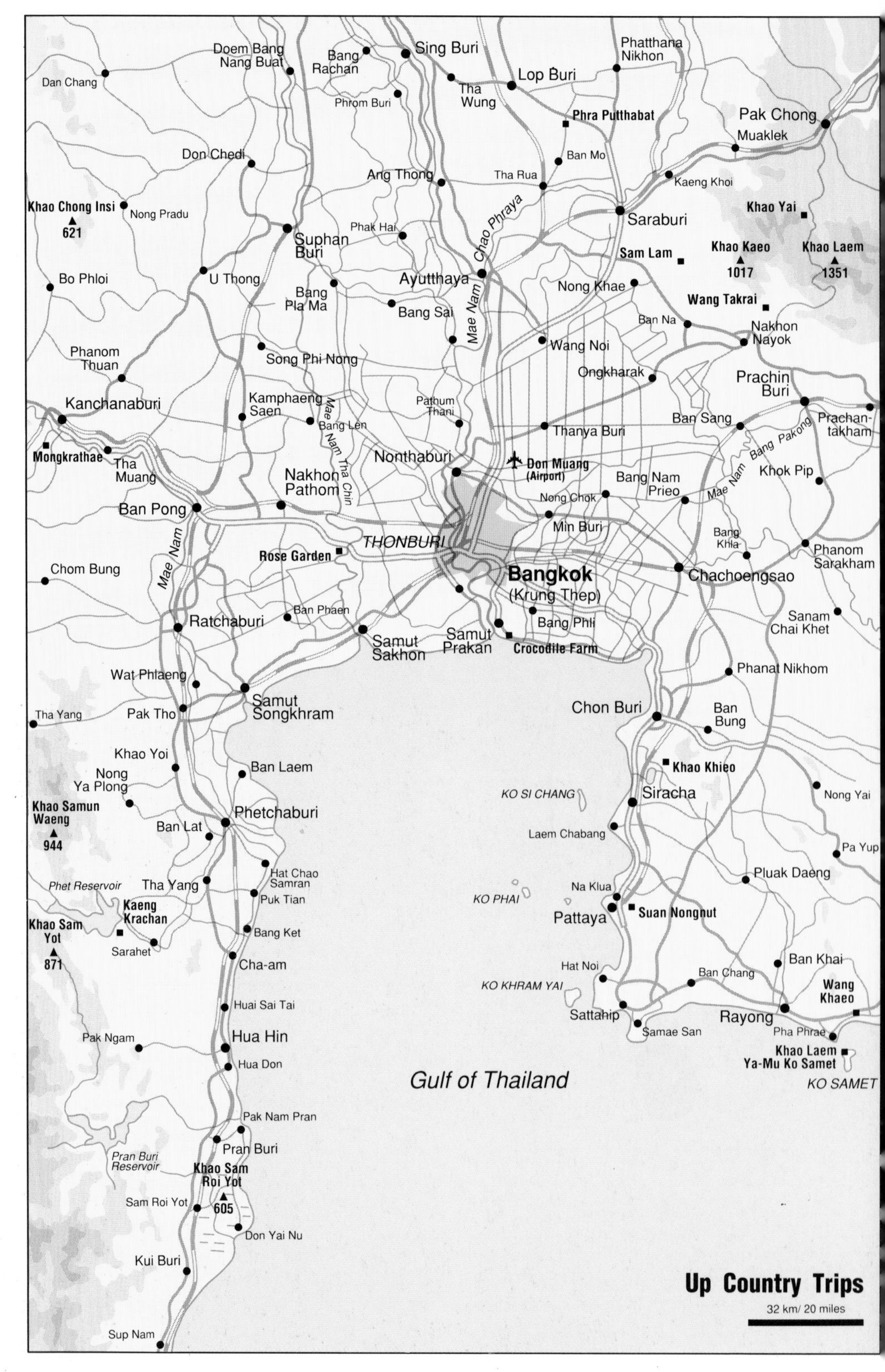
Doem Bang Nang Buat
Bang Rachan
Sing Buri
Lop Buri
Phatthana Nikhon
Dan Chang
Tha Wung
Phrom Buri
Phra Putthabat
Pak Chong
Muaklek
Don Chedi
Ban Mo
Ang Thong
Tha Rua
Kaeng Khoi
Khao Chong Insi
621
Nong Pradu
Saraburi
Khao Yai
Phak Hai
Suphan Buri
Chao Phraya
Sam Lam
Khao Kaeo
1017
Khao Laem
1351
Bo Phloi
U Thong
Ayutthaya
Nong Khae
Bang Pla Ma
Bang Sai
Mae Nam
Wang Takrai
Ban Na
Nakhon Nayok
Phanom Thuan
Song Phi Nong
Wang Noi
Ongkharak
Prachin Buri
Kanchanaburi
Kamphaeng Saen
Mae Nam Tha Chin
Bang Len
Pathum Thani
Ban Sang
Prachantakham
Thanya Buri
Mongkrathae
Tha Muang
Nonthaburi
Don Muang (Airport)
Mae Nam Bang Pakong
Khok Pip
Nakhon Pathom
Bang Nam Prieo
Ban Pong
Nong Chok
Min Buri
Mae Nam
Bang Khla
THONBURI
Rose Garden
Phanom Sarakham
Chom Bung
Bangkok
(Krung Thep)
Chachoengsao
Ban Phaen
Bang Phli
Sanam Chai Khet
Ratchaburi
Samut Sakhon
Samut Prakan
Crocodile Farm
Wat Phlaeng
Phanat Nikhom
Samut Songkhram
Chon Buri
Tha Yang
Pak Tho
Ban Bung
Khao Yoi
Ban Laem
Khao Khieo
Nong Ya Plong
KO SI CHANG
Siracha
Nong Yai
Khao Samun Waeng
944
Phetchaburi
Ban Lat
Laem Chabang
Pa Yup
Hat Chao Samran
Phet Reservoir
Tha Yang
Pluak Daeng
Puk Tian
Na Klua
Kaeng Krachan
KO PHAI
Pattaya
Suan Nongnut
Khao Sam Yot
871
Bang Ket
Sarahet
Cha-am
Hat Noi
Ban Khai
Ban Chang
KO KHRAM YAI
Wang Khaeo
Huai Sai Tai
Sattahip
Rayong
Samae San
Pha Phrae
Hua Hin
Pak Ngam
Khao Laem Ya-Mu Ko Samet
Hua Don
KO SAMET
Gulf of Thailand
Pak Nam Pran
Pran Buri
Pran Buri Reservoir
Khao Sam Roi Yot
605
Sam Roi Yot
Don Yai Nu
Kui Buri
Up Country Trips
32 km/ 20 miles
Sup Nam

though, is the chance to meet and talk with ordinary Thais heading to the same destination. It will likely mean mounds of food passed around and friendly conversation. A car would be faster and give you more mobility but at the sacrifice of interaction with Thais which should be a primary reason for coming to Thailand in the first place.

The 127-meter-tall orange-tiled **Phra Pathom Chedi** is the largest in Asia. Buses leave regularly for Nakhon Pathom, 35 miles (56 km) west of Bangkok, from the Southern Bus Terminal on Charoensanitwong Road in Thonburi. It is not worth making a special trip to see but tours to Damnern Saduak Floating Market generally include the chedi and the Rose Garden in their itinerary.

The **Rose Garden** is a large, landscaped park on the banks of the Tachin River, 20 miles (32 km) west of Bangkok. It offers bungalows and a golf course but many people go there to look at its tropical plants and to enjoy a daily show presenting key elements of village culture like dancing, elephants, Thai boxing, a wedding, a monk ordination ceremony and demonstrations of umbrella making and other types of village crafts.

Most travelers visit the Rose Garden as part of a package tour but if you want to go on your own, Bangkok Sightseeing Travel agency has a bus that leaves the Indra Hotel at 1:30 p.m., returning after the show. Coach cost: 220 baht. The Rose Garden entrance price of 140 baht includes the show. Open daily from 8 a.m. to 6 p.m. The cultural show begins at 3 p.m.

The train on which you can never get lost: That's because it goes to the end of the line, waits a while and comes back. It leaves the Wongwian Yai Railway Station in Thonburi every 30 minutes starting at 5:30 a.m. for an hour's journey through coconut plantations to **Samut Sakhon**, a fishing town on the banks of the Tachin River. It is a pleasant lazy ride with milk stops at

Chinese pagoda at the Ancient City.

every sleepy little hollow. This is not a train ride to get someplace quickly; it is for meshing with the slow rhythms of Thai country life.

From the train station, follow the crowds to the dock for the ferry boat ride across the river to catch the train to **Samut Songkram**. If you tarry in Samut Sakhon, it may be a long wait for the next Samut Songkram train, although it would not be an unpleasant wait because there is much to see in Samut Sakhon's backstreets.

The next segment of the journey takes you past salt flats with windmills lazily turning in the sea breeze to draw salt water into evaporating pans. An hour later, the train pulls into Samut Songkram. Here you can wander the town, have lunch and wait for the return journey (last train at 3:15 p.m.). Or you can walk to the bank of the Maeklong River and hire a long-tailed boat for 500 baht for a two-hour ride to Ratchburi speeding through superb canals overhung with palm trees. From Ratchburi, catch a bus back to Bangkok.

Petchburi is another old royal town. Two hours southeast of Bangkok by car, public bus or train, its main attraction is a lovely hilltop palace built by King Rama IV. A frangipani-lined path leads up a steep hill to the observatory the king built to pursue his passion for astronomy. The observatory commands a superb view of the surrounding countryside. Also, visit **Wat Kampaeng Laeng,** a beautiful old Khmer temple that marks the westernmost penetration by the ancient lords of Angkor Wat. Petchburi can be a trip in itself or a relaxing stop on a journey to the beach resorts of Cha-am and Hua Hin.

The SRT offers a day trip to the royal beach resort of **Hua Hin** to relax on a broad beach, wander in its market watching trawlers unload fish or play a round of golf at its beautiful course. The train leaves Hualampong Station each Saturday and Sunday at 6:35 a.m. and arrives back at 7:35 p.m. Tickets are 75 baht per person.

Koh Si Chang, an island in the Gulf of Thailand, was once Thailand's customs port and with sailors ashore, what a wild and woolly reputation it had. On the south end of the island, King Chulalongkorn built a summer retreat. Today, it is a sleepy little village with little to do but entertain visitors who stroll through the town or catch mini-buses to explore its beaches and wild scenery.

The Canal Tour company offers a single-day boat trip to Koh Si Chang each Saturday and Sunday that leaves from the Tha Chang Wang Luang landing near the Grand Palace at 6:30 a.m. and conveys travelers down the Chao Phya River, into the sea and on to the island. After an hour's stay on the island, the boat continues for another 45 minutes to Koh Larn, off the Pattaya coast, for swimming, leaving the island at 3:15 p.m. and arriving back at Tha Chang at 7:30 p.m.

A ticket costs 195 baht per person and includes two meals. You can get off to stay the night at Koh Larn, returning the

Floating houses on the River Kwai.

following afternoon. Tel. 221-2297 for reservations.

Crocodiles were once the scourge of the waterways, silently cruising through the canals to attack Thais bathing or washing clothes. The canals have been cleansed of them so to see these fearsome beasts up close, travel to the **Crocodile Farm**, the world's largest with more than 30,000 specimens.

The crocodiles aren't kept there out of the goodness of the owner's heart but because their hides can be turned into handsome wallets, briefcases and shoes. Neither does the owner's heart bleed for foreigners since the 80-baht entrance price is eight times that charged Thais, a never-ending source of foreign irritation vented in the Letters to the Editor pages of local English-language newspapers.

There is a show every hour beginning at 9 a.m. during which the lethargic reptiles are "tamed" and a trainer performs feats of derring-do. The best views are at feeding time between 5 and 6 p.m. when the somnolent, leathery beasts erupt in a frenzy like a tableful of boarding house diners. The Farm is located east of the town of Samut Prakan (also called Paknam), an hour east of Bangkok along Sukhumvit Road. Opening hours are 7 a.m. to 6 p.m. Air-conditioned buses numbers 8 and 11 stop at its doorstep. Catch them on Ploenchit or Sukhumvit Roads.

Tour Thailand in a day at the **Ancient City**, whose construction was inspired by a passion for the past and not for commercial gain. On a 200-acre site laid out like a map of Thailand, an art loving millionaire has spent more than 20 years building one-third-sized replicas of the country's most important buildings and monuments.

The Ancient City, also called Muang Boron, is in the vicinity of the Crocodile Farm in Samut Prakarn (Km 33 of the old Sukhumvit Highway). It operates an air-conditioned coach that leaves from its office on the Democracy Monument circle on Rajdamnern Avenue. The 50-baht ticket (25 baht for children) covers coach fare, entry fee and a guide: a real bargain. Open on Saturdays, Sundays and holidays from 8 a.m. to 6 p.m. Book by telephoning 224-1057 or 222-8143.

Prapadaeng-Paknam loop: For the adventurous, there is a trip on local buses to two provincial fishing towns near the mouth of the river. Climb aboard air-conditioned bus number 13 from Sanam Luang which crosses the river and heads south to Prapadaeng. Prapadaeng is populated predominantly by Mons, an ancient people who entered Thailand from Burma long before the arrival of the Thais. It has some interesting old wooden buildings to be found in its backstreets.

If you have the energy, walk to the **Phra Chedi Klang Nam** (Chedi in the Middle of the River) which, until the river shifted its course, was in the middle of the river. It was customary for every monarch traveling in and out of Thailand by sea to stop at the *chedi* to make an offering. It is picturesque

Wat Kampaeng Laeng, Petchburi.

rather than architecturally stunning.

From the Prapadaeng dock, there is a car ferry that crosses the river to the Bangkok shore. From here, take a bus to the Crocodile Farm town of Samut Prakan, Prapadaeng's twin sentinal guarding the entrance to the river. Samut Prakan, or Paknam, (river-mouth), is home port for hundreds of fishing boats that trawl thousands of miles out at sea in search of rapidly-diminishing fish and shellfish. Walk the docks to inhale the briney scents and watch the brawny arms of fishermen sending their catches to Bangkok's markets. Catch air-conditioned buses numbers 8 or 11 for the trip back down Sukhumvit Road into Bangkok.

Overnighters: Also within easy reach of Bangkok are a number of resorts and sights that make interesting stays of two or more days. You can rent a car or use the very comfortable air-conditioned buses operated by the government.

Pattaya is widely regarded as Asia's premier beach resort not because it has the most beautiful beach in the world but because it has developed its facilities to the point that there is simply more to do than anywhere else.

Two hours southeast of Bangkok, it can be a day trip but it is more worthwhile to spend at least one night there Hotels range from luxurious with their own private beaches, to bungalows near the beach for around 600 baht a night, to rooms in shophouses for a few hundred baht a night. Reservations can be made at their Bangkok offices.

If the children are running out of things to do in Bangkok, they'll love Pattaya. Water sports include windsurfing, water skiing, sailing and parasailing where the rider is strapped into a parachute and pulled aloft for a brief bird's eye view of the coastline.

The water is a bit cloudy for snorkeling but scuba diving can be enjoyed at the offshore islands. Equipment can be rented for reasonable prices. There are scuba diving and windsurfing courses

Jomtien Beach, Pattaya.

leading to international certification.

Many hotels have their own tennis courts (bring your own racket and balls); golf is played (with your own clubs) at the Siam Country Club south of the city. There is also horseback riding astride Appaloosa horses at Reo Ranch on the road to the golf course. Outdoor sports include mini-golf and archery. Indoor sports include bowling and a shooting range.

For swimming, most bathers head for nearby Jomtien Beach where the strand is wider and the warm water clearer. Jomtien also has a water theme park, Pattaya Park, with giant water slides and flumes.

Pattaya's range of restaurants nearly rivals that of Bangkok. There are also several fast-food restaurants for the children. The nightlife is somewhat rawer, consisting of open air bars, some of which feature ersatz Thai boxing shows and transvestites dressed to the hilt in glamorous fashions while mouthing the words to hit songs, a new dimension in High Camp.

Air-conditioned buses leave from the Eastern Terminal on Sukhumvit Road across from Soi 63 (also called Soi Ekamai). Round-trip tickets are 90 baht. Thai International also has a terminal in Pattaya where you can catch an air-conditioned coach for a two-hour trip directly to the airport, bypassing Bangkok. It leaves the THAI office at the Royal Cliff Hotel at 6:30 a.m., 1 p.m. and 6:30 p.m. and costs 180 baht. Book in Bangkok at 277-0111, 277-0112; in Pattaya at 423-140, 423-141.

As the name **Khao Khiew Open Zoo** suggests, you and the animals are in the same cage or, in this case, in large compounds. The prickly, clawed and fanged beasts are on islands surrounded by moats to protect them from the visitors. There is also a large walk-in aviary containing some of the most beautiful jungle birds in Asia.

The landscaping of the 200-acre park is a bit bare and its bungalows are a bit spartan but their hillside location pro-

Hua Hin's Railway Station retains much of its early charm.

vides a lovely view of the zoo below and the jungle beyond. The night sounds of birds and strange insects alone would make a stay worthwhile. There is a simple restaurant serving Thai meals.

If going on your own, drive down Highway 3 to Pattaya, turning off at Km 106 onto Highway 3144. Turn left at the T-junction two miles (three km) in and proceed to Km 15. Turn left and drive five miles (eight km) to the zoo. The bungalows are 170 baht/night and hold four persons. There are also large tents for 160 baht/night. Call the Dusit Zoo in Bangkok at 281-0000.

Khao Yai National Park has bungalows (three-bedroom with 10 single beds) ranging in price from 380 to 950 baht (plus 11 percent government tax). Arrange a stay through the Tourism Authority of Thailand by telephoning 282-1143, 281-3041.

In addition to nature hikes through thick jungles, there are observation towers at the edge of savannas. Perch there late in the afternoon and watch the night feeders (sambar and deer) come out to graze. The park also conducts night tours in a truck with a searchlight to catch wild animals feeding. For golfers, there is an 18-hole course with a strong emphasis on rustic, its greens resembling fairway roughs during the hot season.

The Bridge on the River Kwai was filmed in Sri Lanka because of its rugged beauty but if the director had ventured up the River Kwai well beyond the real bridge he would have discovered equally picturesque scenery. There are bamboo forests, teak groves, jungle vegetation, the river itself, caves and hill tribesmen.

There are also bamboo raft bungalows resorts. Jungle Raft Resort offers accommodation, meals, a bus and a guide for a weekend trip that costs 1,550 baht/person. The bus leaves its 1091/121-122 Petchburi Rd. office at 7 a.m., returning to Bangkok at 8 p.m. Tel. 253-5989 for reservations.

To the southwest of Bangkok are beach resorts which serve as alter egos to Pattaya, offering calm rather than frenetic activity. **Cha-am**, two-and-a-half hours south, is a new resort with a single modern hotel, the Cha-am Regent. It offers little more than a chance to flee to the sea but that is enough. A special bus leaves Regent House at 183 Rajdamri Road at 9.30 a.m. daily (180 baht). Tel. 251-0305 for bookings.

Hua Hin is a similar resort with a wide beach whose southern end is occupied by His Majesty's summer palace. Hua Hin offers horseback rides, some water sports, a fishing village to explore and a golf course.

Hua Hin's old Railway Hotel where scenes of *The Killing Fields* were filmed has been renovated but has retained much of its charm. Now called Le Sofitel Central Hua Hin, its bus leaves from the Charn Issara Building at 942 Rama 4 Road at 8 a.m. daily (175 baht) but will pick you up from your hotel. Book by telephoning its Bangkok office at 233-0256. Also in Hua Hin is the Royal Garden Resort whose bus leaves the Indra Hotel at 1 p.m. (300 baht). Tel. 252-4638 for reservations.

Phuket is rapidly becoming a major tourist destination. Abundant natural beauty, a wealth of superb beaches and clean, warm water make it a magnet for sun worshipers. The inland areas comprise hills blanketed in rubber, palm and banana plantations.

Recent development has filled its beaches with a variety of hotels, restaurants and water sports facilities. An hour's flight south of Bangkok, it requires more than a day to see but the journey is well worth it. It is also now served directly from Hong Kong and Singapore or can be made a stopover on a flight from those cities to Bangkok.

Its most popular beach is Patong with the Coral Beach Hotel; north is the Phuket Arcadia at Karon Beach and Dusit Laguna on Bang Thao Bay. Just south is the Phuket Meridien Hotel and at Kata beach is Club Med. At beautiful Nai Harn, the southernmost beach is the luxurious Phuket Yacht Club.

Ko Mak in Phangnga Bay, a popular excursion from Phuket.

TRAVEL TIPS

Getting There

BY AIR

Bangkok is a transportation center for Southeast Asia with service provided by more than 40 regularly-scheduled airlines. There are four international airports at Chiang Mai, Phuket, Hat Yai and Bangkok with service to the capital either direct or via a stopover at one of the other cities.

Thailand's flag carrier, Thai Airways International or THAI serves 43 cities on five continents and enjoys a high reputation for excellence and superb in-flight service. It is not to be confused with Thai Airways, the domestic airline, which operates a network of daily flights to Thailand's major towns aboard a fleet of sleek 737s.

Thailand's principal airport, Don Muang, is located 14 miles (22 km) north of the city. In September 1987 it opened a modern new extension with airbridges which doubled handling capacity and now speeds visitors through immigration formalities, baggage collection and customs. At the airport are currency exchange counters paying bank rates, transportation desks and a desk of the Thai Hotels Association where it is possible to book a hotel room in the city. An airport tax of 120 *baht* (US$4.70) is levied.

BY RAIL

Trains operated by the State Railways of Thailand are clean, cheap and reliable albeit a little slow. There are only two railroad entry points into Thailand, both from Malaysia on the southern Thailand border.

The Malay Mail leaves Kuala Lumpur daily at 7:30 a.m. and 8:20 a.m. and 1:40 p.m., 2:40 p.m., 8:25 p.m. and 10 p.m. It arrives about seven to nine hours later at Butterworth at 1:05 p.m., 5:20 p.m., 8:25 p.m., 9:10 p.m., 5:30 p.m. and 6:40 a.m. respectively. A train leaves Butterworth at 1:55 p.m. everyday, crossing the border into Thailand and arriving in Bangkok at 8:35 a.m. the next day. Air-conditioned first- and second-class sleepers are available. Dining cars serve local food.

First class Butterworth-Bangkok tickets are US$61 (1,555 *baht*) while second class tickets are US$25 (635 *baht*). Trains leave Bangkok's Hualampong Station everyday at 3:15 p.m. for the return journey to Malaysia.

A second, somewhat less convenient but more entertaining train travels from Kuala Lumpur up Malaysia's east coast to the northeastern town of Kota Bharu. A taxi crosses the border to catch the SRT train from the southern Thai town of Sungai Kolok. Trains leave Sungai Kolok at 10:15 a.m. and 10:55 a.m., arriving in Bangkok at 6.35 a.m. and 7.05 a.m. the following day. First-class tickets are US$45 (1,158 *baht*); second-class is US$24.25 (618 *baht*).

BY ROAD

Although Thailand borders four countries, only that with Malaysia is open to road traffic. Drivers will find that all Thai roads are modern and well maintained by comparison with those of its neighbors. The Malaysian border closes at 6 p.m. so plan your itinerary accordingly.

Travel Essentials

VISAS & PASSPORTS

All foreign nationals entering Thailand must have valid passports. Foreign nationals holding valid passports from the following countries will, at the point of entry, be granted gratis a Transit Visa valid up to 15 days: Algeria, Argentina, Australia, Austria, Bahrain, Belgium, Brazil, Brunei, Burma, Canada, Denmark, Egypt, Fiji, Finland, France, Greece, Iceland, Indonesia, Ireland, Israel, Italy, Japan, Jordan, Kenya, Kuwait,

Luxembourg, Malaysia, Mexico, Netherlands, New Zealand, Nigeria, North Yemen, Norway, Oman, Papua New Guinea, Philippines, Portugal, Qatar, Saudi Arabia, Senegal, Singapore, South Korea, Sudan, Spain, Sweden, Switzerland, Tunisia, Turkey, United Arab Emirates, United Kingdom, U.S.A., Vanuatu, Western Samoa, West Germany and Yugoslavia.

If planning a longer stay, a Transit Visa valid for 30 days or a Tourist Visa valid for 60 days must be obtained from a Royal Thai Embassy or Consulate abroad by filing an application, supplying three passport-sized photographs and paying a fee of 200 *baht* (US$7.90) and 300 *baht* (US$ 11.80) respectively. Visas can be extended by applying at the Immigration Division on Soi Suan Plu (8:30 a.m. to 4 p.m., Mon. to Fri.) before the visa's expiration date. The fee is 500 *baht*. The Immigration Department has attempted to streamline operations to speed the extension process but visitors on a round-Asia tour may find it easier to leave for a neighboring country and obtain another tourist visa.

Visitors wishing to leave Thailand and return before the expiry of their visas can apply for a re-entry permit prior to their departure at immigration offices in Bangkok, Chiang Mai, Pattaya, Phuket and Hat Yai. The fee is 500 *baht*. An exit visa, however, is not required.

MONEY MATTERS

The *baht* is the principal Thai monetary unit. It is divided into 100 units called *satangs*. Banknote denominations include the 500 (purple), 100 (red), 50 (blue), 20 (green) and 10 (brown) notes.

While the banknotes are easy to decipher, the coinage is a confusing matter with a variety of sizes and types for each denomination. There are two different five *baht* coins (silver pieces with copper rims), three varieties of one *baht* coin (silver; only the medium-size will fit in a public telephone), a two *baht* coin (silver, nearly the same size as the small one *baht* and small five *baht* coin) and two small coins of 50 and 25 *satang* (both are brass-colored).

The very stable Thai currency is tied to a basket of international currencies heavily weighted in favor of the U.S. dollar. The rate at time of press was 24.4 baht to one dollar. For daily rates, check the *Bangkok Post* or the *Nation Review* newspapers. There is no currency black market.

Both cash and traveler's checks can be changed in hundreds of bank branches throughout the city; rates are more favorable for traveler's checks than for cash. Banking hours are 8:30 a.m. to 3:30 p.m., Monday to Friday, but nearly every bank maintains money-changing kiosks. Hotels generally give poor rates in comparison with banks whose rates are set by the Bank of Thailand.

BANKING SYSTEM

Thailand has a sophisticated banking system with representation by the major banks of most developed foreign countries. Money can be imported in cash or traveler's checks and converted into *baht*. It is also possible to arrange telex bank drafts from one's hometown bank. There is no minimum requirement on the amount of money that must be converted. Money can be reconverted into the currency of your choice at bank counters at the airport. Please refer to the following section for a listing of banks, their addresses and banking services.

Thai Banks

Bank of Asia
191 S. Sathorn Rd.
Tel: 287-2211, 287-2212

Bank of Ayuthya
550 Ploenchit Rd.
Tel: 253-8601, 253-8632

Bangkok Bank
333 Silom Rd.
Tel: 234-3333, 235-5997

Krung Thai Bank
35 Sukhumvit Rd.
Tel: 255-2222, 251-9586

Siam Commercial Bank
1060 New Phetchburi Rd.
Tel: 251-3114, 252-7418

Thai Military Bank
34 Phyathai Rd.
Tel: 246-0020, 245-7503

Thai Farmers Bank
400 Paholyothin Rd.
Tel: 270-1122, 270-1133

Overseas Banks

Bank of America
NT. & SA.
2/2 N. Wireless Rd.
Tel: 251-633

Bank of Tokyo
Thaniya Bldg.
62 Silom Rd.
Tel: 236-0119, 236-9103

Banque Indosuez
142 Wireless Rd.
Tel: 253-3616, 253-0106

Banque Nationale de Paris
Dusit Thani Bldg., 5th. floor,
946 Rama I Rd.
Tel: 236-7928, 236-7929

Bharat Overseas Bank
221 Rajawong Rd.
Tel: 221-8181, 221-8182

Chase Manhattan Bank N.A.
Silom Centre Bldg.
965 Rama I Rd.
Tel: 252-1141, 252-1150

Citibank N.A.
127 S. Sathorn Rd.
Tel: 286-3992, 286-3993

Deutsche Bank (Asia)
Thai Wah Tower
21 S. Sathorn Rd.
Tel: 240-9425, 240-9402

Hongkong & Shanghai Bank
Hongkong Bank Bldg.
64 Silom Rd.
Tel: 233-1904, 233-1905

Mitsui Bank
138 Boonmitr Bldg.
Silom Rd.
Tel: 234-3841, 234-3842

Standard Chartered Bank
946 Rama VI Rd.
Tel: 234-0820, 2344-0823

United Malayan Bank
149 Suapa Rd.
Tel: 221-9191, 221-9192

CREDIT CARDS

American Express, Diner's Club, Mastercard and Visa are widely accepted throughout Bangkok. Many stores will levy a surcharge on their use, the highest (three to five percent) of which is American Express cards. Credit cards can be used to draw emergency cash at most banks. Each card has a local representative office, their addresses and telephone numbers are listed below:

American Express (Thai)
11th floor, Bangkok Bank Bldg.
333 Silom Rd.
Tel: 236-0276, 235-0990
Hours: 8:30 a.m.-5:30 p.m., Mon-Fri.

Diner's Club (Thailand)
11th floor, Dusit Thani Bldg.
946 Rama 4 Rd.
Tel: 233-031, 233-5775
Hours: 8:30 a.m.-5:00 p.m., Mon-Fri.

VISA and Mastercard
Thai Farmers Bank (Head Office)
400 Paholyothin Rd.
Tel: 270-1259, 270-1122
Hours: 8:30 a.m.-3:30 p.m., Mon-Fri.

HEALTH

Visitors entering the kingdom are no longer required to show evidence of vaccination for smallpox or cholera. Persons arriving from Africa must show certificates indicating vaccination against yellow fever.

Concerned about the spread of AIDS, the government, in late 1987, passed a new regulation barring the entry into Thailand of persons with the disease. How the disease was to be detected and the regulation enforced was not clarified.

HYGIENE

Thais place high value on personal hygiene and are aware of the dangers of germs and infections. They do not, however, place such a high priority on keeping the environment clean. However, establishments catering to foreigners are generally careful with food and drink preparation.

Bangkok water is clean when it leaves the modern filtration plant; the pipes that carry it into the city are somewhat less than new and visitors are advised to drink bottled water or soft drinks. Both are produced under strict supervision as is the ice used in large hotels and restaurants. Most streetside restaurants are clean; a quick glance should tell you which are and which are not.

PRECAUTIONS

With its thriving nightlife and transient population, Bangkok is a magnet for the types of diseases one would expect to find in red light districts anywhere. The women (and men) in these service industries are aware of the consequences of carelessness and of not insisting that their partners take precautions, but economic necessity coupled with a Thai reluctance to offend anyone means that there is a great risk of taking home a souvenir one would rather not show to friends and loved ones.

The rule is to assume that there is a good chance of picking up something and to take appropriate measures. With the spread of AIDS worldwide, there is even more reason to be careful. Several massage parlors, mindful of the dangers, now bar foreign patrons and cater only to Thais on the grounds that they reduce their risks.

CUSTOMS

The Thai government prohibits the import of drugs, dangerous chemicals, pornography, firearms and ammunition. Foreigners are allowed to bring with them a maximum equivalent to US$2,000 per person or US$4,000 per family. All higher amounts must be declared at the point of entry.

Foreign guests are allowed to import without tax, one camera with five rolls of film, 200 cigarettes, and one bottle of spirits.

GETTING ACQUAINTED

GEOGRAPHY & POPULATION

Thailand, at whose geographic center Bangkok is situated, lies between 7 and 21 degrees latitude. With a total of 198,000 square miles (514,000 square km), approximately the size of France, the country is said to resemble an elephant with its trunk dangling. It is bordered by Malaysia on the south, Burma on the west, Laos across the Mekong River to the northeast and Cambodia to the east.

The north is marked by low hills with the tallest peak, Doi Inthanon, standing 8,497 feet (2,590 meters) tall. A range of hills divides Thailand from Burma and forms the western boundary of the broad alluvial Central Plain which is the country's principal rice-growing area. The valley's eastern edge rises to the Korat Plateau which defines most of the Northeast. The spine of the southern peninsula is the same range of hills that separates Thailand from Burma, sloping down to the Andaman Sea on the west and the Gulf of Thailand on the east. Thailand has a total of 1,612 miles (2,600 km) of coastline.

Thailand's population is nearly 55 million. A majority of its people are farmers who till alluvial land so rich that Thailand is a world leader in exporting tapioca (No. 1), rice (No. 2), rubber (No. 2), canned pineapple (No. 3), and is a top-ranked exporter of sugar, maize and tin.

Bangkok, the nation's capital, is situated at 14 degrees north latitude. Like Hungary's Buda and Pest, Bangkok is a city divided into halves by a river, the Chao Phya which separates Bangkok and Thonburi. It covers a total area of 604 square miles (1,565.2 square km) of delta land of which no natural area is more than 2 meters above any other. Population totals 5,832,843. Bangkok is +7 hours GMT.

CLIMATE

Most guidebooks suggest that there are three seasons in Thailand – hot, rainy and cool. But to tourists winging in from anywhere north of the 30th parallel, Thailand has only one temperature: hot. Worse, the temperature drops only a few degrees during the night and is accompanied 24 hours a day by high humidity. If not for air-conditioning, Bangkok would be a large omelet frying on the cosmic sidewalk.

This fact has now been officially recognized by the World Meteorological Organization. Average the daytime highs and the nighttime lows and Bangkok emerges as the world's hottest city. Add to it the rains of the monsoon season and what emerges is the world's only 602 square miles (1,565 square km) sauna.

The following temperature ranges give a rough guide to the degree of heat:

- Hot season (March to mid-June) 27°C-35°C (80°F-95°F)
- Rainy season (June to October) 24°C-32°C (75°F-90°F)
- Cool season (November to February) 18°C-32°C (65°F-90°F but with less humidity)

CULTURE & CUSTOMS

Thais are remarkably tolerant and forgiving of the foibles of foreigners but there are a few things which will rouse them to anger.

PATRIOTISM & BUDDHISM

For one, the Royal Family is regarded with a genuine reverence paralleled in few other countries and Thais will react strongly if they consider any member of royalty has been insulted. Ill-considered remarks or refusing to stand for the Royal Anthem before the start of a movie in a theater will earn some very hard stares and perhaps worse.

Similarly, the second pillar of the society, Buddhism, occupies a special place in most Thai hearts. Disrespect towards Buddha images, temples or monks is not taken lightly. Monks have to observe vows of chastity, which require that they not touch women, not even their mothers. When in the vicinity of a monk, try to stay clear to avoid accidentally brushing against him. When visiting a temple, it is acceptable for both sexes to wear long pants but not shorts. Ill-kempt persons are often turned away from major temples.

CUSTOMS TO OBSERVE

The Thai greeting and farewell is "*Sawasdee*," spoken while raising the hands in a prayer-like gesture, the fingertips touching the nose and bowing the head slightly. It is an easy greeting to master and one which will earn you smiles wherever you go.

Thais believe in personal cleanliness. They dress, not richly, but cleanly and neatly. They frown on those who do not share this belief.

From the Hindu religion has come the belief that the head is the fount of wisdom and the feet are unclean. For this reason, it is insulting to touch another person on the head, point your feet at him or step over him. Kicking in anger is worse than spitting at him and will earn you quick retribution.

If you wish to pass someone who is seated at the floor, bow as you walk and indicate with your extended arm pointing down the path you wish to take. Like the Red Sea, the crowd will part to let you through. Similarly, it is believed that spirits dwell in the raised doorsills of temples and traditional Thai houses and that when one steps on them the spirits become angry and curse the building with bad luck.

Twenty years ago, Thai couples would never have thought of holding hands when they walked down the street. That has changed due to Western influence on the young; but, as in many tradition-bound countries of the world, displaying open affection in public is a sign of bad manners.

THAI CONCEPTS

A few Thai concepts will give not only an indication of how Thais think but will smooth your social interaction with them. Thais strive to maintain equanimity in their lives and go to great lengths to avoid confrontation. It is called *kriangjai,* meaning an unwillingness to bother someone superior in rank to you. In many cases, it means not giving you the bad news until too late for fear it might upset you.

Jai yen or "cool heart", an attitude of keeping calm, is a trait admired by Thais. Getting angry or exhibiting a *jai ron* (hot heart) is a sign of immaturity and lack of self-control. Reacting to adversity or disappointment with a shrug of the shoulders and saying *mai pen rai* (never mind) is the accepted response to most situations.

Sanuk means "fun" or "enjoyment" and is the yardstick by which life's activities are measured. If it is not *sanuk*, it is probably not worth doing.

TERMS OF ADDRESS

Thais are addressed by their first rather than their last names. The name is usually preceded by the word *Khun*, a term which honors the person. Thus, Silpachai Krishnamra would be addressed as Khun Silpachai.

You will find some Thais referred to in newspapers with the letters M.C., M.R. or M.L. preceding their names. These are royal titles normally translated as "prince" or "princess". The five-tier system reserves the highest two titles for the immediate Royal Family. Below that come the nobility, remnants of the noble houses of old. The highest of these three ranks is *Mom Chao* (M.C.) followed by *Mom Rachawong* (M.R.) and *Mom Luang* (M.L.)

The title is not hereditary thanks to a unique system which guarantees that Thailand will never become top-heavy with princes and princesses spilling out of the woodwork. Each succeeding generation is born into the next rank down. Thus, the son or daughter of a *Mom Chao* is a *Mom Rachawong*. Soon, Thailand will be a nation of *Nai*, Mister, and *Nang*, Miss or Mrs., a truly democratic realm.

TIPPING

Tipping is not a custom in Thailand although it is becoming more prevalent. A service charge of 10 percent is generally included in restaurant bills and is divided among the staff. A bit extra for the waitress would not go unappreciated. Do not tip taxi or *tuk-tuk* drivers unless the traffic has been particularly bad and he has been especially patient, 10 *baht* would suffice; for a long journey, over 40 *baht*. Hotel roomboys and porters are becoming used to being tipped but will not hover with hand extended if you do not.

ELECTRICITY

Electrical outlets are rated at 220 volts, 50 cycles and accept either flat-pronged or round-pronged plugs.

BUSINESS HOURS

Government offices are open from 8:30 a.m. to 4:30 p.m. Monday through Friday. Business hours are from 8 a.m. or 8:30 a.m. to 5:30 p.m. Monday through Friday. Some businesses are open half days Saturday from 8:30 a.m. to noon. Banks are open from 8:30 a.m. to 3:30 p.m., five days a week but operate money-changing kiosks throughout the city which are open until 8 p.m., seven days a week.

The Central Post Office on New Road between Suriwongse and Siphya Roads opens at 8:30 a.m. and closes at 4:30 p.m. Mondays through Fridays and from 8:30 a.m. to 12:30 p.m. on Saturdays, Sundays and holidays. At the right side of the lobby is a packing service with boxes in various sizes for mailing purposes. A department on the right end of the building is open 24 hours to sell stamps and send telegrams.

Branch post offices are located throughout the city; and many of these usually stay open until 6 p.m. The post office in the Indra Hotel arcade stays open until 8 p.m., seven days a week. Kiosks along some of the city's busier streets sell stamps, aerograms (8 *baht* each) and ship small parcels. Hotel reception counters will send letters for their guests at no extra charge.

Department stores are open from 9:30 a.m. to 8 p.m. seven days a week. Ordinary shops open at 8:30 a.m. or 9 a.m. and close between 6 p.m. and 8 p.m., depending on the location and type of business. Foodland supermarket on Patpong 2 is open 24 hours. Some pharmacies remain open all night.

Small open-air coffee shops and restaurants open at 7 a.m. and close at 8:30 p.m. though some stay open past midnight. Large restaurants generally close at 10 p.m. Most coffeeshops close at midnight; some stay open 24 hours. For a late-night Thai food meal, the markets at Pratunam and Bangrak and wherever bright fluorescent lights are shining stay open until the wee hours.

Banks in Bangkok include Thai institutions and branches of foreign banks. Most are equipped to handle telegraph and telex money transfers and a wide range of money services. Most can change nearly every type of currency. Many operate sidewalk money changing kiosks which are open from 8:30 a.m. to 8 p.m., seven days a week, far beyond normal banking hours of 8:30 a.m. to 3:30 p.m. Monday through Friday.

HOLIDAYS & FESTIVALS

JANUARY

New Year's Day is a day of relaxation after the festivities of the night before. It is a public holiday.

Elephant Round-Up in the northeast Thailand town of Chaiyaphum early in January. Over 100 of the gentle giants show off their unique abilities in this annual event including demonstrations of wild elephant hunts, elephant soccer matches, obedience demonstrations and the spectacular reenactment of medieval wars.

Phra Buddha Chinarat Fair. Late January. Enshrined in Phitsanulok's Wat Phra Si Ratana Mahatat, Phra Buddha Chinarat is one of Thailand's most sacred and delicately-cast Buddha images of the Sukhothai style. The fair includes folk performances and various entertainment.

Don Chedi Memorial Fair in Suphanburi (January 24-31) commemorates the decisive battle won by King Naresuan the Great at Don Chedi, the fair features historical exhibitions, entertainment and local handicraft stalls.

FEBRUARY

Flower Festival held in Chiang Mai between February 3 and 5, this annual event features flower displays, floral floats, beauty contests and it coincides with the period when the province's temperate and tropical flowers are in full bloom.

Dragon and Lion Parade. Held annually in the central Thailand town of Nakhon Sawan (between January and February) by people of Chinese ancestry, the Dragon and Lion procession is a traditional homage-paying rite to the golden dragon deity in gratitude of his benevolence to human beings. The lively parade comprising leading marching bands, golden dragon and lion dances, and deities procession, takes place along the downtown area of the city.

Chinese New Year is not celebrated with the boisterousness of other Asian countries, not even igniting strings of red firecrackers. The temples are a bit busier with wishes made for good fortune in the coming year but otherwise there is nothing to mark the period. Shops close and behind the steel grills, private family celebrations go on for three or four days.

Chinese New Year is not officially recognized as a holiday in Thailand but many shops are closed, often for several days.

Magha Puja, a public holiday in Bangkok and a Buddhist holiday on the full moon night of February 9, marks the spontaneous gathering of 1,200 disciples to hear the Lord Buddha preach. In the evening, Thais gather at temples to hear a sermon by the chief monk of the *wat*. Then, when the moon is rising, they place their hands in a praying position before their faces and, clasping candles, incense and flowers, follow the chanting monks around the *bot* of the *wat* three times before placing their candles and incense in trays at the front of the *bot*. It is a most solemn and moving ceremony.

MARCH

Kite flying is not a festival but it would be difficult to convince kite enthusiasts otherwise. They gather on Sanam Luang in the afternoons as the brisk winds haul their large kites aloft, filling the sky with bright colors.

APRIL

Chakri Day celebrates the founding in 1782 of the dynasty which presently rules Thailand. It is celebrated in the palace but there are no public ceremonies. An official holiday, most Thais celebrate it as a day off from work.

The **Phra Chedi Klang Nam Fair** in April is one of the larger temple fairs of the cool season. It is celebrated at the wat at the

THE PROBLEMS OF A

HEAVY TRAFFIC.

You'll come across massive Thai jumbos at work and play in their natural habitat. In Thailand, elephants are part of everyday rural life.

FALLING MASONRY.

A visit to the ruined cities of Sukhothai or Ayutthaya will remind you of the country's long and event-filled history.

EYESTRAIN.

A problem everyone seems to enjoy. The beauty of our exotic land is only matched by the beauty and gentle nature of the Thai people.

GETTING LOST.

From the palm-fringed beaches of Phuket to the highlands of Chiang Mai there are numerous places to get away from it all.

OLIDAY IN THAILAND.

GETTING TRAPPED.

n bunkers mostly. The fairways, superb club ouses and helpful caddies make a golf trap for layers of all standards.

HIGH DRAMA.

A performance of the 'Khon' drama, with gods and demons acting out a never-ending battle between good and evil, should not be missed.

EXCESS BAGGAGE.

hai food is so delicious you'll want to eat more nd more of it. Of course, on Thai there's o charge for extra kilos in this area.

MISSING YOUR FLIGHT.

In Thailand, this isn't a problem. Talk to us or your local travel agent about Royal Orchid Holidays in Thailand.

Thai
We reach for the sky.

river's edge at Prapadaeng 9 miles (15 km) south of Bangkok on the Thonburi side of the river.

Songkran is a public holiday which in the past was the traditional Thai New Year until royal decree shifted the date to January 1 to accord with the rest of the world. It most closely resembles the Indian festival of "Holi" which occurs at the same time. Songkran is a time of wild revelry, a chance for the normally placid Thais to let off steam. The central event is the sprinkling of water on one's friends to bless them but this usually turns into a boisterous throwing of buckets of water on passersby.

In recent years, Bangkok residents have become much more subdued in their celebration of Songkran but while it is now safe for a visitor to ride an open-windowed bus down the street, he is advised to be prepared when walking in markets and, oddly, on Patpong where it is celebrated.

To see Songkran at its most riotous, travel down the western bank of the Chao Phya River on April 17 to the town of Phrapadaeng. There, no one is safe; but in the April heat, who cares – a dousing is cool relief from the burning rays of the sun.

MAY

Labor Day (May 1) is a public holiday.

Coronation Day (May 5) is a private royal affair and a public holiday.

The Plowing Ceremony is a colorful antique tradition celebrated only in Bangkok. Held at Sanam Luang, it is presided over by King Bhumibol and marks the official start of the rice planting season. Crimson-clad attendants lead bullocks, drawing an old-fashioned plow, around a specially prepared ground. The lord of ceremonies, usually the Minister of Agriculture, follows behind, scooping rice seed out of baskets held by pretty maidens and sowing it in the furrows left by the plow, all to the accompaniment of blaring conch shells and drums.

Visakha Puja, a public holiday on the full moon night of May, that commemorates the birth, enlightenment and death of Buddha. The three things are all said to have happened on the same day. Visakha Puja is celebrated like Magha Puja with a triple circumambulation around the temple as the moon is rising.

JUNE

International long-boat races under the Rama 9 Bridge with participants from around the world. Held from June 24-25.

JULY

Asalaha Puja on the full moon night of July is the third most important Buddhist holiday and marks the occasion when Buddha preached to his first five disciples. It is celebrated on the full moon night in similar manner to Magha Puja and Visakha Puja. It also marks the beginning of the 3-month Lenten season. Tradition says that Buddha was approached by farmers who asked that he bar monks from going on their morning alms rounds for a period of three months because they were trampling on the rice shoots they had just planted. They offered instead to take food to the monks at the temple during this period, a practice which has been followed ever since.

Candle Festival (July 17-19) in the northeast town of Ubon celebrates commencement of Phansa with a lovely spectacle where some beautifully embellished beeswax candles are ceremoniously paraded before being presented to temples.

Tourism Festival with performances by artists from around the country. August 9-20 in Bangkok.

AUGUST

Her Majesty Queen Sirikit marks her birthday (August 12) by religious ceremonies and private celebrations. It is a public holiday.

SEPTEMBER

On the first day of the eighth lunar month, Chinese celebrate the **Moon Festival**. They place small shrines laden with fruit, incense and candles in front of their houses to honor the moon goddess. It is a lovely festival, the highlight of which are the utterly scrumptious cakes shaped like a full moon. They are specially prepared, often by chefs flown in from Hong Kong, and found no other time of the year.

Phichit Boat Races (September 2 and 3) is the famous regatta featuring long boat races. The low-slung, wooden boats are raced with great gusto.

The **Chinese Vegetarian Festival** last held in October, is a subdued affair by comparison with the firewalkers of the Phuket island version. Enormous amounts of vegetarian food, Chinese opera performances and elaborate offerings are made at various Chinese temples around the city. A superb photography opportunity. Only those wearing all white attire are allowed in the area of the altar, so dress appropriately.

OCTOBER

Ok Pansa (October 14) marks the end of the 3-month Lenten season and the beginning of the Kathin season when Buddhists visit *wats* to present monks with new robes and other necessities. Groups will rent boats or buses and travel long distances to spend a day making gifts to monks of a particular *wat*. If you are invited, by all means go because it is a day of feasting and fun as well.

Chulalongkorn Day (October 23) honors King Rama V (1868-1910) who led Thailand into the 20th century. On this public holiday students lay wreaths before his statue in the plaza at the old National Assembly building in an afternoon ceremony.

NOVEMBER

Golden Mount Fair held the first week of November is one of the noisiest of temple fairs. Carnival rides, food concessions, variety performances and product stalls are the main attractions.

The **Little Royal Barge** Festival at Wat Nang Chee in Phasi Charoen early in November is a smaller version of the grand Royal Barge procession but it is still marked by more gaiety in small towns.

Loy Krathong, one of the most beautiful festivals anywhere in Asia, is on the full moon night of November. It is said to have been started in Sukhothai in the 13th century. A young queen, Nang Nopamat, is said to have floated a small boat laden with candles and incense downstream past the pavilion where her husband was talking with his friends. Whatever the origins, it has grown to be one of the country's most enchanting festivals, a night when Thais everywhere launch small candle-laden boats into the rivers and canals to ask blessings. The tiny dots of light and shimmering water are mesmerizing.

Long-boat races have become increasingly popular in the past few years and it is not unusual to open a newspaper during November and find that yet another race is being staged somewhere in the vicinity of Bangkok. The biggest in Bangkok is that held at the Royal Orchid Sheraton Hotel Boat on a weekend day near the end of November. It is colorful and exciting and provides superb photo opportunities for someone with a telephoto lens.

The **Phra Pathom Chedi Fair** at the world's biggest stupa in Nakhon Pathom, 35 miles (56 km) west of Bangkok is another temple fair, and is regarded as one of the most exciting.

DECEMBER

Trooping of the Colors (December 3). The royal regiments dressed in brilliantly-colored costumes pass in review before the King. Held on the plaza before the old National Assembly building, the Trooping of the Colors is the most impressive of martial ceremonies equivalent to the Changing of the Guard in London.

His Majesty King Bhumibol celebrates his birthday (December 5) with a ceremony at Wat Phra Kaew only for invited officials and guests and with a private party. It is a public holiday.

Constituition Day (December 10) is a public holiday in Thailand.

Christmas will soon be a Thai holiday if the merchants have any say in the matter. If endless repetitions of Christmas carols in department stores bludgeon everyone into acceptance of it, it will take about a year or two before it becomes an official holiday.

But **New Year's Eve** on December 31 is a public holiday. From the last week of December through the first week of January, dancers and performers from all over Thailand gather in Bangkok for the Cultural Identity Festival. At a venue which changes every year, village houses are built and demonstrations of village crafts are displayed while dancers perform their region's special dances. The highlight is a big parade of floral floats and everyone in his local dress.

RELIGIOUS SERVICES

ANGLICAN

Christ Church
11 Convent Rd.
Tel: 234-3634
Services: 8 a.m., 10 a.m.

Assembly of God
196 Soi Yasoop 1
Ekamai Rd.
Tel: 391-4387
Service: 6 p.m.

BAHAI

Bahai Faith
77 Soi Langsuan
Ploenchit Rd.
Tel: 252-5355
Services: 8 a.m., 5 p.m.

BAPTIST

Calvary Baptist Church
88 Soi 2, Sukhumvit Rd.
Tel: 251-8278
Services: 9 a.m., 10:15 a.m.

CATHOLIC

Holy Redeemer Church
123/19 Soi
Ruam Rudi Wireless Rd.
Tel: 253-0305, 253-8411
Mass: 7 a.m., 9 a.m., 5:30 p.m.

Assumption Cathedral
23 Oriental Lane New Rd.
Tel: 234-8556, 234-4592
Mass: 7:30 a.m., 8:30 a.m., 10 a.m.

St. Louis Church
215/2 S. Sathorn Rd.
Tel: 211-0220
Mass: 6 a.m., 8 a.m., 10 a.m., 5:30 p.m.

Evangelical Church
42 Soi 10,
Sukhumvit Rd.
Tel: 251-9539
Services: 10:30 a.m., 6 p.m.

HINDU

Thamsapha Association
50 Soi Wat Prok,
New Rd.
Tel: 211-3840
Services: 7 a.m. to 10 p.m.

INTERNATIONAL CHURCH

73 Soi 19, Sukhumvit Rd.
Tel: 253-3353
Services: 8 a.m.-9:15 a.m.

JEWISH ASSOCIATION OF THAILAND (ASHKENAZI)

121 Soi 22,
Sukhumvit Rd.
Tel: 258-2195
Services: Fri. 6:30 p.m.

EVEN CHEN JEWISH ASSOCIATION (SEPHARDIC)

Soi 3, Mahasek Rd.
Services: Sat. at 9:30 a.m.

MORMON

72 Chulintr Lane,
Soi 21, Sukhumvit Rd.
Tel: 258-3585, 258-3586
Services: 9 a.m., noon

MUSLIM

Sha-Roh-Tal Islam Mosque
133 Soi 1 Sukhapiban Rd.
Tel: 328-8950
Services: 12:30 p.m.-2 p.m.

SEVENTH DAY ADVENTIST

Bangkok Sanitarium Church
430 Phitsanuloke Rd.
Tel: 281-1422
Services: 8 a.m. to noon

Seventh Day Adventist Chinese Church
1325 Rama 4 Rd.
Tel: 215-4529
Services: 10:30 a.m., noon

SIKH

Wat Sirikurusing Saha
565 Chuckrapetch Rd.
Tel: 221-1011
Services: 6 a.m.-5 p.m.

COMMUNICATIONS

TELECOMMUNICATIONS

Bangkok has a sophisticated communications system, not that it always works; the lines have a way of getting jammed, like the traffic, especially after a heavy rain. Most hotels have telephones, telegrams, telexes and FAX facilities. Hotel operators can place international telephone calls within minutes; many hotel rooms have installed IDD for convenience. If the hotel lacks such facilities, one can place long distance calls at an annex to the General Post Office located on the ground floor of Nava Building on Soi Braisanee across a lane to the north of the GPO itself.

NEWSPAPERS

With television and radio stations broadcasting in Thai, the English-language morning newspapers are the foreigner's lifelines to the outside world. The *Bangkok Post* and the *Nation Review* are considered among the best and most comprehensive dailies in Asia. The *Asian Wall Street Journal* and the *International Herald Tribune* dailies are available at most bookstalls after 4 p.m. Newsstands in major hotel gift shops carry air-freighted, and therefore expensive, (at least 50 *baht* per copy), editions of British, French, German and Italian newspapers. News sellers on Sukhumvit Soi 3 also offer Arabic newspapers.

RADIO & TELEVISION

AM radio is devoted entirely to Thai-language programs. FM frequencies include several English-language stations with the latest pop hits. Radio Thailand offers 4 hours of English-language broadcasts each day on the 97 MHz frequency. Of value to visitors is a daily English-language program of travel tips broadcast at 6:40 a.m., with news at 7 a.m., 8 a.m., 12:10 p.m., 12:30 p.m., 6:35 p.m. and 7 p.m. In addition, a French-language program of general interest topics and news is broadcast from 11:30 a.m. to noon every day.

Bangkok has four color television channels, three of which offer American, Japanese and European programs dubbed in Thai. At 8 p.m., all channels broadcast news beamed by satellite from Europe. The English-language soundtrack is supposed to be broadcasted simultaneously on FM radio but for inexplicable reasons is frequently not transmitted. The FM frequencies are listed in the newspapers.

EMERGENCIES

SECURITY & CRIME

In the unlikely event you should become the victim of a criminal attack, you must be taken to a **Police Hospital**, normally the one at Rajprasong intersection. Those finding you after an incident may take you to an ordinary hospital and, being a foreigner, an exception may be made for you and you will be treated.

In Bangkok, the police emergency number is 191. There are also Tourist Police assigned specially to assist travelers. They are located at the Tourist Assistance Center at the Tourism Authority of Thailand headquarters at No. 4 Rajdamnern Nok Avenue and can be reached by telephoning 195 or 221-6206, 221-6207. They also maintain a booth on the Lumpini Park corner of the Rama 4 and Silom Roads intersection. Most members of the force speak English.

MEDICAL SERVICES

Hospitals in Bangkok are of high standards, some of the best in the region. They boast highly-sophisticated equipment and excellent care. Refer to the listing below for a more detailed run-down on hospitals, special clinics and other medical services. Prices normally won't pose a strain on one's finances.

Bangkok's first-class hotels also have doctors on call for medical emergencies. Should you be outside the hotel, however, Bangkok has ambulances and emergency wards the equivalent of any major Western city. Intensive care units of most hospitals are fully equipped and staffed by doctors to handle any emergency quickly and competently. If you are hospitalized, you will find that nursing care is generally superior to that of Western hospitals because there is a higher staff to patient ratio. Many doctors have trained in Western hospitals and even those who have not, speak good English. There are many developing countries where a visitor has cause for concern should he fall ill; in Bangkok, he can put all those worries aside.

Bangkok Adventist Hospital
430 Phitsanuloke Road
Tel: 281-1422, 282-1100

Bangkok Christian Hospital
124 Silom Road
Tel: 233-6981, 233-6907

Bangkok Nursing Home
9 Convent Road
Tel: 233-2610

Samitivej Hospital
133 Soi 49, Sukhumvit Road
Tel: 392-0011, 392-0061

The above are all excellent; the latter three have Western doctors on their rosters or staff, however, the Thai physicians are also their equal.

CLINICS

For minor problems, there are numerous clinics and dentists around Bangkok. Venereal disease clinics are probably the most open in the world with large signs and newspaper advertisements proclaiming their services.

Medical Clinics
There are many polyclinics in Bangkok with specialists in several fields. The **British Dispensary** located at 109 Sukhumvit Road (between Sois 5 and 7, tel: 252-8056) has three British doctors on its staff.

VD Clinics
These doctors have seen it all so there is no reason to be shy or embarrassed. Very professional, very thorough treatment ensures you return home with a clean bill of health. **VD International** at 588 Ploenchit Road (Tel: 250-1969) is one of many who are very competent.

Dental Clinics
Dental clinics are almost as numerous as medical clinics. One clinic with a long-standing reputation is the **Dental Polyclinic** at 211-3 New Petchburi Road, Tel: 314-5070.

Chiropractor
Bangkok has only one chiropractic clinic and it utilizes the Japanese method (no bone-cracking as practised in the West but firm massages to ease pinched nerves back into place). It is open 9 a.m. to 6 p.m. Monday to Saturday, 9 a.m. to noon on Sundays. Down Soi Vichan at No. 51 off Silom Road across from the Victory Hotel. Call 234-2649 for an appointment.

Snake Bites
The chances of being bitten by a poisonous snake in Bangkok or its environs are negligible but if it should occur, most clinics will have anti-venom serum on hand. If they cannot acquire any, travel to the **Saowapha Institute** (**Snake Farm**) at 1871 Rama IV Road. They maintain sera against the bites of six types of cobras and vipers.

OTHER SERVICES

Counseling: The Community Services of Bangkok is a volunteer organization made up of foreigners to provide information to families living in Bangkok. They operate a Hotline and are always willing to help travelers with problems who have nowhere else to turn. They also have a Counseling Service for those in mental distress. Telephone them at 258-5663.

Pharmaceuticals are produced to the highest standards and pharmacies must have a registered pharmacist on the premises. Most pharmacy personnel in the shopping and business areas speak English.

Emergency Repairs: Shoe repairs and key grinding services are performed at Mr. Minit booths on the ground floor of the Robinson Department Store at the Silom and Rama 4 Road intersection and in the sub-basement of the Chidlom branch of Central Department Store at the Ploenchit Road, Soi Chidlom intersection.

GETTING AROUND

MAPS

Bookshops in Bangkok carry a variety of maps designed to help one find his way around. Among the best are those put out by APA and numerous local publishers. The most accurate is the one published by Siam Book Store with no title other than "*Especially for Tourists*" which costs 50 *baht*. Like others of its ilk, it outlines the routes for both ordinary as well as air-conditioned buses.

CULTURAL MAPS

There are also a number of specialized maps. The Association of Siamese Architects puts out a series of four colorful hand-drawn Cultural Maps with details and information on Bangkok, the Grand Palace, the Canals of Thonburi and Ayutthaya.

CANAL MAPS

D.K. Books issues an English-language book of canal maps by Geo.-Ch. Veran under the title *50 Trips into the Canals of Thailand* which details journeys using the express and long-tailed commuter boats which operate on the rivers and canals. The French-language edition called *La Thailande en Bateau pour 10 Frs par Jour* is a packet of two maps and two explanatory booklets which are easier to carry.

MARKET MAPS

Nancy Chandler's *Market Map* has been a standby for years for its colorful cartoon maps of all of Bangkok's major markets. Its author, a well-traveled lady with a sense of humor, has filled the margins with useful information designed to make any market trip fun.

HISTORY MAPS

For history buffs, the Jim Thompson House sells old maps of Siam which double up as handsome wall decorations when framed.

FROM THE AIRPORT

The journey along the expressway into the city can take from 30 to 45 minutes depending on the traffic conditions. Some hotels have limousines to pick up guests but otherwise the traveler is on his own.

AIR-CONDITIONED MINI-BUSES

Thai Airways International operates a transport service into city to hotels or private residences on a round-the-clock basis. Air-conditioned limousines are the most convenient transportation to town and cost just 300 *baht*. THAI air-conditioned mini-buses cost 100 *baht* per passenger and leave the airport every 30 minutes. Because they have to fight traffic to deliver their passengers at various hotels around the city, they can take considerable time to get you to your hotel. It might be worth shelling out extra for a limousine if you arrive at the airport during the rush hour. There is also a THAI Shuttle Minibus that operates between the Airport and the City Terminal at the Asia Hotel on Phya Thai Road at 30-minute intervals between 7 a.m. and 9 p.m. It costs 60 *baht* per person.

TAXIS

Recently introduced at the airport is a taxi queue. Air-conditioned taxis charge 180 *baht* to nearly every point in the city. A clerk at a counter near the door between the Arrival Lounge and the street issues written instructions on your destination and the price. Hand this paper to the taxi driver and pay him the price noted on it. If you think the price too high or are going a shorter distance, you can walk out to the main highway and flag down a taxi. Remember, taxis are not metered, one must bargain for the fare. A sharp bargainer can ride to town in air-conditioned comfort for as little as 150 *baht*.

For economy minded travelers, five air-conditioned buses – Nos. 3, 4, 10, 13, and 29 – stop in front of the airport. The trip into town costs just 15 *baht*. The last buses leave about 8 p.m. (except for No. 4 which stops running at 7 p.m.).

For the very economy-minded, a train leaves from the station across the highway every hour until 8:13 p.m. for Hualampong Station in the center of Bangkok. The 40-minute journey costs 5 *baht*.

For the return trip to the airport, THAI limousine has three in-town offices at 485 Silom Rd. (Tel: 235-4365, 235-4366), Montien Hotel (Tel: 233-7060), and Asia Hotel (Tel: 215-0780). Most major hotels have air-conditioned limousines. Taxis make the trip for 150-200 *baht* depending on traffic conditions.

PUBLIC TRANSPORT

TAXIS & TUKS-TUKS

Bangkok taxis are reliable, air-conditioned conveyances through the city's streets but the drivers' command of English is often less than perfect. This presents a problem not only in conveying to him your destination but bargaining the price as well.

Do not step into a taxi without having first agreed on a price. The price can fluctuate depending on the hour of the day and the amount of traffic, rain, and the number of one-way streets he must negotiate. A sample fare for 9 a.m. between the Dusit Thani Hotel and the Grand Palace or between the Oriental Hotel and the Jim Thompson House would be 60 *baht*. The base fare for all journeys is 30 *baht*. Taxi drivers do not charge you an extra fee for baggage stowage or extra passengers and there is no tipping.

If the English fluency of taxi drivers is limited, that of *tuk-tuk* (also called *samlor*) drivers is even less. *Tuk-tuks* are the bright blue and yellow three-wheeled taxis whose name comes from the noise their two-cycle engines make. They are fun for short trips but choose a taxi for longer journeys. A *samlor* driver on an open stretch of road can seldom resist racing and the resultant journey can be a hair-raising experience. For very short trips, the fare is 10 *baht*.

BUSES & MINI-BUSES

Bangkok buses come in three varieties: air-conditioned, ordinary, and the green mini-buses. They operate every two or three minutes along more than 100 routes and are an excellent way to see the outer areas of the city. Bus maps give the routes for both types of buses.

Buses are especially useful during rush hours when traveling up one-way streets like Sukhumvit Road because they can speed along specially-marked bus lanes going against on-coming traffic. Conductors prowl through the aisles collecting fares and issuing tickets. Unfortunately, destinations are only noted in Thai so a bus map is needed. Most routes cease operation around midnight though some (Nos. 2 and 4) run all through the night.

There are more than a dozen air-conditioned bus routes through the city. Fares for the big blue and white buses are 5 *baht*.

Ordinary buses come in two varieties: red and white (3 *baht*) and blue and white (2 *baht*). Aside from the price, there is no difference in service routes. Both can be very crowded (it is a sight to see one listing heavily to one side while students cling to the open doors. Their route numbers correspond with those of ordinary buses since they ply the same routes. Their drivers are the cowboys of the road and usually drive in very colorful fashion. Most drivers have decked out their buses with stereo sets; some even have television sets though on bumpy roads the reception is less than perfect.

BOATS

White express boats with red trim run regular routes at 20-30 minute intervals up and down the Chao Phya River, going all the way to Nonthaburi 6 miles (10 km) north of the city. They begin operation at 6 a.m. and cease at 6:30 p.m. Fares are 5 *baht* for short distances.

Ferries cross the river at dozens of points and cost 50 *satang* per journey. They begin operation at 6 a.m. and stop at midnight.

Bangkok is not one of the easiest cities to find your way around but, luckily, there is plenty of help.

PRIVATE TRANSPORT

LIMOUSINES

Most major hotels have their own air-conditioned limousine services. Although the prices are about twice those of ordinary taxis, they offer the convenience of English-speaking drivers, door-to-door service and the elimination of unnecessary bargaining with taxi drivers.

RENTAL CARS

Avis, Hertz and several local agencies offer late model cars with or without drivers and with insurance coverage for Bangkok and up-country trips. Prices for a chauffeured Mercedes Benz average 4,000 *baht* per day (2,500 *baht* for self-drive vehicle) and 2,200 *baht* for a chauffeured Toyota (1,800 *baht* for self-drive) plus gasoline costs (8.90 *baht* per liter for Premium at the time of publication). An average of 2,000 *baht* is required as deposit. An International Driver's Licence is valid in Thailand.

Avis
10/1 North Sathorn Road
Tel: 233-0397
Open daily 8 a.m. to 9 p.m., its desk at the Dusit Thani Hotel is open 24 hours.

Hertz
987 Ploenchit Road
Tel: 253-6251
Open from 8 a.m. to 5 p.m.

Grand Car Rent
144/3-4 Silom Road
Tel: 234-9956
Open from 8 a.m. to 9 p.m.

WHERE TO STAY

HOTELS

FIRST-CLASS (1,500 BAHT UP)

Asia
296 Phya Thai Rd.
Tel: 215-0780, 215-0787
650 rooms. European, Chinese, Japanese, Thai restaurants, coffeeshop, two pools, health club, Thai International limousine service. 1,936-2,178 *baht*/night. Near the city's biggest shopping malls.

Central Plaza
1695 Paholyothin Rd.
Tel: 541-1234
607 rooms. Pool, restaurants, coffeeshop, discotheque. 2,200-18,400 *baht*/night. Midway between airport and town, across from Chatuchak Park.

The Dusit Thani Hotel
946 Rama 4 Rd.
Tel: 233-1130
525 rooms. Thai, Chinese, European restaurants, tea room, coffeeshop, pool, health club, rooftop restaurant with panoramic view of the city. Across from Lumpini Park, in close proximity to business and entertainment centers.

Hilton International
N. Wireless Rd.
Tel: 253-0123, 253-0671
389 rooms. Four restaurants, pool, poolside bar, gardens, health club, beauty salon, coffeeshop. A centrally-located luxury hotel set in a beautiful garden.

Imperial
6 Wireless Rd.
Tel: 254-0111, 252-1555
400 rooms. Five restaurants, pool, two saunas, tennis and squash courts, nightclubs, garden. 2,210-2,470 *baht*/night. Near shopping areas.

Indra Regent
120/126 Rajprarob Rd.
Tel: 251-1111
500 rooms. Pool, nightclub, Chinese, Thai, European restaurants, coffeeshop. 1,936-7,260 *baht*/night. In heart of market area.

The Landmark Hotel
138 Sukhumvit Rd.
Tel: 254-0404, 254-0424
415 rooms. Pool, squash courts, sauna, a choice of Chinese, Japanese or French cuisine at its restaurants, discotheque, nightclub, coffeeshop.

Le Meridien President
(formerly the "President")
135/26 Gaysorn Rd.
Tel: 253-6550, 253-0444
420 rooms. Pool, restaurants, piano lounge, coffeeshop. Quiet city-center elegance.

The Menam
2074 New Road
Tel: 289-0352, 289-0353
727 rooms. Pool, tennis and squash courts, sauna, health club, beauty salon, European, Japanese, Chinese, Thai restaurants, coffeeshop, cocktail lounge. 1,700-9,000 *baht*/night. Luxury on the river a bit out of city center.

The Montien Hotel
54 Suriwong Rd.
Tel: 233-7060, 234-8060
500 rooms. Pool, Chinese and European restaurants, nightclubs, discotheque. First-class accommodations situated in the heart of the city and at the edge of the entertainment district.

The Oriental
48 Oriental Ave., New Rd.
Tel: 236-0400, 236-0420
398 rooms. Two pools, French, Italian, Thai, and seafood restaurants, coffeeshop, tea salon, terrace restaurant. Located at the river's edge, The Oriental is the queen of Bangkok's hotels and is frequently voted the best in the world; has the reputation of having been patronized by famous novelists Joseph Conrad and Somerset Maugham.

Rama Gardens
9/9 Vibhavadi Rangsit Rd.
Tel: 579-5400
364 rooms. Two swimming pools, four restaurants, lobby lounge, nightclub, spacious gardens with long jogging paths, health club. 1,573-9,680 *baht*/night. Quiet, sylvan, 8 minutes from airport.

The Regent Bangkok
(formerly the "Bangkok Peninsula")
155 Rajdamri Rd.
Tel: 251-6127
400 rooms. French and Thai restaurants, nightclub, tea in lobby, pool, health club. Luxury right in the heart of Bangkok.

Royal Orchid Sheraton
Captain Bush Lane, Siphya Road
Tel: 234-5599
780 rooms. Pool, sauna, Italian and English restaurants, riverside coffeeshop. 1,600-12,000 *baht*/night. Superb comfort in super riverside location.

Shangri-la Hotel
89 Soi Wat Suan Plu, New Rd.
Tel: 236-7777
697 rooms. Pool, a wide choice of restaurants including European, Chinese, Japanese, French and Thai, lobby lounge, cocktail lounge. The Shangri-la Hotel is Bangkok's most recent riverside luxury hotel and is deemed one of the city's finest.

Siam Inter-Continental Hotel
Rama I Rd.
Tel: 253-0355, 253-0356
Pool, health club, restaurants, coffeeshop, poolside bar, tennis courts, driving range, putting green, outdoor workout area, long jogging paths, mini-zoo. Set amidst 10 acres of gardens, the hotel is a cool oasis rivalled by none.

Tawana Ramada
(formerly the "Sheraton")
80 Suriwongse Rd.
Tel: 233-5160, 233-5161
265 rooms. Pool, restaurants, cocktail lounge, discotheque, health club. 1,800-14,000 *baht*/night. Immediate access to business and entertainment districts.

MODERATE (1,000-1,499 BAHT)

Airport Hotel
333 Chert Wudthakas Rd.
Don Muang
Tel: 566-1020, 566-1021
300 rooms ringed around a garden and pool, 24-hour coffeeshop, three restaurants, video lounge. Linked to the airport by a skybridge and bus shuttle service. 690-1,936 *baht*/night. Closest Bangkok hotel to airport.

Ambassador
Soi 11, Sukhumvit Rd.
Tel: 251-5170
980 rooms. Pool, health club, exotic bird garden, European, Japanese, Chinese, Thai and seafood restaurants and huge "food market" with a variety of Asian cuisines, 3 bars, 2 coffeeshops, 24-hour room service. 1,000-10,000 *baht*/night. In busy shopping district.

Bangkok Palace
1091/336 New Petchburi Road
Tel: 253-0510
670 rooms. Pool, Thai, European, and Japanese restaurants, coffeeshop, videotheque, night club, discotheque, sauna. 1,200-1,400 *baht*/night. Near lively Pratunam market.

Erawan
494 Rajdamri Rd.
Tel: 252-9129
250 rooms. Japanese, Chinese, Swiss, French restaurants, pool, coffeeshop, post office. 1,430-1,650 *baht*/night. Heart of city, Thai government-owned.

Impala
9 Soi 24, Sukhumvit Rd.
Tel: 259-0053, 253-0054
200 rooms. Pool, sauna, health club, restaurants, coffeeshop. 1,385-1,667 *baht*/night. Quiet lane near busy Sukhumvit Rd.

Mandarin
662 Rama 4 Rd.
Tel: 234-1390, 234-1391
350 rooms. Pool, restaurants, nightclub, 24-hour coffeeshop. 1,200-6,000 *baht*/night. Near city center.

Manohra
412 Suriwong Rd.
Tel: 234-5086, 234-5087
250 rooms. Pool, restaurants, discotheque, 24-hour coffeeshop. 1,331-1,876 *baht*/night. Within walking distance of GPO and river.

Narai
222 Silom Rd.
Tel: 233-3350, 233-3351
500 rooms. Pool, Italian coffeeshop, revolving roof restaurant with European and Asian cuisines. 400-5,000 *baht*/night. In the center of the business district.

Royal River Hotel
670/805 Charoensanitwong Road
Tel: 433-0046, 433-0047
404 rooms. Pool, tennis court, sauna, Thai, Chinese, Japanese, French restaurants, coffeeshop. 1,400-15,000 *baht*/night. First Bangkok hotel on western bank of river.

Silom Plaza
320 Silom Rd.
Tel: 236-0333
209 rooms. Pool, Japanese, Chinese, French, European, Thai restaurants, discotheque, health club, cocktail lounge, coffeeshop. 1,331-2,299 *baht*/night. At the foot of Silom near the river.

Windsor
Soi 20, Sukhumvit Rd.
Tel: 258-1527, 258-0160
250 rooms. Pool, tennis court, restaurants, cocktail lounge, beauty salon, coffeeshop. 1,200-6,000 *baht*/night. Comfortable off-Sukhumvit hostelry.

BUDGET (600-999 BAHT)

Ariston
19 Soi 24, Sukhumvit Road
Tel: 259-0960
152 rooms. 24-hour coffeeshop, pool. 968-1,089 *baht*.

Bangkok Center
382 Rama 4 Rd.
Tel: 235-1799
225 rooms. Coffeeshops and restaurants, no pool. 600-3,200 *baht*/night. Near Chinatown and Hualampong railway station.

Dorchester
21 Soi Kotoey, Pratipat Rd.
Tel: 270-0904
80 rooms. Thai and European restaurant, pool, coffeeshop. 612-956 *baht*/night. Near Weekend Market.

First
2 Petchburi Rd.
Tel: 252-5011, 251-7040
218 rooms. European, Chinese, Thai restaurants, 24-hour coffeeshop, pool. 700-1,540 *baht*/night. On a busy street near Pratunam market.

Golden Dragon
20/21 Ngarmwongwan Rd.
Tel: 589-5148, 589-5141
112 rooms. Restaurant, coffeeshop, pool. 600-1,800 *baht*/night. 15 minutes from the airport.

Grace
12 Soi 3, Sukhumvit Rd.
Tel: 253-0671, 243-0680
550 rooms. Seafood and other restaurants, pool, 24-hour coffeeshop known for its exotic clientele. 600-1,540 *baht*/night. Favored by an Arab clientele.

Majestic
97 Rajdamnern Ave.
Tel: 281-5000
Pool, garden, nightclub, restaurants. Near UN offices, royal palace and government ministries.

Manhattan
Soi 15, Sukhumvit Rd.
Tel: 252-7141, 252-7149
205 rooms. Swimming pool, beer garden, Chinese, European, Japanese, Korean and Thai restaurants, 24-hour coffeeshop, disco, cocktail lounge. 700-4,000 *baht*/night. Off Sukhumvit Rd.

New Nana
4 Soi Nana (Soi 4), Sukhumvit Rd.
Tel: 252-0121
344 rooms. Pool, restaurants, 24-hour coffeeshop, bar. 611-655 *baht*/night. In heart of bar area.

Peninsula
295/3 Suriwong Rd.
Tel: 234-3910
114 rooms. Restaurants, coffeeshop, cocktail lounge. 622-799 *baht*/night. Economical; 10 minutes from the river.

Rajah
Soi 4, Sukhumvit Rd.
Tel: 251-8563, 251-8564
450 rooms. Pool, European, Chinese and Thai restaurant, coffeeshop. 968-1,889 *baht*/night. Large and comfortable.

Siam
1777 New Petchburi Rd.
Tel: 252-4967, 252-4968
120 rooms. Pool, restaurant, cocktail lounge, coffeeshop. 666-1,066 *baht*/night. Modest and inexpensive.

Trocadero
343 Suriwong Rd.
Tel: 234-8920, 234-8921
138 rooms. Pool, bar, coffeeshop. 611-3,333 *baht*/night. Popular with Asian and Middle Eastern visitors; perhaps the tiniest pool in Asia.

Victory
322 Silom Rd.
Tel: 233-9060
125 rooms. Pool, restaurant, coffeeshop. 644-1,332 *baht*/night. At the foot of Silom, minutes from the river.

INEXPENSIVE (200-599 BAHT)

Century
9 Rajprarob Rd.
Tel: 245-1755, 245-3271
96 rooms. Western, Chinese, Japanese restaurant, coffeeshop. 540-1,800 *baht*/night. Near Pratunam market.

City Inn
Behind Mahatun Building,
Ploenchit Road.
Tel: 254-2070
30 rooms. 24-hour coffeeshop. 500-700 *baht*. New concept in city hotels with basic rooms and services only.

Continental
971/16 Paholyothin Rd.
Tel: 278-1598
120 rooms. European, Asian and Thai cuisines, pool, coffeeshop. 450-1,550 *baht*/night. On northern edge of town near Weekend Market.

Federal
27 Soi 11, Sukhumvit Rd.
Tel: 253-0176
93 rooms. Restaurants, pool coffeeshop. 400-480 *baht*/night. Down a quiet side street.

Florida
43 Phya Thai Rd.
Tel: 245-4552, 254-2190
107 rooms. European and Thai restaurant, coffeeshop, pool, free car service from airport. 400-500 *baht*/night. Near shopping malls.

Fortuna
19 Soi 5, Sukhumvit Rd.
Tel: 251-5127
110 rooms. Japanese, European, Chinese, Thai restaurants, coffeeshop, nightclub, Japanese nightclub. 500-1,000 *baht*/night. In quiet lane off busy road.

Honey
31 Soi 19, Sukhumvit Rd.
Tel: 253-0646, 253-0647
75 rooms. Restaurant, 24-hour coffeeshop, pool. 340-990 *baht*/night. Offers economical comfort.

Liberty
215 Sapan Kwai, Pratipat Rd.
Tel: 271-0150, 271-0876
209 rooms. Pool, restaurant, bar, coffeeshop. 290-360 *baht*/night. At edge of town on road to airport.

Malaysia
54 Soi Ngam-Duplee, Rama 4 Rd.
Tel: 286-3582, 286-7263
120 rooms. Pool, restaurant, bar. 250-450 *baht*/night. Budget travelers' paradise.

Metro
1902 New Petchburi Rd.
Tel: 314-4741
88 rooms. Pool, restaurant, 24-hour coffee-

shop, bar. 300-400 *baht*/night. At edge of town.

Miami
2 Soi 13, Sukhumvit Rd.
Tel: 253-0369, 252-7379
123 rooms. Pool, restaurants, coffeeshop, bar. 165-300 *baht*/night. Economical accommodations off busy Sukhumvit Rd.

Miramar
777 Mahachai Rd.
Tel: 222-1720
150 rooms. Restaurant, bar coffeeshop. At the edge of Chinatown.

Morakot
2802 New Petchburi Rd.
Tel: 314-0761
120 rooms. Pool, restaurant, bar, coffeeshop, discotheque. 250-650 *baht*/night. On the eastern edge of town.

New Empire
572 Yawaraj Rd.
Tel: 234-6990
140 rooms. Chinese restaurant that offers European and Thai food, coffeeshop, free transportation to/from airport. 190-370 *baht*/night. Heart of Chinatown.

New Fuji
299-301 Suriwong Rd.
Tel: 234-5364
Caters to middle-class Japanese businessmen, no pool, restaurant. 600-750 *baht*. Some of the best, least expensive meals in town.

Park
6 Soi 7, Sukhumvit Rd.
Tel: 252-5111, 252-5112
128 rooms. Pool, lobby lounge, beer garden, European and Chinese restaurants, bar. 500-850 *baht*/night. Inexpensive, quiet.

Prince
1537/1 New Petchburi Rd.
Tel: 251-3318
210 rooms. Pool, restaurants, cocktail lounge, coffeeshop. 396-600 *baht*/night. Around the corner from the Soi 3 entertainment district.

Rajsubhamitra
(also known as "R.S. Hotel")
269 Larn Luang Rd.
Tel: 281-3644
142 rooms. Pool, European, Chinese and Thai restaurants. 320-500 *baht*/night. Unpretentious but comfortable. Monthly rates. Favored by U.N. officials on long stays.

Ramada
1169 New Road.
Tel: 234-8971
48 rooms. Restaurant, cocktail lounge, tea lounge, coffeeshop. 363-605 *baht*/night. Unassuming, near river.

Reno
40 Soi Kasemsan 1, Rama I Road.
Tel: 215-0026, 215-0027
67 rooms. Pool, restaurants, coffeeshop. 250-350 *baht*/night. Across from National Stadium.

Rex
762/1 Sukhumvit Rd.
Tel: 259-0106, 259-0107
131 rooms. Pool, restaurant, coffeeshop. 450-1,800 *baht*/night. Near the far end of Sukhumvit Rd.

Rose
118 Suriwong Rd.
Tel: 233-7695
105 rooms. Restaurant, 24-hour coffeeshop. 460-680 *baht*/night. Long-favored by frequent visitors.

Royal
2 Rajdamnern Ave.
Tel: 222-9112, 222-9113
297 rooms. Pool, restaurant, coffeeshop. 508-823 *baht*/night. A venerable old hotel, the closest of all to the Grand Palace.

Suriwongse
31/1 Suriwong Rd.
100 rooms. Restaurant, coffeeshop. 300-400 *baht*/night. Unpretentious accommodation for habitués of nearby Patpong Road.

Swan
31 New Road
Tel: 233-8444
64 rooms. Pool, coffeeshop. 180-450 *baht*/night. Popular with journalists.

Thai
78 Prachatipat Rd.
Tel: 282-2831, 282-2832
100 rooms. Pool, European and Chinese restaurant, coffeeshop. 520-620 *baht*/night. One of city's oldest hotels, popular with aid workers; near U.N.

Viengtai
42 Tani Rd.
Tel: 281-5788, 282-8672
200 rooms. Pool, restaurant, coffeeshop. 520-620 *baht*/night. Another old veteran; near U.N.

World
1996 New Petchburi Rd.
Tel: 314-4340
101 rooms. Facilities include pool, restaurant, bar. 280-320 *baht*/night. Unassuming but comfortable.

GUEST HOUSES

A host of guest houses line Khaosarn Road in Banglampoo. Prices range from 60 to 300 *baht*/night. For the budget traveler.

Small hotels in the vicinity of the Malaysia Hotel also offer the traveler good budget accommodations.

Bangkok Christian Guest House
123 Soi Saladaeng 2, Silom Rd.
Tel: 233-2206
30 rooms, 380 *baht*. Has dining room with meals.

P. S. Guest House
9 Prasumeru Road
Tel: 282-3932/2

Swiss Guest House
3 Convent Rd.
Tel: 234-3729
20 rooms. 250-500 *baht*. Only breakfast available.

YMCA
27 S. Sathorn Rd.
Tel: 286-5136
50 rooms; some cottages available. Sports facilities, European, Chinese and Thai restaurant. 250-550 *baht*/night.

UP-COUNTRY HOTELS

Except for Pattaya, Hua Hin, Cha-am, Phuket and Chiang Mai, up-country hotels are not up to the standards of Bangkok. They are clean and comfortable, offering both air-conditioned and fan-cooled rooms. Most have coffeeshops.

AYUTTHAYA

Thai Sena
286 Senanawin 2 Road
17 rooms

U-Thong
86 U-Thong Road
Tel: 251-136
65 rooms. Pool, coffeeshop.

CHA-AM

Beach Garden Hotel Cha-am
949/21 Cha-am Beach
Tel: (032) 471-334
Bangkok office: 175-177 Suriwong Rd.
Tel: 233-6886, 234-7287.
230 rooms, 48 cottages. Four pools, fishing park, coffeeshop, golf course.

The Cha-Am Methavalai Hotel
220 Ruamchitr Rd.
Cha-am, Petchburi
Tel: (032) 471-145, 471-028
Bangkok office: Tel: 215-1316, 215-3317, 280-2581
Telex: 22158 Metha TH.
118 rooms, all sea fronted. Two pools and a jacuzzi.

The Regent Cha-am
849/21 Cha-am Beach
Tel: (032) 471-483
Bangkok office: 183 Rajdamri Rd.
Tel: 251-0305
504 rooms. Restaurant, coffeeshop, pool, golf course. A luxury hotel on the beach.

CHIANG MAI

Chiang Mai Orchid
100-102 Huay Kaew Rd.
Tel: (053) 222-099
Bangkok office: 2nd floor, Metropolis Bldg.
395/2 Silom Rd.

Tel: 245-3973, 245-3974
274 rooms. Pool, disco, sauna, restaurants. Modern amenities near the heart of Chiang Mai.

Dusit Inn
112 Changklang Rd.
Tel: (053) 251-044
Bangkok office: Dusit Thani Hotel
946 Rama 4 Rd.
Tel: 233-1130
206 rooms. Pool, disco, restaurants. Near the famed night market.

Rincome
301 Huay Kaew Rd.
Tel: (053) 221-044
Bangkok office: 15th floor, Amarin Tower, 500 Ploenchit Rd.
Tel: 252-6045.
162 rooms. Pool, tennis court, jogging track, restaurants. Set in gardens in a nice, quiet area.

HUA HIN

Hotel Sofitel Central Hua Hin
1 Damnernkasem Rd.
Tel: (032) 512-021, 512-022
Bangkok office: 23rd floor,
Wall Street Tower
33/57 Suriwong Rd.
Tel: 233-0256, 233-0974
152 rooms, 42 villas (64 rooms). Pools, tennis courts, mini-golf, three restaurants and bars.

The Royal Garden Resort
107/1 Petchkasem Rd.
Tel: (032) 511-881
Bangkok office: 17 Soi 11, Sukhumvit Rd
Tel: 255-8822, 255-8823
Restaurant, coffeeshop, pool.

Royal Garden Village
43/1 Petchkasem Beach Rd.
Tel: (032) 512-413, 512-414
Bangkok office: 17 Soi 11,
Sukhumvit Rd.
Tel: 255-8822, 255-8823

LOPBURI

Asia Lopburi
1/17-18 Surasak Rd.
Tel: 411-892
111 rooms.

Taipei
24/6-7 Surasongkram Rd.
Tel: 411-514
105 rooms.

PATTAYA

There are 120 or so hotels in Pattaya; only those in the top ranks are listed here. All have air-conditioned rooms, restaurants, coffee-shops, pools and shopping arcades.

Dusit Resort
Nak Lua Rd.
240 Pattaya Beach Rd.
Tel: (038) 429-901
Bangkok office: 233-9376
500 rooms. North end of Pattaya beach, lovely view.

Montien Pattaya
Beach Rd.
Tel: (038) 428-155, 428-156
Bangkok office: 233-7060
305 rooms. Center of resort.

Nipa Lodge
North Pattaya Beach Rd.
Tel: (038) 428-195, 428-321
Bangkok office: 252-6118, 252-6045
150 rooms. Pretty garden layout.

Orchid Lodge
Nak Lua Rd.
Tel: (038) 428-161, 428-323
Bangkok office: 252-6118
234 rooms. Large gardens.

Pattaya Palace
Beach Rd.
Tel: (038) 428-152, 428-487
Bangkok office: 233-9376
260 rooms. Nice, open air lobby.

Royal Garden Resort
Beach Rd.
Tel: 428122, 429926
Bangkok office: 255-8822

142 rooms. Resort center location.

Siam Bayshore
Beach Rd.
Tel: (038) 428-678, 428-679
Bangkok office: 221-1004, 233-1784
265 rooms. At southern end of beach.

Siam Bayview
Beach Rd.
Tel: (038) 428-728, 428-729
Bangkok office: 221-1004, 233-1784
251 rooms. Middle of resort.

Just south of the hill marking the end of Pattaya beach are these:

Asia Pattaya
Cliff Rd.
Tel: (038)428-602, 428-603
Bangkok office: 251-0808
312 rooms. Overlooks western sea.

Royal Cliff Beach Resort
Cliff Rd.
Tel: (038) 421-421, 421-422
Bangkok office: 282-0999
700 rooms. Pattaya's luxury hotel.

On adjacent Jomtien Beach are quite a number of bungalows:

Sugar Hut
Jomtien Beach
Tel: (038) 231-039
24 fan-cooled bungalows.

PETCHBURI

Khao Wang
174/1-3 Rachaviti Rd.
Tel: (032) 425-167
49 rooms.

PHUKET

Amanpuri
Tel: (076 311-396, 311-397, ext 064
Bangkok office: 155 Rajdamri Rd,
Tel: 250-0746

Cape Panwa Sheraton Hotel
Laem Panwa Beach
Tel: (076) 391-123, 391-124
Bangkok office: 233-8989
142 rooms, 7 suites, 6 bungalows. Tennis courts, Hilltop pool, conference facilities. Thai and Continental restaurants.

Club Andaman
Tel: (076)321-102, (076)321-361-2

Club Mediterranée
Kata Beach
Tel: (076) 214-830
Bangkok office: Ground floor, Peninsula Plaza, 153 Rajdamri Rd.
Tel: 253-0108
300 rooms. Pool, tennis courts, volleyball, basketball, watersport facilities, cabaret, restaurants. The second Club Med to be opened in Asia.

Coral Beach
104 Moo 4, Patong Beach
Tel: (076) 321-106
Bangkok office: 15th floor, Amarin Tower, 500 Ploenchit Rd.
Tel: 252-6045
207 rooms. Pool, tennis courts, squash court, badminton court, watersport facilities, fitness center, restaurants. Superb setting above Patong Bay.

Dusit Laguna Resort Hotel
390 Srisunthorn Rd., Talang District
Tel: (076) 311-320
Bangkok office: Dusit Thani Hotel,
946 Rama 4 Rd.
Tel: 233-1130, ext. 2870
240 rooms. Pool, tennis courts, putting green, restaurants. In a beautiful setting on Bang Thao Bay.

Holiday Inn Phuket
Patpong Beach
Tel: (076) 321-020
Bangkok office: 12th floor,
Wall Street Tower,
33/57 Suriwong Rd.
Tel: 234-0847, 236-7245

Karon Villa
Tel: (076) 212-709

Kata Inn 85
Kata Thani Hotel
Kata Noi Beach
Tel: (076) 214-824, 214-825

Le Meridien Phuket
Relax Bay
Tel: (076) 321-480, 321-479
Bangkok office: 15th floor,
Maneeya Center Bldg.
518/3 Ploenchit Rd.
Tel: 254-8147, 254-8148
470 rooms. Fresh water and salt water pool, fitness center, watersports facilities, restaurants. On its own private bay.

Patong Beach Hotel
Tel: (076) 321-301-2, 321-304-6

Pearl Village
Bangkok office: 64/12 Soi 20
Sukhumvit Rd.
Tel: 260-1022, 260-1023

Phuket Arcadia
Karon Beach
Tel: (076) 381-038-9, (076) 381-040-44
Bangkok office: Room 904, 9th floor,
Central Chidlom Tower
Soi Somkid, Ploenchit Rd.
Tel: 254-7091, 254-0921
255 rooms. Pool, tennis courts, putting green, fitness center, restaurants. The biggest hotel on one of Phuket's finest beaches.

Phuket Cabana
94 Patpong Beach
Tel: (076) 321-138, 321-139

Phuket Island
73/1 Ratsada Rd.
Tel: (076) 212-676

Phuket Yacht Club
23/3 Vises Rd.
Nai Harn Beach
Tel: 251-4707
108 rooms. Pool, tennis courts, watersports facilities, restaurants. Phuket's most luxurious hotel overlooking a superb beach.

FOOD DIGEST

THAI CUISINE

Apichart Restaurant
Pinklao Rd.
Tel: 424-2242
Soi 62, Lard Prao Rd.
Tel: 538-2890

Baitarl
3 Soi 33, Sukhumvit Rd.
Tel: 258-5711

Bussaracum
35 Soi Pipat 2, Convent Rd.
Tel: 235-8915
Dusit Thani Hotel branch
Tel: 233-1130, ext. 2699
Extremely popular with local connoisseurs of classical Thai cuisine; pleasant, informal atmosphere.

Cabbages and Condoms
8 Soi 12, Sukhumvit Rd.
Tel: 252-7349
Tasty dishes to support the numerous family planning projects.

D'Jit Pochana
62 Soi 20 Sukhumvit
Tel: 258-1597
Two branches:
1082 Paholyothin Rd.
Tel: 279-5000-2 and
New Paholyothin Rd.
Tel: 531-2716, 531-1645
Has a good reputation for Thai dishes; moderate prices.

Khunying
55 Soi 63, Sukhumvit Rd.
Tel: 391-5769

Krua Sathorn
181 S. Sathorn Rd.
Tel: 286-7528

Laicram
11/1 Soi. 49, Sukhumvit Rd.
Tel: 392-5864 and
120/12 Soi 23, Sukhumvit Rd.
Tel: 258-9616
Variety of Thai dishes at moderate prices.

Lemongrass
5/1 Sukhumvit Soi 24
Tel: 258-8637
High-class; medium prices.

Nathong Restaurant
84 Rachadapisek Rd.
Tel: 246-2160, 246-2161

Salathip
Shangri-la Hotel
Tel: 236-7777, ext. Salathip
Superb Thai dining on the river's edge.

Sara Jane's Larb Lang Suan
36/2 Soi Lang Suan
Tel: 252-6572
Delicious Northeastern dishes.

Sorn Dang (at the Democracy Monument)
78/2 Rajadamnern Rd.
Tel: 224-3088
One of the oldest restaurants in town, well-known for good Thai food. American Express card not accepted.

Spice Market
The Regent Hotel
Tel: 251-6127
Beautifully-decorated restaurant, with good food which is aimed more at Western than Thai palates.

Thai Room
37/17 Patpong 2 Rd.
Tel: 233-7920
Serving Thai, Mexican, Chinese and European food. Oldest restaurant in the city.

Thanying
10 Pramuan Rd., Silom
Tel: 236-4361
Serves excellent Thai food. Set in very pleasant surroundings.

Toll Gate
245/2 Soi 31 Sukhumvit
Tel: 258-4634
Good, simple Thai food, exquisitely presented; a set meal is served offering a variety of tastes. American Express card is not accepted here.

Whole Earth Cafe
93/3 Soi Lang Suan
Tel: 252-5574
Features Thai vegetarian fare; comfortable and friendly. Also has meat dishes which are equally tasty.

SEAFOOD

Dusit Rimtarn Seafood Restaurant
Supakarn Shopping Center
Sathorn Bridge
Tel: 437-9671
One of Bangkok's newer restaurants with a view of the river. Seafood and other Thai and Chinese cuisine superbly prepared under the supervision of the Dusit Thani Hotel.

Kaloang Sea Food and Restaurant
127/41 Leab-Menam Rd., (River Side)
Chongnonthri Yanna
Tel: 294-1488, 294-1799

Kungluang Sea Food
1756 K. Pinklao-Nakornchaisri Rd.
Bangkoknoi
Tel: 424-8367

Lord Jim's
Oriental Hotel
Tel: 234-9920
Top-quality restaurant noted for its good atmosphere, excellent food and service; expensive prices.

Moon Shadow
145 Gaysorn Rd.
Tel: 253-7553
Wide selection of seafood dishes.

Sea Food Market
388 Sukhumvit Rd., (opp. Soi Asoke)
Tel: 391-6256
Pick out the seafood of your choice from a vast variety on ice and they cook it to your taste; very informal and amusing.

Sea Food Restaurant
1980 New Petchburi Rd.
Tel: 314-4312
Still remains the favorite of many locals; moderate prices.

The Hibicus
The Landmark Hotel
Tel: 254-0404, 254-0424
Polynesian Cuisine.

Talay Thong
Siam Inter-Continental Hotel
Tel: 253-0355
High quality dining, decor and service.

THAI DINNER & CULTURAL SHOWS

Baan Thai
7 Sukhumvit Soi 32
Tel: 258-5403
Pleasant atmosphere in a group of old Thai houses in a tropical garden. Open daily 5:30 p.m. with Thai dancing starting at 9 p.m.

Maneeya Lotus Room
518/4 Ploenchit Rd.
Tel: 251-0382
Open daily. Lunch 10 a.m. to 2 p.m. Nightly 7 p.m. with Thai classical dance performance at 8:15 p.m.

Sala Rim Nam
Oriental Hotel
Tel: 437-6211
Located in a beautiful, temple-like building across the river from the Oriental; particularly good Thai dancing. Free boat service from Oriental Hotel landing.

Sala Thai
Indra Hotel
Tel: 251-1111
Attractive reproduction of a classic building on an upper floor of the hotel.

Silom Village Trade Center
286 Silom Rd.
Tel: 235-8760
Has open-air and indoor restaurants, traditional food stalls, Thai Cultural Show presented every Sat. & Sun. from 12:45 a.m. and Thai classical dance shows daily at 8 p.m. Informal atmosphere.

UP-MARKET FOOD CENTERS

Ambassador Food Center
Ambassador Hotel
Credit cards not accepted.

Mahboonkrong Food Center
6th floor,
Mahboonkrong Shopping Center
Credit cards not accepted.

OUTDOOR THAI RESTAURANTS

When giving instructions to the taxi driver, tell him "Suan Aahaan" (garden restaurant) before giving him the name of one of the restaurants below.

Baanbung
32/10 Soi Intramara 45
Tel: 277-8609, 277-7563

Buatong
30 Rajadapisek Rd.
Tel: 245-5545

Khunluang
560 Asoke-dindeang Rd.
Tel: 246-3273

Nan Chao
68 Rajadapisek Rd.
Tel: 246-2145, 246-2147
American Express card not accepted.

Rajada
99/10 Soi Neam-uthit
Rajadapisek Rd.

Tham Nak Thai
131 Ratchada Pisek Rd.
Tel: 276-1810
According to the Guinness Book of Records this is the largest restaurant in the world. Waitresses on roller skates serve food from all regions of Thailand; very popular with tourists.

Wangkaew
74-74/1 Rajadapisek Rd.
Tel: 245-8499, 246-2050
Credit cards not accepted.

RIVERSIDE RESTAURANTS

Baan Khun Luang
131/4 Khaw Rd.
Tel: 241-0521
Also offers Chinese and Japanese cuisine in riverside setting.

Dusit Rimtam Seafood Restaurant
Supakarn Shopping Center
(at Thonburi side of Sathorn Bridge)
Tel: 437-9671, 437-9672

Rimnam
11/1 Cherng Sapan
Prapinklao, Pinklao Rd.
Tel: 424-1112

Sala Rim Nam
Oriental Hotel,
48 Oriental Avenue, New Rd.
Tel: 437-6211

Salathip
Shangri-la Hotel
89 New Rd.
Tel: 236-7777

Savoey
River City
23 Yotha Rd.
Tel: 237-0077, 237-0078, ext. 1216

DINNER CRUISES

Tassaneya Nava
Contact World Travel Service at:
Oriental Hotel.
Tel: 236-1920
600 *baht* per person for a Thai meal. Two trips per night: 6 p.m. to 8 p.m., 8 p.m. to 10 p.m. Passengers have to board at River City Shopping Center pier.

BARGAIN BUFFETS

Bangkapi Terrace
Ground floor, Ambassador Hotel
Soi 11 Sukhumvit Rd.
Tel: 254-0444, ext. 3202

D'Jit Pochana
1082 Paholyothin Rd.
Tel: 279-5000, 279-5001

Lord Jim's
Oriental Hotel
48 Oriental Avenue New Rd.
Tel: 236-0400, ext. 173

Maenam Terrace
Shangri-la Hotel
89 New Rd.
Tel: 236-7777

Moon Palace
Windsor Hotel
8-10 Soi 20 Sukhumvit Rd.
Tel: 258-0160, ext. 173; 258-0165

Tiara
Dusit Thani Hotel
946 Rama 4 Rd.
Tel: 233-1130

Villa Norden
1 Soi 20 Sukhumvit Rd.
Tel: 258-1496

ASIAN RESTAURANTS

BURMESE

Mandalay
75/5 Soi 11, Sukhumvit Rd.
Tel: 250-1220
Extensive menu, good food and lovely decor; medium prices.

CHINESE

Chiu Chau
Ambassador Hotel
Tel: 254-0400, ext. 1541
Delicacies from the Southern Chinese province of Chiu Chau (Guangchao).

Coca Noodles
8 Soi Tantawan
Suriwong Rd.
Tel: 236-9323
Specializes in Chinese, sukiyaki and noodle dishes.

Galaxy Theater and Restaurant
19 Rama 4 Rd.
Tel: 235-5000
Featuring singers and exotic floor shows from all over Asia; good food.

Golden Dragon
108-114 Sukhumvit Rd.
Tel: 251-4553
Cantonese food; good dim sum lunches.

Grand Shangri-la
58/4 Thaniya Rd.
Tel: 234-2045
Northern Chinese cooking.

Hoi Tien Lao
762 Laadya Rd. on Thonburi bank of river opp. Royal Orchid Sheraton Hotel.
Tel: 437-1121
Cantonese food; one of Bangkok's oldest and most popular Chinese restaurants.

Hong Teh
Ambassador Hotel
Tel: 254-0444
A favorite amongst local gourmets for banquet entertaining.

Jade Garden
Montien Hotel
Tel: 234-8060
Southern Chinese dishes prepared by Hong Kong chefs.

Kilane Restaurant
Soi 1 Siam Square
Tel: 252-0322
Cantonese banquet fare elegantly conceived by master chefs from Hong Kong.

Maple Leaf (Fung Lin)
90/36-40 Rajaprarop Rd.
(in the O.A. Theater complex)
Tel: 245-6799, 245-7731

Mayflower
Dusit Thani Hotel
Tel: 233-1130
One of Bangkok's elegant places with local Chinese food fanciers.

Ming Palace
Indra Hotel
Tel: 251-1111
Southern Chinese dishes.

New Great Shanghai
648 Sukhumvit Rd.
Tel: 258-7042
Good Shanghai style; medium prices. Credit cards not accepted.

Nguan Lee
101/25-26 Soi Lang Suan
Ploenchit Rd.
Tel: 251-8366, 252-3614
Covered market; real atmosphere.

Royal Kitchen
N. Sathorn Rd.
Tel: 233-1495
More elegant and expensive than others.

Scala Restaurant
Scala Theater
Siam Square
Tel: 250-1633
Specializes in Peking Duck.

Scala Sharks-fins Restaurant
Siam Square Soi 1
Tel: 252-0322
Specializes in sharks-fin soup.

Shang Palace
Shangri-la Hotel
Tel: 236-7777, ext. 1350 & 1358
Cantonese and Szechuan specialities. The *dim sum* is a real treat; restaurant has an elegant decor.

Silom Restaurant
793 Silom Rd.
Tel: 236-4442
One of the oldest Chinese restaurants in town; northern Chinese dishes. Credit cards not accepted.

Silver Palace Restaurant
5 Soi Pipat, Silom Rd.
Tel: 235-5118
Well known for the variety of its delicious *dim sum* menu.

Sui Sian
The Landmark Hotel
Tel: 254-0404, 254-0424
Cantonese specialities

Tai-Pan
Imperial Hotel
Tel: 254-0111, ext. 1473
Presents fine Cantonese fare amidst elegant surroundings.

Tien Tien Restaurant
105 Patpong 1 Road
Bangrak
Tel: 234-8717, 234-6006

Tienlong
50 Soi Lang Suan
Ploenchit Rd.
Tel: 251-3048
Dim sum luncheon but the menu offers specialty items, including a choice of vegetarian dishes.

PHILIPPINES

Little Home Bakery
3rd floor, Mah Boonkrong Center
Tel: 217-9441
Good Philippino cuisine.

INDIAN/ARABIC/MUSLIM

Akbar Restaurant
1/4 Soi Nana Nua
Sukhumvit
Tel: 253-3479
Northern Indian food; medium prices.

Aladdin
4/6 Soi Nana Nua
Sukhumvit
Tel: 253-5582
Arabic and Indian food; inexpensive.

Amber
21/3 Sukhumvit Soi 4,
Tel: 252-5102
Southern Indian food; also Lebanese.

Cafe India
460/8 Surawong Rd.
Tel: 233-0419
Northern Indian cooking, in handsomely-decorated surroundings.

The Cedar
138 Soi 49
Sukhumvit Road
Tel: 392-7399
Superb Lebanese meals. Credit cards are not accepted.

Himali Cha Cha
1229/11 New Rd.
Tel: 235-1569
Northern cuisine by a master chef named Cha Cha; ask him what he recommends from the daily menu.

Moghul Room
1/16 Sukhumvit Soi 11
Tel: 253-4465, 253-6091
Good food, inexpensive.

Muslim Restaurant
1217 New Rd.
Tel: 233-1010, 253-6989
Muslim food; inexpensive.

Nana Fondue
6/2-3 Soi 3
Sukhumvit Rd.
Tel: 253-4061, 253-6091

Omar Khayyam
Soi 3 Sukhumvit
Tel: 251-6565
Arabian food; medium prices.

INDONESIAN

Bali
20/11 Ruamrudee Village
Soi Ruam Rudee, Ploenchit Road
No telephone. Customers can savor the best of Javanese cuisine at extremely economical prices.

JAPANESE

Benkey
Royal Orchid Sheraton Hotel
Tel: 234-5599
The restaurant is noted for its exquisite Japanese cuisine served in an ambience of quiet elegance; a place for refined tastes.

Daikoku
960/1 Rama 4 Rd.
Tel: 233-1495
Good Japanese cuisine, casual atmosphere, nice decor.

Fuji Japanese Restaurant
(Mall branch closed)
3rd floor, Central Plaza
Tel: 541-1111, ext. 3513

Genji
Hilton International Hotel
Tel: 253-0123, ext. 8141
Excellent cuisine, high-class; expensive.

Hakata
4 Soi 39 Sukhumvit
Tel: 258-8351
Japanese owner, informal atmosphere; reasonable prices.

Hanaya
683 Siphya Rd.
Tel: 234-8095
(also Amarin Plaza branch, 4th floor, Tel: 253-9648). A favorite with local Japanese; clean and unpretentious.

Kiku-No-Hana
The Landmark Hotel
Tel: 254-0404, 254-0424

Miraku
Imperial Hotel
Tel: 252-3080
Superb Japanese dishes plus decor and surroundings; medium prices.

Mizu's
32 Patpong Rd.
Tel: 233-6447
One of the oldest Japanese restaurants in the city.

Nippon Tei
139/4 Gaysorn Rd.
Tel: 253-7563

Shochiku
62/9 Soi Thaniya
Silom Rd.
Tel: 233-9694
Popular because it has a reputation for good food and service.

Shogun
Dusit Thani Hotel
Tel: 233-1130
Locals come for the sashimi; elegant atmosphere; expensive.

Sushi Tsukiji
Thaniya Rd., Silom
Tel: 234-2414

Teikoku
Imperial Hotel
Tel: 254-0111, ext. 1496
Superb Japanese dishes plus decor and surroundings; medium prices.

Tokugawa
Ambassador Hotel
Tel: 254-0444, ext. 1569
The teppanyaki is delicious and fun to watch being made.

KOREAN

Arirang House
106 Silom Rd. (at the end of Patpong 3 across from Convent Rd.)
Tel: 234-7869
Wide selection of Korean food; inexpensive prices.

First Korean
543 Silom Rd.
Tel: 234-2636
One of the oldest and best if you want to sample fine Korean cuisine.

Korea House
57/23 Wireless Rd. (behind Hoburger on corner with Ploenchit Rd.)
Tel: 252-2584
Good, simple Korean cooking served in an informal atmosphere. Very popular with local residents.

Koreana Restaurant
446-450 Soi 7 Siam Square
Tel: 252-9398
Kim Chi, barbecued beef, and all that; not much in the way of atmosphere but popular with local Koreans.

VIETNAMESE

Cherie Kitchen
593/13 Soi 33/1 Sukhumvit
Tel: 258-5058
Extensive menu, good food and service; medium prices.

Le Chancelier
70/1 Soi 1 Sukhumvit,
Tel: 251-8933
Very good Vietnamese dishes; medium prices.

Le Dalat
51 Soi 23, Sukhumvit Rd.
Tel: 258-9298
One of the best in town.

Saigon Bakery
285/2-3 Silom Rd.
Good food and bakery; inexpensive.

Vietnam
82-4 Silom Rd.
Tel: 234-6174
Northern Vietnamese style; inexpensive.

Vietnam Restaurant
70/1 Soi 1 Sukhumvit.
Tel: 251-8933
Serves very good Vietnamese dishes; medium prices.

CONTINENTAL CUISINE

ENGLISH & GRILL

Angus Steak House
9/4-5 Thaniya Rd.
Tel: 234-3590
Specializes in grill dishes.

Captain Bush Grill
Royal Orchid Hotel
Tel: 234-5599
Elegant English dining. Decor suggests an old sailing ship; extensive Continental menu and charcoal grill.

Copper Pan
8 Sukhumvit Soi 33
Tel: 258-0668
Has a casual atmosphere and inexpensive.

Fireplace Grill
President Hotel
Tel: 252-9880
Renowned for its excellent food and service. Top quality restaurant with good atmosphere without being overly formal.

Gourmet Gallery
6/1 Soi Promsri (which joins Sois 39 and 41)
Sukhumvit Rd.
Tel: 391-4811
Casual atmosphere, good music.

Hamilton's
Dusit Thani Hotel
Tel: 233-1130
High quality dining, decor and service.

La Brasserie
Regent Hotel
Tel: 251-6127
Elegant atmosphere, excellent food and service.

La Rotonde Grill
Narai Hotel
Tel: 233-3350
One of the region's best; rotating restaurant atop the hotel with a spectacular view of downtown Bangkok.

Le Gourmet Grill
Montien Hotel
Tel: 234-8060
An intimate, quiet restaurant with excellent food and good service.

Neil's Tavern
58/4 Soi Ruam Rudee
Tel: 251-5644
Recommended for good steaks and seafood; medium prices.

Prime Beef
71/1 Soi 11/1 (behind Ambassador Hotel)
Tel: 253-2443

Savoury
60 Pan Rd.
Tel: 236-4830
Extensive continental food menu.

TGI Friday
491/14-15 Silom Plaza,
Silom Rd.
Tel: 234-0544
Good food with live jazz, medium prices.

The Cup
2nd floor, Peninsula Plaza
Tel: 252-4568
Gourmet lunches only, closes 6.30 p.m.

Tiara
Dusit Thani Hotel
Tel: 233-1130, ext. 2499
On the top floor of the hotel, offering a superb view of the city.

T'wai
59 Soi 31, Sukhumvit Rd.
Tel: 258-4250
A simple menu of home-cooked dishes, well prepared and tasty. One of the city's only wine bars.

FRENCH

Avenue One
Siam Intercontinental Hotel
Tel: 253-0355
French Nouvelle cuisine, combined very well with European and Oriental.

Chez Jean la Grenouille
220/4 Soi 1 Sukhumvit
Tel: 252-0311
Has a good reputation. Medium prices. Its manta ray in beer sauce is superb.

Diva
1575/1 New Petchburi Rd. (near Soi 3)
Tel: 255-3783

Georges Paineau
Imperial Hotel,
Tel: 252-0450
Attractive restaurant with a noted French chef in charge.

Hugo
Central Plaza Hotel
Tel: 541-1234

La Brasserie
Regent Hotel
Tel: 251-6127
Elegant atmosphere, recommended for its excellent food and service.

La Paloma
26/2 Mahaesak Rd.
Tel: 233-3853
Good food and a quiet atmosphere; moderate prices.

La Tache
Shangri-la Hotel
Tel: 236-7777, ext. La Tache
One of Bangkok's latest French restaurants; delicious food; elegant atmosphere.

Le Bistro
Ambassador Hotel,
Tel: 251-0404
Good food and service, nice decor; medium prices.

Le Bistrot
20/17-19 Soi Ruam Rudee
Tel: 252-9651
A very good find for lovers of simple, brasserie-type French food.

Le Cristal
Regent Hotel
Tel: 251-6127
A place for one to see and be seen; unique Franco-Siamese interior.

Le Normandie Grill
Oriental Hotel
Tel: 236-0400, ext. 3380
One of the finest restaurants in the world, with a spectacular view of the river. High class; jacket and tie required. Expensive.

Le Metropolitain
135/6 Gaysorn Rd.
Tel: 252-8364
Good simple French cooking in an informal atmosphere. Very popular with the locals; medium prices.

Ma Maison
Hilton International Hotel
Tel: 253-0123, ext. 8026
Elegant but relaxed atmosphere with a garden view. Noted for its superb food and excellent service.

GERMAN

Bier-Kutsche
7 Soi 3 Sukhumvit
Tel: 253-2063
Good food yet inexpensive.

By Otto
250 Sukhumvit Rd. (between Sois 12-14)
Tel: 252-6836
Bavarian food; inexpensive.

Haus Munchen
4 Soi 15 Sukhumvit
Tel: 252-5776
Casual atmosphere, nice decor.

Singha Bier Haus
179 Soi 21, Sukhumvit Rd.
Tel: 258-3951
A faithful re-creation of a Bavarian beer house, with a German chef.

Wienerwald
274/1 opp. Soi 19
Sukhumvit Rd.
Tel: 252-3240
German and Austrian cuisine; inexpensive prices.

HUNGARIAN

Nick's No. 1
17 Soi 16, Sukhumvit Rd.
Tel: 259-0135
Bangkok's oldest Hungarian restaurant in a new location; eccentric atmosphere.

ITALIAN

Giorgio's
Royal Orchid Sheraton Hotel
Tel: 234-5599
Good food, enhanced by spectacular views of the Chao Phya River flowing by just outside.

Italian Pavillion
19 Soi Nana Tai
Tel: 250-1550
Attractively decorated, with a lovely garden; Bangkok's first real Italian restaurant.

L'Opera
Soi 39 Sukhumvit
Tel: 258-5605
Medium prices and serves very good food. Warm, friendly atmosphere.

Libra
36 Soi 18 Sukhumvit
Tel: 258-1327
Good pasta. Friendly atmosphere

Paesano
96/7 Soi Ton Son, Ploenchit
Tel: 252-2834
Good food, casual atmosphere prevalent; medium prices.

Pan Pan
591 Sukhumvit (corner Soi 33)
Tel: 258-9304
Also Lang Suan branch, 45 Soi Lang Suan. Good pizza, gelati, cake and ice-cream. Casual atmosphere.

Pepino
Shangri-La Hotel
Tel: 236-7777, ext. Pepino

Pizzeria
Narai Hotel,
Tel: 233-3350
Unpretentious, even spartan, but serving some of the best Italian food in Bangkok.

Rossano's
Soi 16 Sukhumvit
Tel: 258-1849
Good food selection, medium prices.

Trattoria da Roberto
37/9 Plaza Arcade
Patpong 2 Rd.
Tel: 233-6851
Very good Italian food right in the middle of Bangkok's bar belt.

MEXICAN

El Gordo's
130/8 Silom Rd. (in lane opposite Bangkok Bank's head office building)
Tel: 234-5470
Mexican specialities in an old Mexican atmosphere. Superb Margueritas.

SCANDINAVIAN

Rode Orm
440/2 Suriwong Rd.
Wide range of dishes; medium prices.

The Two Vikings
2 Sukhumvit Soi 35
Tel: 258-8843
Bangkok's first really elegant restaurant and still one of the best. Recommended dishes: Gravadlaks, Smoked Eel, and Danish Layer Cake.

Villa Norden
Sukhumvit 20
Good food; wine and spirits. Inexpensive.

TEA ROOMS

Author's Lounge
Oriental Hotel
Tel: 236-0400, ext. 3364

Library 1918
Dusit Thani Hotel
Tel: 233-1130

Little Home Bakery
3rd floor, Mah Boonkrong Center
Tel: 217-9441

Lobby Lounge
The Regent Hotel
Tel: 251-6127

FAST FOOD

A & W Family Restaurant
Six locations:
- Pantip Plaza Shopping Center, Petchburi Rd.
- 197/1 Silom Rd.
- Central Plaza Lard Prao Soi 7
- Siam Square
- Laksi
- Pattaya.

Dairy Queen
Robinson Department Store
Silom Branch, 1st floor.

Kentucky Fried Chicken
Four branches:
- Ploenchit Rd.
- Siam Square
- Silom Rd. at the corner of Thaniya Rd.
- Central Plaza Lard Prao.

McDonalds
Three locations:
- Amarin Plaza on Ploenchit Rd.
- The Mall, Ramkamhaeng
- Silom Rd. opp. Patpong Rd.

Pizza Hut & Swenson's Ice Cream
Six branches:
- Siam Square; Gaysorn Rd., Tel: 251-6800
- Suriwong; Mahboonkrong
- Central Lard Prao
- Sukhumvit at Soi 51, Tel: 258-7182
- Siam Jusco, Tel: 246-4456
- Surawongse, Tel: 235-0525

DRINKNG NOTES

PUBS

Bobby's Arms
Patpong 2
Tel: 233-6828
Customers can enjoy English food in a pub atmosphere; inexpensive.

Brown Sugar
231/20 Soi Sarasin,
Rajadamri Rd.
Tel: 250-0103

Vinothek
61/2 Soi Lang Suan,
Tel: 253-6170

SHOPPING

SHOPPING AREAS

Rather than specializing in a single product, most Bangkok shops sell a variety of items. These are some of the exceptions which are recognized for the quality of their items. They are listed alphabetically.

ANTIQUES

Asian Heritage
57 Soi 23, Sukhumvit Rd.
Tel: 258-4157
Located in a private house and full of pretty things which have been carefully selected by the owner.

Elephant House
67/12 Soi Phra Phinit
Soi Suan Plu, South Sathorn Rd.
Tel: 286-5280
Branches: Regent Hotel, River City.
Some of the best Burmese antiques and lacquerware can be found in these stores. Owned by a Burmese.

Golden Triangle
Room 301, River City Complex
Tel: 237-0077, 237-0078, ext. 301
Antique silver and textiles, ikat and other Hilltribe fabrics.

Lotus
Parichart Court
Regent Hotel
Tel: 250-0732
Quality antiques in a wide range of styles.

Monogram
Author's Lounge and arcade

NeOld
149/2-3 Suriwong Rd.
Tel: 235-8352, 235-8916
Wide range of decorative items from lacquerware to furniture.

Oriental Hotel
Tel: 235-2603
First antique dealer to open in Bangkok; offers good array of Thai, Burmese and Chinese items.

Peng Seng
942/1-4 Rama IV Rd.
Tel: 234-1285, 236-8010
Highly-regarded by local collectors; particularly good for statuary and porcelains.

Rama
30/1 Oriental Plaza
Tel: 235-7991, 235-9907
Very large selection of Burmese, Thai, and Chinese items.

Thai House Antiques
720/6 Sukhumvit Rd.
Tel: 258-6287
Inexpensive items, with an interesting selection of furniture; some old, some beautifully reproduced.

EXPORT PERMITS FOR ANTIQUES

While some shopkeepers know the exact Fine Arts Department regulations regarding antiques, many do not and often are more concerned with making a sale than in protecting the customer from having the piece confiscated. Moreover, the laws pertain not to the sale of antiques but to their export. In part, the problem lies in the interpretation of the laws. The laws are fairly precise in their stipulations, but it is difficult to determine the age, provenance and the category of a piece. Hence, ignorance and confusion reign.

The Department prohibits the export of all Buddha images, and images of other deities and fragments (such as hands or heads) of images dating from before the 18th century.

It requires that all antiques and art objects, regardless of type or age, be registered with the Fine Arts Department. Since the process is time-consuming, the shop will usually do this for you. In most cases you can trust the shop to handle it properly so you will not encounter any problems later. If you decide to handle it yourself, take the piece to the Fine Arts Department on Na Prathat Road across from Sanam Luang together with two postcard-sized photos of it. You will be charged an export fee of 50-200 *baht* depending on the piece.

Fake antiques do not require export permits but Airport Customs officials are not art experts and may mistake it for a genuine piece. If it looks authentic, you may want to clear it at the Department beforehand to avoid problems later.

BASKETS/WICKERWARE/RATTAN

A number of small shops on Mahachai Road near the intersection of Luang Road in the vicinity of Bangkok prison offer a range of practical and decorative items.

BRASSWARE & BRONZEWARE

Chieng Heng Collection
320 River City Shopping Complex
Tel: 237-0077, ext. 320, 335
A wide range of brass ornaments and bronzeware for all tastes.

Leela Art Gallery
993-5 Ploenchit Rd.
Tel: 252-5479, 252-1240
Large bronze items; extremely handsome.

New Charming Souvenir
135/11 Gaysorn Rd.
Tel: 271-6357
Cutlery and gift items.

S. Samran Thailand Co.
302-8 Petchburi Rd.
Tel: 215-8941
Factory shop. They can also custom make wooden chests for cutlery.

CERAMICS

Celadon House
18/17 Soi 21, Sukhumvit Rd.
Tel: 258-3920, 259-7744
Glazed stoneware; dinner sets, lamps, and decorative items, from Chiang Mai.

Ceramic Decor
231/18 Sarasin,
off Rajdamri Rd.
Tel: 252-1350
Very special; large glazed water jars, garden seats, reproductions of Chinese blue-and-white porcelain.

Domino House
137 Gaysorn Rd.
Tel: 253-7551
Good selection of blue and white pottery.

Jada (1969)
135-135/1 Gaysorn Rd.
Tel: 253-7606
Attractive selection of blue and white pottery; mostly larger items.

Lotus Ceramics
Soi 3/1 Sukhumvit Rd.
Tel: 253-0044
Wide ranges of Benjarong ware.

COTTONS

Khomapastr
52/10 Suriwong Rd.
Tel: 236-7998
Very attractive printed cottons by the yard and in made-up items.

FURNITURE

Jujak
30/226 Lard Prao Soi 87
Tel: 530-0187, 538-2689
Among one of the oldest furniture-makers in Bangkok.

Peter
157/1 Soi Mahadlekluang 2
Tel: 252-5236
Noted as one of the first in Bangkok to make fine Western furniture out of local teak and rosewood.

Pure Design
30 Soi Ruamrudee
Tel: 251-5485
Highly imaginative furniture in both wood and rattan; also some antiques.

Scanthai
66 Soi 21 Sukhumvit Rd.
Tel: 258-3599
"Danish modern" style furniture in natural oiled teak.

Sweet Home
155/11-2 Soi Asoke, Sukhumvit
Tel: 258-3419, 258-3420
Finely-crafted furniture; particularly good for Chinese reproductions.

HANDICRAFTS

Anong Gallery
2nd floor, Oriental Plaza
Tel: 235-7991, 234-1320-9
2nd floor, Peninsula Plaza
Tel: 252-3070
Variety of refashioned hilltribe embroidered dresses.

Central Department Store
Chidlom Branch
Ploenchit Rd.
A wide selection including hilltribe handicrafts, basketware, wooden carvings, etc.

Chitralada Shop
4th floor, Oriental Plaza Arcade
Tel: 234-1321, 234-1322, ext. 61
Outlets for H.M. Queen Sirikit's nationwide handicraft projects; brocade and tie-dye silks, finely-woven basketry, etc.

Hilltribe Foundation
195 Phyathai Rd
Tel: 251-9816
Under the patronage of H.R.H. the Princess Mother, the Foundation is located in the grounds of Srapatoom Palace. Offers hilltribe embroideries and jewelry.

House of Handicrafts
Parichart Court
The Regent Bangkok Hotel
Tel: 250-0724
Large array of hilltribe items, Burmese lacquerware, mudmee silk and other fabrics.

Jada (1969) Co. Ltd.
135-135/1 Gaysorn Rd.
Tel: 253-7606
Excellent range of teak goods and assorted handicrafts; reasonable prices.

Motif
296/7 Silom Rd.
Tel: 233-1203
Thai cotton mats, bags, cushions, stuffed animals, rag dolls, pottery, etc.

Narayana Phand Co Ltd.
The Mall, 127 Rajdamri Rd.
Tel: 252-4670, 252-4671
Thai government gift shop that stocks every kind of handicraft at fixed prices.

Pagoda
48 Oriental Lane,
Tel: 236-0400, ext. 3368
Basketry, wood-carvings, umbrellas, etc.; good place if you are looking for souvenirs to send home.

Scandia
769 Sukhumvit Rd. (near Soi 43)
Tel: 258-7279
Wooden trays, salad bowls, Thai blue-and white porcelain; interesting designs.

Silom Village
286/1 Silom Rd.
Tel: 235-87601
Many separate handicraft shops in this charming shopping complex; good for several hours of wandering.

Thai Home Industries
35 Oriental Lane
Tel: 234-1736
Rather gloomy looking but with unexpected surprises; good for wooden spirit houses, bronzeware, stone rubbings, etc.

JEWELRY & SILVERWARE

Alex & Co.
14/1 Oriental Lane
Tel: 234-3908
Branch in Dusit Thani Hotel. Expert workmanship, long-established store. Wide selection of silver items.

Bua Laad
Ground floor, Peninsula Plaza
Rajdamri Rd.
Tel: 253-9760, 253-9761
Situated right next to The Regent of Bangkok Hotel.

J.P. Inter Gems
1009-1011 Silom Rd.

Johnny's Gems
199 Fuengnakorn Rd.
Tel: 222-1706
Jewelry, bronzeware, brassware, Thai silk and Thai handicrafts. Very reliable. Will provide transport to and from shop.

Kim
Oriental Plaza
Tel: 234-1321, 234-1322, ext. 50
Offers a good selection of well-designed costume jewelry.

Lotus
Parichart Court
The Regent Hotel
Tel: 250-0732

Moradok
Room 302 River City Complex,
Tel: 237-0077, 237-0078, ext. 302
Extremely handsome silver accessories, most of them antique.

Phet-Uthai
127 Rajaprasong
Shopping Mall
Tel: 252-4715
Wide variety of jewelry sets.

Prakaiphetch Gems
942/132, 4th floor,
Charn Issara Tower
Tel: 2345-0048, 234-0050
Will design or make your own design.

Sincere Jewelry
Oriental Hotel
Tel: 233-6959
Exquisitely-designed brooches, necklaces, bracelets and rings.

Supermarket of Gems
987 Silom Rd.
Tel: 235-1257
Reliable quality stones.

Thai Nakorn
79 Prachatipatai Rd.
Tel: 281-6285
Silversmith to the Royal Household and Government Ministries, nielloware.

Tok Kwang
224-6 Silom Rd.
Tel: 233-0658
Good quality, especially pearls, one of the town's best for craftsmanship.

Yves Joaillier
Charn Issara
3rd floor, 942/83
Rama 4 Rd.
Tel: 233-3292, 234-8122
Quality designed jewelry in precious and semi-precious stones set in gold.

LEATHERWARE

Ballet Shoes
133/8-9 Gaysorn Rd.
Tel: 253-7580
Made-to-order and ready-made shoes in various designs. Repairs; make handbags.

Chao Phya Bootery
266-268 Sukhumvit Rd.
Tel: 251-3498
Ready-made and custom-made. Also available are ready-made coats, bags, boots, belts, wallets, suitcases and briefcases.

Oriental Leathers
Oriental Hotel
Author's Lounge.
Tel: 236-0400, ext. 3362
Handbags, belts, wallets, watch-straps in leather and crocodile.

Patou
95/250 Rajadamri Rd.
Tel: 251-7991, 251-3971
Fashion shoes and bags, under licence to make Charles Jourdan shoes to original patterns, for both men and women.

Ragazze
3rd floor, Rajadamri Arcade;
2nd floor, Central Plaza;
3rd floor, Siam Centre.
Ready-made casual shoes, bags and belts.

Siam Bootery
294-4 Sukhumvit Rd. (opp. Soi 19)
Tel: 251-6862
Leather jackets, ready-made and made-to-order shoes and boots, briefcases, etc.

Srisoonthorn Shoe Shop
174/1 Sukhumvit. (near Soi 8)
Tel: 253-4461
Large selection of reptile skin and leather shoes in large sizes.

Tony Leather
300-302 Sukhumvit Rd. (opposite Soi 19)
Tel: 251-6861
Men's, women's and children's shoes, made-to-order, good quality leather.

PAINTINGS

Art Resources
Parichart Court, The Regent of Bangkok
Tel: 250-0723
Quality paintings and collectable items.

C.V.N. Exotic
131/3-4 Sukhumvit Rd. (between Soi 7-9)
Tel: 253-0361, 253-7730
Wide selection of good contemporary paintings by local artists.

Four A. Gallery
207 Silom Rd.
Tel: 235-1860
One of many Bangkok galleries with a portrait artist in residence.

Phetburi Gallery
1787/9 New Petchburi Rd.
Tel: 251-2426
Extensive selection of contemporary paintings and some sculpture.

Surawongse Galleries
287/25-6 Suriwong Rd.
Tel: 233-5533;
Oriental d'Art

Maenam Mall in The Oriental Hotel
Tel: 235-7988;
4th floor, River City Shopping Center
Tel: 237-0077, ext. 412, 348.
Paintings and sculpture.

Visual Dhamma
44/28 Soi Asoke
Tel: 277-4017
Specializes in paintings that combine modern and traditional Buddhist themes.

READY-TO-WEAR (WOMEN'S)

Choisy
9/25 Suriwong Rd.
Tel: 234-0290
Classic designs in silk available from the Jim Thompson Company.

Design Thai
304 Silom Rd.
Tel: 235-1553
Silk and cotton dresses and shirts.

Designers' Showcase
115/1 Suriwong Rd.
Tel: 236-2806
Mostly cotton dresses in casual styles; also attractive costume jewelry.

Duangjai Bis
2nd floor, Charn Issara Bldg.
942 Rama 4 Rd.
Tel: 234-2519
Innovative clothes designed by a young Thai designer.

Exotic Siam Boutique
Oriental Hotel, Author's Lounge
Tel: 236-0400, ext. 3371
Silk and cotton dresses, jackets, caftans, and casual wear; also stocks hilltribe fashions and accessories.

Galeries Lafayette
Peninsula Plaza, Rajadamri Rd.
Tel: 253-9790-4
Casual and formal wear in a good range of sizes. A branch of the Paris original.

Jaspal
2nd floor, Siam Centre;
Ground floor, Amarin Plaza;
3rd floor, Rajadamri Arcade.
Exclusive day and evening wear.

Jim Thompson Thai Silk
9 Suriwong Rd.
Tel: 234-4900
Silk and cotton dresses, shirts and caftans.

John Fowler
Ploenchit Arcade
Tel: 252-9650
and 285/1 Silom Rd., (corner Convent Rd.)
Tel: 234-3778
Ethnic-wear plus a range of T-shirts with original screen print designs in beautiful, vibrant colors.

Kai
Hilton Hotel arcade, Wireless Rd.;
2nd floor, Charn Issara Bldg.;
942 Rama 4 Rd.
Tel: 235-9107;
1st floor, Peninsula Plaza
Tel: 235-9752;
3rd floor, Mahboonkrong Center
(called "Kai Junior"; for teenagers).
Designer garments.

Khanitha
3rd floor, Room 362, Siam Center
Tel: 251-2933, ext. 362;
Oriental Plaza
Tel: 234-1321, ext. 16;
Regent of Bangkok Hotel
Tel: 250-0734;
River City, 2nd floor.
Tel: 237-0077, 237-0078 ext. 262.
Selection of superb women's wear in a variety of styles.

Noriko
566 Ploenchit Rd., (corner of Soi Ruam Rudee)
Tel: 251-7712
also, 919/1 Sukhumvit Rd.
Tel: 258-7963
Designer clothes, good range and quality.

World Boutique
392/10-11 Siam Square, Soi 5
Tel: 251-9995
Elegant apparel in a variety of materials.

SILK (THAI SILK)

Anita Thai Silk
294/4-5 Silom Rd.
Tel: 234-2481
Large range of Thai silk, cottons, voile; furnishings and gift items.

Design Thai
304 Silom Rd.
Tel: 235-1553
Silk by the yard, ready-to-wear, some cottons available too.

Jagtar Thai Silk
137/3 Sukhumvit Rd.
Tel: 252-3854, 255-7380
Silk by the yard, dresses and accessories.

Jim Thompson's Thai Silk Co.
9 Suriwong Rd.
Tel: 234-4900-4
The oldest and most famous; silk in bolts, made-up items from cushion covers to clothing, cottons.

Khanitha
3rd floor, Room 362 Siam Center;
Ground floor, Oriental Plaza;
Parichart Court, Regent Hotel;
2nd floor, River City.
Fine silk apparel.

Star of Siam
Oriental Hotel Arcade
Tel: 236-0-400, ext. 3370
Silk by the yard, ready-to-wear.

T. Shinawatra Thai Silk
94 Soi 23 Sukhumvit Rd.
Tel: 258-0295
Choose from a range of silks and cottons in various weights and designs.

Thai Pan
35/6 Suriwong Rd.
Tel: 236-6679
Plain and printed silk and cotton by the yard, ready-made dresses, shirts and numerous other gift items.

Your Silk
Bangkok Hilton arcade, 2 Wireless Rd.
Tel: 235-0123
Thai silk and gift items.

TAILORS (MEN)

Adam's Tailor
Charn Issara Tower
942, Rama 4 Rd.
Tel: 233-0807

Art's Tailor
62/15-6 Thaniya Rd.
Tel: 234-0874
or 39 Rajprasong Shopping Centre
Tel: 251-0239

Central Tailor
182/1 Silom Rd.
Tel: 234-4136

Montien Tailor Shop
52/13 Suriwong Rd.
Tel: 235-3733

Perry's Tailor
60/2 Silom Rd.
Tel: 233-9236

TAILORS (WOMEN)

K.S. Wong Hong Kong Lady Tailor
4/6 Soi 5 Sukhumvit Rd.
Tel: 250-0118
High quality.

Nusra
2nd floor, Peninsula Plaza
155 Rajdamri Rd.
Tel: 252-1947
Good work, also has ready-to-wear.

Pradith Tip
260 Sukhumvit Rd. (between Sois 12-14)
Tel: 252-8411
Bikinis and swimsuits made to measure; also maternity swimsuits.

Usa
392/32 Soi 20
Sukhumvit Rd.
Tel: 258-1418
Good work.

CRAFT FACTORIES TO VISIT

Bangkok Dolls
85 Soi Rajatapan, Makkasan
Tel: 245-3008

Hand-made, authentic in detail, these dolls reproduce the clothing and ornaments of the hilltribe people as well as classical dancers depicting *Ramakien* figures.

Blue & White Potteries
Surachai Nuparwan
Oom Noi, Samut Sakhon
On the way to the Rose Garden, left hand side of road. Small family business, excellent art work, good quality and prices. Open daily, 8 a.m. to 10 p.m.

Bronze Factory
S. Samran, 304
Petchburi Rd.
Tel: 215-8941, 215-8849.
This is the showroom address. When you are there ask to be taken across the road to watch the craftsmen work on bronze and buffalo horn cutlery.

Gold Leaf Factory
Off Rajadamnern Klang Avenue, behind Post Office. The official shop is at 321 Prasumane Road, opposite Wat Bovornivet. Well worth a visit. Watch the practice of an ancient craft: gold being beaten to tissue paper thinness.

Nielloware
Thai Nakorn Company
79 Prachatipatai Rd.
Tel: 281-7867, 281-3526
Telephone for an appointment.

Thai Silk Weaving
Shinawatra's factory
Tel: 258-0925
Can be seen at 94 Soi 23, Sukhumvit Rd.

LANGUAGE

ORIGINS & INTONATION

For centuries, the Thai language, rather than tripping from foreigners' tongues has been tripping them up. Its roots go back to the hills of southern China from whence the Thais originated but are overlaid by Indian influences. From the original settlers come the five tones which seem designed to frustrate Westerners, one sound with five different tones to mean five different things.

When you mispronounce, you don't simply say a word incorrectly, you say another word entirely. It is not unusual to see a semi-fluent foreigner standing before a Thai running through the scale of tones until suddenly a light of recognition dawns on his companion's face. There are misinformed Westerners who will tell you that tones are not important. These people do not communicate with Thais, they communicate *at* them in a one-side exchange that frustrates both parties.

THAI NAMES

From the languages of India have come polysyllabic names and words, the lexicon of literature. Thai names are among the longest in the world. Every Thai first and surname has a meaning. By learning the meaning of the name of everyone you meet, you would acquire a formal, but quite extensive vocabulary.

There is no universal transliteration system from Thai into English which is why names and street names can be spelled three different ways. For example, the surname Chumsai is spelled Chumsai, Jumsai and Xoomsai depending on the family. This confuses even the Thais. If you ask a Thai how you spell something, he may well reply "how do you want to spell it?"

PHONOLOGY

The way Thai consonants are written in English often confuses foreigners. An "*h*" following a letter like "*p*", and "*t*" gives the letter a soft sound; without the "*h*" the sound is more explosive. Thus, "*ph*" is not pronounced "*f*" but as a soft "*p*". Without the "*h*", the "*p*" has the sound of a very hard "*b*". The word Thanon (street) is pronounced "tanon" in the same way as "Thailand" is not meant to sound like "Thighland." Similarly, final letters are often not pronounced as they look. A "*j*" on the end of a word is pronounced "*t*"; "*l*" is pronounced as an "*n*". To complicate matters further, many words end with "*se*" or "*r*" which are not pronounced.

Vowels are pronounced like this: ***i*** as in *sip*, ***ii*** as in *seep*, ***e*** as in *bet*, ***a*** as in *pun*, ***aa*** as in *pal*, ***u*** as in *pool*, ***o*** as in *so*, ***ai*** as in *pie*, ***ow*** as in *cow*, ***aw*** as in *paw*, ***iw*** as in *you*, ***oy*** as in *toy*.

In Thai, the pronoun "I" and "me" use the same word but it is different for males and females. Men use the word *phom* when referring to themselves; women say *chan* or *diichan*. Men use *khrap* at the end of a sentence when addressing either a male or a female i.e. *pai* (f) *nai*, *khrap* (h) (where are you going? sir). Women add the word *kha* to their statements as in pai (f) *nai*, *kha* (h).

To ask a question, add a high tone *mai* to the end of the phrase i.e. *rao pai* (we go) or *rao pai mai* (h) (shall we go?). To negate a statement, insert a falling tone *mai* between the subject and the verb i.e. *rao pai* (we go), *rao mai pai* (we don't go). "*Very*" or "*much*" are indicated by adding *maak* to the end of a phrase i.e. *ron* (hot), *ron maak* (very hot).

Listed below is a small vocabulary intended to get you on your way. The five tones have been indicated by appending letters after them viz. high (h), low (l), middle (m), rising (like asking a question) (r), and falling (like suddenly understanding something as in "ohh, I see") (f).

NUMBERS

One
Nung (m)

Two
Song (r)

Three
Sam (r)

Four
Sii (m)

Five
Haa (f)

Six
Hok (m)

Seven
Jet (m)

Eight
Pat (m)

Nine
Kow (f)

Ten
Sip (m)

Eleven
Sip Et (m, m)

Twelve
Sip Song (m, r)

Thirteen
Sip Sam (m, r) and so on

Twenty
Yii Sip (m, m)

Thirty
Sam Sip (f, m) and so on

100
Nung Roi (m, m)

1,000
Nung Phan (m, m)

DAYS OF THE WEEK

Monday
Wan Jan

Tuesday
Wan Angkan

Wednesday
Wan Phoot

Thursday
Wan Pharuhat

Friday
Wan Sook

Saturday
Wan Sao

Sunday
Wan Athit

Today
Wan nii (h)

Yesterday
Mua wan nii (h)

Tomorrow
Prung nii (h)

When
Mua (f) *rai*

GREETINGS & OTHERS

Hello, goodbye
Sawasdee (a man then says *khrup*; a woman says *kha*; thus *sawasdee khrup)*

How are you
Khun sabai dii, mai (h)

Well, thank you
Sabai dii, Khapkhun.

Thank you very much
Khapkhun Maak.

May I take a photo?
Thai roop (f) *noi, dai* (f) *mai* (h)

Never mind
Mai (f) *pen rai*

I cannot speak Thai
Phuut Thai mai (f) *dai* (f)

I can speak a little Thai
Phuut Thai dai (f) *nit* (h) *diew*

Where do you live?
Khun yoo thii (f) *nai* (r)

What is this called in Thai?
An nii (h), *kaw riak aray phasa Thai*

How much?
Thao (f) *rai*

DIRECTIONS & TRAVEL

Go
Pai

Come
Maa

Where
Thii (f) *nai* (r)

Right
Khwaa (r)

Left
Sai (h)

Turn
Leo

Straight ahead
Trong pai

Please slow down
Cha cha noi

Stop here
Yood thii (f) *nii* (f)

Fast
Raew

Hotel
Rong raam

Street
Thanon

Lane
Soi

Bridge
Saphan

Police Station
Sathanii Dtam Ruat

USEFUL PHRASES

Yes
Chai (f)

No
Mai (f) *chai* (f)

Do you have.....?
Mii....mai (h)

Expensive
Phaeng

Do you have something cheaper?
Mii arai thii thook (l) *kwa, mai* (h)

Can you lower the price a bit?
Kaw lot noi dai (f) *mai* (h)

Do you have another color?
Mii sii uhn mai (h)

Too big
Yai kern pai

Too small
Lek kern pai

Do you have bigger?
Mii arai thii yai kwa mai (h)

Do you have smaller?
Mii arai thii lek kwa mai (h)

OTHER HANDY PHRASES

Hot (heat hot)
Ron (h)

Hot (spicy)
Phet

Cold
Yen

Sweet
Waan (r)

Sour
Prio (f)

Delicious
Aroy

I do not feel well
Mai (f) *sabai*

FURTHER READING

Chakrabongse, Prince Chula. *Lords of Life*. London: Alvin Redman, 1960. A history of the Chakri kings.

Coedes, George. *The Indianized States of Southeast Asia*. Translated by Susan Brown Cousing and edited by Walter F. Vella, Honolulu: East-West Center Press, 1968. Well-written scholarly work.

Hall, D.G.E. *A History of South-East Asia*. Third edition. London: Macmillan, 1968. The classic text.

Moffat, Abbot Low. *Mongkut, the King of Siam*. Ithaca, New York: Cornell University Press, 1961. Superb history of one of Asia's most interesting 19th-century men.

Van Beek, Steve. *Bangkok Only Yesterday*. Hong Kong: Hong Kong Publishing, 1982. Anecdotal history of Bangkok illustrated with old photos.

Vella, Walter F. *Chaiyo!* Honolulu: University of Hawaii Press, 1979. The life and times of King Vajiravudh (1910-1925).

Wyatt, David K. *Thailand: A Short History*. Thai Wattana Panich/Yale University Press, Bangkok/London., 1984. Concise and well-written.

Seidenfaden, Erik. *The Thai Peoples*. Bangkok: Siam Society, 1967. Solid work by long-time resident.

Skinner, G. William. *Chinese Society in Thailand*. Ithaca, New York: Cornell University Press, 1957. An insight into an important part of Bangkok's history.

Bunnag, Jane. *Buddhist Monk, Buddhist Layman*. Cambridge: Cambridge University Press, 1973. Gives an account of the monastic experience.

Dhani Nivat, Prince. *A History of Buddhism in Siam*. Bangkok: Siam Society, 1965. Prince Dhani Nivat is one of Thailand's most respected scholars.

Diskul, M.C. Subhadradis. *Art in Thailand: A Brief History*. Bangkok: Silpakorn University, 1970. Diskul is the Dean of the Fine Arts University.

Rajadhon, Phya Anuman. *Essays on Thai Folklore*. Bangkok: D.K. Books. A description of Thai ceremonies, festivals and rites of passage.

Van Beek, Steve. *The Arts of Thailand*. Hong Kong, Travel Publishing Asia, 1985. Lavishly illustrated, includes the minor arts.

Warren, William. *The House on the Klong*. Tokyo: Weatherhill. The story of the Jim Thompson House.

Wray, Joe and Elizabeth, Clare Rosenfeld, and Dorothy Bailey. *Ten Lives of the Buddha; Siamese Temple Paintings and Jataka Tales*. Tokyo: Weatherhill, 1974. Well-illustrated, valuable for understanding Thai painting and the Tosachat (Jataka Tales).

Amranand, Pimsai. *Gardening in Bangkok*. Bangkok: Siam Society. This is a good piece of work on plants although could use more photographs.

Cooper, Robert and Nanthapa. *Culture Shock: Thailand*. Singapore: Times Books, 1982. Very useful look at Thai customs and how to avoid faux pas; written and illustrated in highly amusing manner.

Hollinger, Carol. *Mai Pen Rai*. Boston: Houghton Mifflin. Expatriate life in the 1950s.

Ingram, J.C. *Economic Change in Thailand 1830-1970*. Palo Alto, California: Stanford University Press, 1971.

Segaller, Denis. *Thai Ways*. Bangkok: Thai Wattana Panich, 1979. A collection of columns on Thai customs by a long-time resident .

Segaller, Denis. *More Thai Ways*. Bangkok: Allied Newspapers, 1982. More reprinted columns.

Stockmann, Hardy. *Thai Boxing*. Bangkok: D.K. Books, 1979. Excellent, well-illustrated book detailing the basics of Thai boxing.

Warren, William. *The Legendary American*. Boston: Houghton Mifflin. Presents the intriguing story of American Thai silk king Jim Thompson.

USEFUL ADDRESSES

TOURIST INFORMATION

Planning a trip to Bangkok can be made easier if you contact a travel agent or an office of the Tourism Authority of Thailand. These offices offer promotional brochures, maps and videotapes of the country's multitude attractions.

The Tourism Authority of Thailand is the Thai government's official tourism promotion organization. Its office at No. 4 Rajmdanern Nok Avenue has brochures on various attractions and personnel to answer questions. Call 282-1143, 282-1144 for more information.

Numerous publishers issue travel magazines that give current information on events and attractions that is usually reliable. The Nation newspaper's *Saen Sanuk* tourism newspaper is issued each Friday as part of the morning edition.

Listed below are some of the countries in Europe and Asia Pacific region with offices of the Tourism Authority of Thailand.

ASIA PACIFIC

Australia
12th floor, Royal Exchange Bldg.
56 Pitt St., Sydney 2000
Tel: (02) 227-549, 227-540
Cable:THAITOUR SYDNEY
Telex: 23467 THAITC AA

Hong Kong
Room 401, Fairmont House
8 Cotton Tree Drive, Central
Tel: (5) 868-0732, (5) 868-0854
Cable: HKTHAITOUR
Telex: 63092 HKTAT HX

Japan
Hibiya Mitsui Bldg.,
1-2, Yurakucho 1-Chome

Chiyoda-ku, Tokyo 100
Tel: (03) 580-6776, (03) 580-0237
Cable: THAITOUR TOKYO
Telex: 333964 TATTYO

Hirano-machi Yachiyo Bldg.
5th floor, 2-8-1 Hirano-machi
Higashi-ku, Osaka 541
Tel: (06) 231-4434
Telex: J64675
FAX: (06) 231-4337

Malaysia
c/o Royal Thai Embassy
206 Jalan Ampang, Kuala Lumpur
Tel: 248-0958
Telex: TATKL 31089 (MA)

Singapore
c/o Royal Thai Embassy
370 Orchard Rd., Singapore 0923
Tel: 235-7901, 235-7694
Cable: THAITOUR SINGAPORE
Telex: 39428 TATSIN RS

EUROPE

France
90 Avenue des Champs-Elysees
75008 Paris
Tel: 4562-8656, 4562-8748
Cable: THAITOUR PARIS
Telex: 650093 TATPAR F

Italy
Ente Nazionale
Per II Tourismo-Thailandese
Via Barberini 50, 00187, Rome
Tel: (06) 474-7410, (06) 474-7660
Telex: 626139 TAT I

England
49 Albemarle St.
London WIX 3FE
Tel: (01) 499-7670, (01) 499-7679
Cable: THAITOUR LONDON
Telex: 298760 THAI TRG, TAT/LON

U.S.A.
5 World Trade Center, Suite 2449
New York, N.Y. 10048
Tel: (212) 432-0433
Cable: THAITOUR NEW YORK
Telex: 667612 TAT UW
3440 Wilshire Blvd.
Suite 1101, Los Angeles, CA 90010
Tel: (213) 382-2353, 382-2354
Cable: THAITOUR LOS ANGELES
Telex: 686208 TTC LSA

West Germany
Bethmannstr, 58/IV., D-6000
Frankfurt/M.1
Tel: (069) 295-704, (069) 295-804
Cable: THAITOUR FRANKFURT/M
Telex: 413542 TAFRA D

AIRLINE OFFICES

Of the airlines listed here, only those with an asterisk before their names offer regularly-scheduled flights to Bangkok. The others maintain ticketing offices for flights in other parts of the world.

***Aeroflot Soviet Airlines**
183 Mezzanine floor, Regent House
Rajdamri Rd., Bkk 10500
Tel: 251-0617-9,
Airport: 523-6921

Air Canada
c/o World Travel Service
1053 New Rd.
Tel: 233-5900, 233-5901, ext. Air Canada

***Air France**
Ground floor,
Charn Issara Bldg.
942/51 Rama 4 Rd.
Tel: 234-1333
Airport: 523-7302, 523-7303

***Air India**
16/F Amarin Plaza Bldg.
500 Ploenchit Rd.
Tel: 256-9614, 256-9615-9
Airport: 535-2121-2

***Air Lanka**
942/34-35 Rama 4 Rd.
(Charn Issara Bldg.)
Ground floor,
Tel: 236-0159, 236-9292
Airport: 535-2330-2

Air New Zealand
c/o World Travel Service
1053 New Rd.
Tel: 233-5900 ext. Air New Zealand

***Alia Royal Jordanian Airlines**
Yada Bldg.
56 Silom Rd.
Tel: 236-0030
Airport: 535-2152, 535-2153

***Alitalia**
138 Silom Rd.
Tel: 233-4000-4, 234-5253

American Airlines
Maneeya Bldg.
518/2 Ploenchit Rd.
Tel: 251-1393, 251-4521

***Bangladesh Biman**
Ground and 6th floors.
Chongkolnee Bldg.
56 Suriwongse Rd.
Tel: 235-7643-4, 234-0300-9
Airport: 531-0022, ext. 2151

***British Airways**
942/81 Rama 2/F 4 Rd.
(Charn Issara Bldg.)
Tel: 236-8655-8
Airport: 531-0022, ext. 143

British Caledonian
Maneeya Bldg.
518/2 Ploenchit Rd.
Tel: 251-1393, 251-4521

***Burma Airways**
208 Suriwongse Rd.
Tel: 234-9692, 233-3052
Airport: 523-7420

***Canadian Airlines**
International Maneeya Bldg., 6/F
518/2 Ploenchit Rd.
Tel: 251-4521, 251-1393
Airport: 531-0022, ext. Canadian Airlines

***Cathay Pacific Airways**
5F/(Charn Issara Bldg.)
942/136 Rama 4 Rd.
Tel: 233-9825, 233-9826

***China Airlines**
4th floor, Peninsula Plaza
153 Rajdamri Rd.
Tel: 253-5733, 253-4241-4
Airport: 523-7300

Delta Airlines
Dusit Thani Bldg.
946 Rama 4 Rd.
Tel: 233-8530, 233-8531

***Dragonair**
Airland Co., Ltd
866 Ploenchit Rd.
Tel: 254-7468-9

Eastern Airlines
20/10-11 Rajdamri Rd. (Bangkok Bazaar)
Tel: 253-9097, 253-9098

***Egypt Air**
120 Silom Rd.
Tel: 233-7601-3
Airport: 523-7334

***Finnair**
518/2 Maneeya Bldg.
Ploenchit Rd.
Tel: 251-5445, 251-5012
Airport: 535-2104, 535-2105

***Garuda Indonesian**
944/19 Rama 4 Rd.
Tel: 233-3873
Airport: 523-8865

***Gulf Air**
G/E Maneeya-Center Bldg.
518/5 Ploenchit Rd.
Tel: 254-7931
Airport: 535-2313

Hawaiian Airlines
Maneeya Bldg.
518/2 Ploenchit Rd.
Tel: 251-1393, 251-4521

***Indian Airlines**
2/1-2 Decho Rd.
Tel: 233-3890, 233-3891
Airport: 535-2420

***Iraqi Airways**
Ground floor, ASC Bldg.
325-329 Silom Rd.
Tel: 233-5950-5
Airport: 535-2310

***Japan Air Lines**
Wall Street Tower, M/F
33/33-34 Suriwong Rd.

Tel: 234-9111
Airport: 535-6922

***KLM Royal Dutch Airlines**
2 Patpong Rd.
Tel: 235-5150-4, 235-5155-9
Airport: 523-7277

***Korean Airlines**
3/F Dusit Thani Bldg.
946 Rama 4 Rd.
Tel: 234-9283-7
Airport: 523-7320

***Kuwait Airways**
159 Rajdamri Rd.
Tel: 251-5855-9
Airport: 532-6993
ext. Kuwait Air

***Lao Aviation**
Ground floor, New Bldg.
193 Sathorntai
Saint Louis 3
Tel: 286-9244
Airport: 523-8271-3

***Lot Polish Airlines**
485/11-12 Silom Rd.
Tel: 235-2223-7
Airport: 523-2399

***Lufthansa German Airlines**
331/1-3 Silom Rd.
Tel: 234-1350-9
Airport: 535-2211

***Malaysian Airlines**
98-102 Suriwong Rd.
Tel: 234-5871-5
Airport: 523-7270

***Northwest Orient Airlines**
4th floor, Peninsula Plaza
153 Rajdamri Rd.
Tel: 253-4822
Airport: 523-2413

***Pakistan International Airlines**
52 Suriwongse Rd.
Tel: 234-2961-4
Airport: 535-2127-8

Pan American
Maneeya Bldg.
518/2 Ploenchit Rd.
Tel: 251-4521

***Philippine Airlines**
56 Suriwong Rd.
Tel: 233-2350
Airport: 523-9086, 523-6928

***Qantas Airways**
11th floor, 942/51
Rama 4 Rd. (Charn Issara Bldg.)
Tel: 236-0102
Airport: 523-0640

***Royal Brunei Airlines**
942/42 Rama 4 Rd.
2/F (Charn Issara Bldg.)
Tel: 234-0007

***Royal Nepal Airlines**
Yada Bldg.
56 Silom Rd.
Tel: 236-0030
Airport: 535-2346

***Sabena Belgian Airlines**
11th floor, CCT Bldg.
109 Suriwong Rd.
Tel: 233-2020-3
Airport: 523-7274

***SAS Scandinavian Airlines System**
412 Rama I Rd.
Tel: 253-8333
Airport: 523-8853

***Saudi Arabian Airlines**
Ground floor, CCT Bldg.
109 Suriwong Rd.
Tel: 236-0112
Airport: 523-9047-8

***Singapore Airlines**
12th floor, Silom Center Bldg.
2 Silom Rd.
Tel: 236-0440, 236-0303
Airport: 523-7299

***Swissair**
1 Silom Rd.
Tel: 233-2930-4, 233-2935-8
Airport: 523-2371

***Tarom Romanian Air Transport**
89/12 Rajdamri Rd.
(Bangkok Bazaar)
Tel: 253-1681, 253-1682

***Thai Airways** (domestic service)
6 Larn Luang Rd.
Tel: 280-0070, 280-0080
Airport: 523-8271, 523-8272

***Thai Airways International**
Head office
89 Vibhavadi Rangsit Rd.
Tel: 513-0120-36

Silom Office
485 Silom Rd.
Tel: 234-3100-19, 233-3810

Rajawong office
45 Anuwong Rd.
Tel: 224-9602, 224-9603

Asia Hotel office
296 Phya Thai Rd.
Tel: 215-0787, 215-0788
Airport: 523-6121

Trans World Airlines
942/147 Rama 4 Rd.
12/F (Charn Issara Bldg.)
Tel: 233-7290, 233-7291

***Union de Transports Ariens (UTA)**
942/51 Rama 4 Rd.
(Charn Issara Bldg.)
Tel: 234-1330, 234-1331
Airport: 523-7302, 523-7303

***United Airlines**
16/F Regent House
183 Rajdamri Rd.
Tel: 253-0558-9
Airport: 535-2231-2

***Vietnam Airlines**
83/1 Wireless Rd.
Tel: 251-7202

Western Airlines
Dusit Thani Bldg.
946 Rama 4 Rd.
Tel: 234-7876, 234-7877

INFORMATION SERVICES

For reading or reference, stop in at one of the following. All carry books in English on Thailand.

A.U.A.
179 Rajdamri Rd.
Tel: 252-8953
Open 8:30 a.m. to 6 p.m. (Mon.-Fri.), 9 a.m. through 1 p.m. on Sat. Sponsored by the U.S. Information Service.

British Council
428 Siam Square
Soi 2
Tel: 252-6136
Open 10 a.m. to 7 p.m. (Tue.-Fri.), 10 a.m. through 5 p.m. Sat.

Neilson Hayes
195 Suriwong Rd.
Tel: 233-1731
Open 9:30 a.m. to 4 p.m. (Mon.-Sat.), and from 9:30 a.m. to 12:30 p.m. on Sun.

Siam Society
131 Soi 21
Sukhumvit Road
Tel: 258-3491
Open 9 a.m. to 5 p.m. (Tue.-Sat.)

BOOKSTORES

Bangkok has many good bookstores with a wide selection of books for information and for entertainment. If you want to read about something you have encountered in Bangkok or a good, light read, try one of these many bookshops. Alternatively, try your hotel bookstore.

Asia Books
221 Sukhumvit Road
(between Sois 17 and 19)
2nd floor, Peninsula Plaza and
Ground floor, Landmark Hotel Plaza.
Art books, coffee table books, travel books and bestsellers.

D.K. Books
Basement CCT Bldg. (behind Lido Theater)
109 Suriwong Rd.
Tel: 236-2899
The most complete bookstore in Bangkok

with books in English on nearly every subject under the sun.

COOKING SCHOOLS

Bussaracum Restaurant
35 Soi Pipat off Convent Rd.
Tel: 235-8915
Ten-day course, Mon. through Fri., 9 a.m. to noon or 1 p.m. to 4 p.m. 3,800 *baht*/person. One of Bangkok's best Thai food restaurants teaches 21 different dishes, appetizers and sweets.

The Thai Cooking School
Oriental Hotel
48 New Rd.
Tel: 437-3080
Five-day course, Mon. through Fri., 9 a.m. to noon. 7,500 *baht*/person. Learn to prepare ten of the finest of Thai dishes taught by master chef, Chalie Amatyakul.

YMCA
13 South Sathorn
Tel: 286-2329
Five-day course, Tue.; two hours each Sat. from 1 p.m. to 3 p.m. 700 *baht*/person. One of the longest-established cooking schools in Bangkok teaches ten basic Thai dishes.

COMMUNITY ORGANIZATIONS

Alliance Francaise
29 S. Sathorn Rd.
Tel: 213-2122, 213-2123
Open Mon.-Fri., 8 a.m.-7:30 p.m.; Sat., 9 a.m.-7 p.m.

American Chamber of Commerce
140 Wireless Rd.
Tel: 251-1605, 251-9266
Open Mon.-Fri., 8:30 a.m.-noon and 1 p.m.-4:30 p.m.

British Chamber of Commerce
Room 604 Bangkok Insurance Bldg.
302 Silom Rd.
Tel: 234-1140, 234-1169
Open Mon.-Fri., 8 a.m.-noon and 1 p.m.-4:30 p.m.

British Council
428 Soi 2 Siam Square
Rama I Rd.,
Tel: 252-6136, 252-6111
Open Mon.-Fri., 8:30 a.m.-4 p.m.

Franco-Thai Chamber of Commerce
104 Wireless Rd.
Tel: 251-9385
Open Mon.-Fri., 8:30 a.m.-noon and 2 p.m.-4:30 p.m.

German-Thai Chamber
699 Klongboonma Bldg.
Silom Rd.
Tel: 236-2396
Open Mon.-Fri., 9 a.m.-noon.

Goethe Institute
Soi Attakamprasit
S. Sathorn Rd.
Tel: 286-9002-4, 281-7211 or 281-7526
Open Mon.-Fri., 8 a.m.-5 p.m.; Sat., 8 a.m.-noon.

Japanese Chamber of Commerce
15th floor, Amarin Tower
500 Ploenchit Rd.
Tel: 256-9170, 256-9171
Open Mon.-Fri., 9 a.m.-5 p.m.; Sat., 9 a.m.-noon.

INTERNATIONAL ORGANIZATIONS

Foreign Correspondents
Club of Thailand
23rd floor, Dusit Thani Hotel
Tel: 233-1130, ext. 2970
Open Mon.-Fri.: Noon to midnight; Sat.: Noon to 6 p.m.

Lions Chaophaya
(Bangkok) Association
10 Soi Soomvijai
New Pethburi Rd.
Tel: 258-9037
Meetings the last Thursdays of the month. Foreign members welcome.

Rotary Club
Bangkok Rotary
Hilton Hotel
Tel: 251-1360
Meetings on Thursdays at 12:30 p.m. Bangkok South Rotary, Montien Hotel, Tel: 234-8060, ext. 260. Meetings on Fridays are held at 12:30 p.m. Bangkapi Branch, Siam Intercontinental Hotel, Tel: 253-0355.

Meetings on Tuesdays are held at 12:30 p.m. Foreign members are also welcome; English is the medium.

EMBASSIES & CONSULATES

All of the embassies are open from Monday through Friday inclusive unless otherwise stated.

Argentine Embassy
20/85 Promitr Villa
Soi 49/1 Sukhumvit
Tel: 259-0401, 259-0402
Office hours: 8:30 a.m.-2 p.m.
Visa hours: 8:30-noon

Australian Embassy
37 S. Sathorn Rd.
Tel: 287-2680
Office hours: 8 a.m.-12:30 p.m., 1:30 p.m.-4 p.m.
Consular hours are between 8:15 a.m.-noon.

Austrian Embassy
14 Soi Nanta, off Soi Attakarnprasit
S. Sathorn Rd.
Tel: 286-3011, 286-3037
Office hours: 8:30 a.m.-noon and 1 p.m.-4 p.m. (Mon.-Fri.); 9 a.m.-noon (Sat.)

Belgian Embassy
44 Soi Pipat
Silom Rd.
Tel: 233-9370, 233-0840
Office hours: 8:30 a.m.-1:30 p.m.

Bangladesh Embassy
8 Soi Charoenmitr
Soi 63, Sukhumvit Rd.
Tel: 391-8069, 391-8070
Office hours: 8:30 a.m.-4:30 p.m. (Mon.-Thur.); 8:30 a.m.-noon on Fri.

Bolivian Embassy
148/4 Nang Linchee Rd.
Tel: 286-2410
Office hours: 10 a.m.-2 p.m.

Brazilian Embassy
9th floor, Maneeya Center Bldg.
518/5 Ploenchit Rd.
Tel: 252-6023, 252-6043
Office hours: 8 a.m.-4 p.m.
Visa hours: 9 a.m.-2 p.m.

British Embassy
1031 N. Wireless Rd.
Tel: 253-0191, 253-0192
Office hours: 8 a.m.-noon, 1:30 p.m.-4:30 p.m.
Consular hours: 8 a.m.-noon

Brunei Embassy
14th floor, Orakan Bldg.
26/50 Soi Chidlom, Ploenchit Rd.
Tel: 251-5766, 251-5767
Office hours: 8:30 a.m.-noon, 1:30 p.m.-4:30 p.m.

Bulgarian Embassy
64 Soi Charoenmit 63
Sukhumvit Rd.
Tel: 381-1385
Office hours: 9 a.m.-2 p.m.

Burmese Embassy
132 N. Sathorn Rd.
Tel: 233-2237, 234-2258
Office Hours: 8:30 a.m.-12:30 p.m. and 1 p.m.-4:30 p.m. (Mon.-Thur.); 8:30 a.m.-11 a.m., 1 p.m.-5 p.m. (Fri.)

Canadian Embassy
11th floor, Boonmitr Bldg.
138 Silom Rd.
Tel: 234-1561, 234-1568
Office hours: 7:30 a.m.-12:15 p.m. and 1 p.m.-4:15 p.m. (Mon.-Thur.) and 7:30 a.m.-1 p.m. (Fri.)

Chilean Embassy
15 Soi 61, Sukhumvit Rd.
Tel: 391-4858, 391-8443
Office hours: 9 a.m.-5 p.m.
Visa hours: 9 a.m.-2 p.m.

Chinese Embassy
57/2 Rajadapisek Rd.
Tel: 245-7032, 245-7033
Office hours: 9 a.m.-noon, 2 p.m.-5 p.m.

Czechoslovakian Embassy
Rm. 705, Silom Center Bldg.
197/1 Silom Rd.
Tel: 234-1922, 233-4535
Office hours: 8 a.m.-1 p.m.

Danish Embassy
10 Soi Attakarnprasit
S. Sathorn Rd.

Tel: 286-3930, 286-3943
Office hours: 7:30 a.m.-3 p.m. (Mon.-Thur.) and 7:30 a.m.-12:30 p.m. (Fri.)

Dominican Consulate
96/9 Chakrapadipong Rd., Pomprap
Tel: 281-4345, 281-4745
Office hours: 9 a.m.-3 p.m.

Egyptian Embassy
49 Soi Ruam Rudee
Ploenchit Rd.
Tel: 253-0161, 253-8138
Office hours: 9 a.m.-3 p.m.
Consular hours are 10 a.m.-noon

Finnish Embassy
16th floor, Amarin Plaza Bldg.
500 Ploenchit Rd.
Tel: 256-9306, 256-9307
Office hours: 8 a.m.-noon, 1 p.m.-3:15 p.m.

French Embassy
35 Soi Rongpasi
(Customs House Lane)
Charoenkrung Rd.
(New Road)
Tel: 234-0950, 234-0951
Office hours: 8:30 a.m.-noon, 1 p.m.-5 p.m.

German Embassy
9 S. Sathorn Rd.
Tel: 286-4223, 286-4224
Office hours: 8:30-noon

Greek Consulate
3rd fl., President Travel Service Bldg.
412/8-9 Soi 6, Siam Square
Rama I Road
Tel: 251-5111, 251-5112
Office hours: 9 a.m.-noon, 1:30 p.m.-3:30 p.m.

Hungarian Embassy
28 Soi Sukchai
off Soi 42, Sukhumvit Rd.
Tel: 391-2002, 391-2003
Office hours: 8:30 a.m.-2 p.m.
Visa hours: 9 a.m.-noon (Mon., Wed., Fri.)

Iceland Embassy
59 Soi Nawin
Chuaploeng Rd.
Tel: 249-1300, 249-1253
Office hours: 10 a.m.-2 p.m.

Indian Embassy
46 Soi 23, Sukhumvit Rd.
Tel: 258-0300, 258-0301
Office hours: 8:30 a.m.-1 p.m., 1:30 p.m.-5 p.m.

Indonesian Embassy
600-602 Petchburi Rd.
Tel: 252-3135, 252-3136
Office hours: 7:30 a.m.-noon, 1:30 p.m.-3:30 p.m.
Consular hours are 8 a.m.-noon

Iranian Embassy
602 Sukhumvit Rd. (between Soi 22 and 24)
Tel: 259-0611, 259-0613
Office hours: 8:30 a.m.-2:30 p.m.
Visa hours: 8 a.m.-4 p.m.

Iraqi Consulate
47 Pradipat Rd.
Tel: 278-5335, 278-5336
Office hours: 8:30 a.m.-2:30 p.m.

Ireland Embassy
205 Rajawong Rd.
Tel: 223-0876
Office hours: 9:30 a.m.-5:30 p.m.

Israeli Embassy
31 Soi Lang Suan,
Ploenchit Rd.
Tel: 252-3131, 252-3132
Office hours: 8 a.m.-4 p.m. (Mon.-Thur.), 8 a.m.-3 p.m. (Fri.)
Consular hours: 8 a.m.-1 p.m.

Italian Embassy
399 Nang Linchee Rd.
Tel: 286-2054, 286-2055
Office hours: 9 a.m.-1 p.m.

Japanese Embassy
1674 New Petchburi Rd.
Tel: 252-6151, 252-6159
Office hours: 8:30 a.m.-noon

Jordanian Consulate
47 Soi 63, Sukhumvit Rd.
Tel: 391-7142
Office hours: 9 a.m.-noon

Korean Embassy
Sathornthani Bldg.
90 N. Sathorn Rd.

Tel: 234-0723, 234-0724
Office hours: 8:30 a.m.-noon, 1:30 p.m.-4:30 p.m.

Laotian Embassy
193 S. Sathorn Rd.
Tel: 286-0010, 286-3362
Office hours: 8 a.m.-noon, 2 p.m.-4:30 p.m.

Malaysian Embassy
35 S. Sathorn Rd.
Tel: 286-7190, 286-1392
Office hours: 8:30 a.m.-noon, 1 p.m.-4 p.m.

Mexican Consulate
1 Siam Yamaha Bldg.
Din Daeng Rd.
Tel: 245-1415, 245-7820, ext. Mexican Consulate
Office hours: 8:30 a.m.-noon, 1 p.m-3 p.m.

Nepalese Embassy
189 Soi Puengsuk
Soi 71, Sukhumvit Rd.
Tel: 391-7240, 390-2985
Office hours: 8 a.m.-noon, 1:30 p.m.-4:30 p.m.

Netherlands Embassy
106 Wireless Rd.
Tel: 254-7701
Office hours: 9 p.m.-noon

New Zealand Embassy
93 Wireless Rd.
Tel: 251-8165, 252-8995
Office hours: 8 a.m.-noon, 1:30 p.m.-4 p.m.

Norwegian Embassy
20th fl., Chokchai Bldg.
690 Sukhumvit Rd.
Tel: 258-0531, 259-1010
Office hours: 9 a.m.-3 p.m. (Mon.-Thur.), 9 a.m.-1 p.m. (Fri.)

Oman Consulate
7th fl., Aswinwichit Bldg.
134/1-2 Silom Rd.
Tel: 236-7385, 236-7386
Office hours: 8:30 a.m.-noon
Visa hours: 8:30 a.m.-11 a.m.

Pakistan Embassy
31 Soi 3, Sukhumvit Rd.
Tel: 253-0288, 253-0289
Office hours: 8:30 a.m.-4 p.m.
Consular hours: 8:30 a.m.-noon

Panama Consulate
Rm. 704, Prapavit Bldg.
28/1 Surasak Rd.
Tel: 234-8309, 234-8311
Office hours: 9 a.m.-3:30 P.M.

Peruvian Consulate
10 Soi 3, Moo Baan Seri 1
Tel: 314-1054, 314-3752

Philippines Embassy
760 Sukhumvit Rd. (opp. Soi 47)
Tel: 259-0139, 259-0140
Office hours: 9 a.m.-noon, 2 p.m.-4 p.m.

Polish Embassy
61 Soi Prasarnmit off Soi 23
Sukhumvit Rd.
Tel: 258-4112, 258-4113
Office hours: 9 a.m.-noon, 1 p.m.-3 p.m.

Portuguese Embassy
26 Captain Bush Lane
New Rd.
Tel: 233-7610, 234-2123
Office hours: 9 a.m.-2 p.m.

Romanian Embassy
39 Soi 10, Sukhumvit Rd.
Tel: 251-7881, 251-2242
Office hours: 8 a.m.-5:30 p.m.

Saudi Arabian Embassy
10th floor, Sathornthani Bldg.
90 N. Sathorn Rd.
Tel: 235-0875
Office hours: 9 a.m.-3 p.m.

Senegal Embassy
2/092 Muang Thong Nivet 1
Chaeng Wattana Rd.
Tel: 573-1976
Consulate: 394/14 Samsen Rd.
Tel: 281-6451.
Office and Consular hours: 8:30 a.m.-noon, 1 p.m.-4:30 p.m.

Singapore Embassy
129 S. Sathorn Rd.
Tel: 286-2111, 286-1434
Office hours: 8:30 a.m.-noon, 1 p.m.-4:30 p.m.

Spanish Embassy
104 Wireless Rd.
Tel: 252-6112, 252-8368
Office hours: 8:30 a.m.-3:30 p.m.
Consular hours: 8:30 a.m.-noon

Sri Lanka Embassy
48/3 Soi 1, Sukhumvit Rd.
Tel: 251-8399
Consulate: 1/7-8 Soi 10, Sukhumvit Rd.
Tel: 251-0803
Office and Consular hours: 8 a.m.-3:45 p.m. (Mon.-Thur.), 8 a.m.-2 p.m. (Fri.)

Swedish Embassy
11th floor, Boonmitr Bldg.
138 Silom Rd.
Tel: 234-3891, 234-3892
Office hours: 8 a.m.-12:30 p.m.

Swiss Embassy
35 N. Wireless Rd.
off Ploenchit Rd.
Tel: 253-0156, 253-0157
Office hours: 9 a.m.-noon

Turkish Embassy
153/2 Soi Mahadlek
Luang I, Rajdamri Rd.
Tel: 251-2987, 251-2988
Office hours: 8:30 a.m.-4 p.m.
Consular hours: 8:30 a.m.-1 p.m.

United Arab Republic Embassy
49 Soi Ruam Rudee
Ploenchit Rd.
Tel: 253-0161
Office hours: 9 a.m.-3p.m.

U.S.A. Embassy
95 Wireless Rd.
Tel: 252-5040, 252-5049
Office hours: 7:30 a.m.-noon, 1 p.m.-4:30 p.m.

U.S.S.R. Embassy
108 N. Sathorn Rd.
Tel: 234-9824, 234-2012
Office hours: 7:30 a.m.-4:15 p.m. (Mon.), 7:30 a.m.-3:15 p.m. (Tue.-Fri.)

Vatican Holy See
Apostolic Nunciature
217/1 S. Sathorn Rd.
Tel: 211-8709, 211-8519
Office hours: 8:30 a.m.-5:30 p.m. (Mon.-Fri.), 8:30 a.m.-noon (Sat.)

Vietnamese Embassy
83/1 Wireless Rd.
Tel: 251-7203, 251-5836
Office hours: 8:30 a.m.-4:30 p.m.

Yugoslavia Embassy
28 Soi 61, Sukhumvit Rd.
Tel: 391-9090, 391-9091
Office hours: 8:30 a.m.-4:30 p.m.

ART/PHOTO CREDITS

Photographs	
154, 168	**Apa Photo Agency**
148	**Lloyd, R. Ian**
149	**Reichelt, G.P.**
12/13, 14/15, 16/17, 18/19, 22, 25, 27, 30, 33, 34, 35, 36, 38, 39, 40, 41, 45, 46/47, 48, 50, 51, 52, 53, 54, 56, 57, 58, 59, 60, 61, 62, 63, 64, 65, 66, 67, 69, 70/71, 72/73, 74/75, 76, 77, 78/79, 80, 82, 83, 84, 86L, 86R, 87L, 87R, 88, 89, 90, 91, 92, 93, 94, 95, 96, 98, 100R, 101, 102, 103, 104, 105L, 105R, 106, 107, 108, 110, 111, 112, 115, 116, 118, 119, 120, 121, 122/123, 124, 125, 126/127, 128/129, 130, 131, 133, 134, 135, 136, 138, 139, 141, 142, 143, 144, 145, 146, 147, 150, 152, 153, 156, 159, 160, 161, 163, 164, 166, 167, 169, 170, 171L, 171R, 172/173, 174, 175, 177, 179, 181, 183, 184/185, 186, 188, 190, 191, 192L, 192R, 193, 197, 198, 199, 201, 202, 203, 205, 207	**Tettoni, Luca Invernizzi**
20/21, 42/43, 44, 97, 100L, 113, 117, 137, 140, 155, 158, 176, 182, 194/195, 204	**Van Beek, Steve**
Illustrations	**Geisler, Klaus**
Visual Consulting	**Barl, V.**

INDEX

A

B

C

D

E

F

G

H

I

J

K

L

M

N

O

P

R

S

T

U – V

W – Y